SCIENTIFIC THOUGHT IN POETRY

SCIENTIFIC THOUGHT IN POETRY

BY

RALPH B. CRUM

AMS PRESS, INC.
NEW YORK
1966

AMS PRESS, INC.
New York, N.Y. 10003
1966

PN
1059
.S3
C7
1966

Manufactured in the United States of America

PREFACE

By the title *Scientific Thought in Poetry,* I do not presume to imply that I am in any sense offering a solution to the vexed question of the relationship of science and poetry. The most that I can hope for this study is that it may subsequently prove to be a step in that direction.

My interests were first enlisted in the problem by reading Dr. A. H. Thorndike's volume *Literature in a Changing Age.* I began to wonder in greater detail just what influence the biological theories of Darwin might have had upon the poets of his age and subsequently. Obviously, before arriving at an answer to that question it was necessary to examine the effects of earlier scientific thinking upon the poets. In this connection Erasmus Darwin proved an interesting figure, but still the relationship of scientific thought to poetry seemed very obscure. My studies led me from the eighteenth and nineteenth centuries, through the seventeenth and sixteenth, thence to the Middle Ages, and finally to the Roman and Greek poets.

I hope that, by considering in chronological order some of the poems which have concerned themselves in any way with science, I might be able to point out a steady progression or growth of scientific thought in poetry. With such a hypothesis in mind, I examined much of the work of Lucretius, Virgil and Dante; of Chaucer and other medieval writers, Italian, French and English; and the works of later writers from the time of Spenser to John Davidson in the twentieth century. As a result I came to feel that the phrase "growth of scientific thought in poetry" would be a misnomer. The idea, for example, that Tennyson is more thoroughly imbued with science than Lucretius will not bear very close scrutiny. It became increasingly evident that before anything like a true historical account of the relations of science and poetry could be written, more details about the individual authors would be necessary.

In this study, therefore, I have limited the scope of my survey to noting primarily the effect of science on the ideas of the several poets discussed, and especially as those ideas have been reflected in their verse. Undoubtedly science has also exerted an effect upon the art of their poetry, but that relationship will be considered only incidentally.

After some preliminary reflections about the meaning of the terms "scientific thought" and "poetry" and about some of the views that have been held regarding this relationship, we shall turn to an examination of the more important figures who have reacted definitely towards that conflict which has long been waging between science and poetry.

To attempt to acknowledge the kindness and courtesy that has been accorded me while gathering my material and while writing the book I should have to catalogue a list of names which would include many on the Library staffs of the Columbia University Library, the New York Public Library, and the Library of the University of California. For valuable criticism of some of the earlier drafts of the work I owe much to Professor J. B. Fletcher and Professor W. W. Lawrence. For reading the manuscript and making helpful suggestions I wish especially to thank Professor Charles Sears Baldwin and Dr. Henry W. Wells. My chief debt of gratitude, however, is due Professor Ashley H. Thorndike whose written word first inspired this line of thought and whose subsequent encouragement and advice at every stage has made the completion of the work possible.

R.B.C.

UNIVERSITY OF WICHITA
Wichita, Kansas
April, 1931

CONTENTS

I.	Science and Poetry.....................	1
II.	Pre-Newtonian Science in Poetry: Lucretius	25
III.	Poetry and the New Science.............	40
IV.	Poetry Solemnly Surveys the Newtonian World Machine	61
V.	Poetry Advances a Step towards the Conception of the World Machine: Voltaire and André Chénier.....................	81
VI.	Poetry Smiles at a Growing World: Erasmus Darwin	110
VII.	Poetry Champions Evolution: Goethe.....	131
VIII.	Nature Red in Tooth and Claw: Tennyson's Problem	157
IX.	The Poet's Dilemma—Reason or Mysticism	191
X.	In Conclusion: John Davidson..........	228
Bibliography		239
Index		243

Chapter I

SCIENCE AND POETRY

The question whether science can have any relationship at all to poetry is one which has been frequently discussed throughout the course of literary criticism. Especially has this query come to the fore during the latter part of the nineteenth century and the first quarter of the twentieth, as the general interest in science and in scientific achievement has steadily advanced. Prominent among the recent treatments of the subject is that of I. A. Richards of Cambridge University, in his little volume, *Science and Poetry*.[1] He states the problem cogently from the twentieth-century point of view. In sum and substance it seems to be this: Poetry arose at a time when the greater part of mankind held the magical view of the universe (i.e., a belief in a world of Spirits and Powers which control events, which can be evoked, and to some extent controlled, by human practices.)[2] Since then, and more especially in our time, science has tended to weaken the magical view of nature and to make men regard it more and more from the point of view of statistics and mathematics. Obviously, then, if poetry is going to maintain the magical view for its own, it can no longer bear such a vital relation to life as it has borne in the past. On the other hand, if it is to hold such an intimate relationship, then poetry, too, must change its point of view and become, in brief, more scientific. Can it do this and yet remain poetry? Or must poetry, if it is to continue to exist, address itself to the unintelligent portion of

[1] N.Y., 1926.
[2] *Ibid.*, p. 58.

humanity? Professor Richards declares, in looking over the vast body of verse, that in its best manifestations it consists of two streams—the intellectual and the emotional—and of these two, it is the emotional stream which he regards as of greater importance. Hence the only way which science can enter into poetry is through our emotions (i.e., "the play of our interests"). In brief, the intellectual factor must be emotionalized.

Various other opinions concerning the relationship of science and poetry have of course been advanced, in the nineteenth and twentieth centuries, by critics, poets, and scientists. These opinions have ranged over such a wide field that they have covered very nearly all the possible relations that could conceivably exist. They might, in fact, be classified as follows: (1) those that regard science and poetry as mutually exclusive; (2) those which place science as inimical to poetry; and (3) those that make one complementary to the other.

(1) Let us suppose, for the sake of argument, that science and poetry are mutually exclusive. There is no denying the fact that much poetry bears no apparent relation to science. Indeed, many a poem may be cited which is as free from scientific nomenclature, thought, and purpose as though science had never existed; but this scarcely needs demonstration, it is so entirely patent. On the other hand, it ought to be noted in this connection that the great abundance of such poetry, especially in the second half of the nineteenth century, is due to some extent, at least, to a reaction against the scientific temper and all that is implied by it. The whole Pre-Raphaelite movement might be cited as an example, and also the aesthetic cult of "art for art's sake." Thus, from the idea of science and poetry being mutually exclusive, we come easily to the idea:

(2) That science and poetry are inimical to each other. If this is true and science continues to advance as it has advanced for the past hundred years, then poetry, as some pessimistic writers have long maintained, must be regarded as doomed.

Coleridge, it will be recalled, regarded science as the antithesis of poetry; and Poe believed that a poem should be written solely for the poem's sake. Many of the Romanticists looked upon the interests of the poet and the scientist as entirely irreconcilable. Keats's well known toast in execration of Newton for destroying the poetry of the rainbow is an example. These poets feel—and surely not without cause—that the analytical method of the scientist tends to destroy beauty of expression, while the procedure of generalizing and abstracting deprives poetry of its concrete and sensuous qualities. This is also the attitude of the philosophers Schopenhauer and Croce.

Furthermore, poetry is recognized as being freer than science —by Hegel, Schopenhauer, and Dewey—and as refusing to be bound down by the regularity and the necessity which characterize science. The poet insists upon the right of moving from one field to another at will, without explaining his meaning, but seeing and reporting things just as they impress him.

Shakespeare's lines are doubtless a true description of how much poetry is produced:

> The poet's eye, in a fine frenzy rolling,
> Doth glance from heaven to earth, from earth to heaven,
> And as imagination bodies forth
> The form of things unknown, the poet's pen
> Turns them to shapes, and gives to airy nothing
> A local habitation and a name.

But can it be said that all poetry is produced in this way? Is it true that imagination, "bodies forth the forms of things unknown"? If the poet happens to be well grounded in science, for example, will not his imagination be colored somewhat by that science?

In brief, although it is a fact that much poetry does exclude science, and a great deal of it is inimical, is there not left a remnant, at least, which does bear a more intimate relationship to science?

(3) Many critics, feeling that such a relationship does exist,

have defined it as complementary. Thus for Hegel poetry is a naïve expression of philosophy; and for Croce it is a form of philosophy in embryo. Hegel, however, like Goethe, suggests that beauty is the manifestation of a hidden idea, thus endowing poetry with prophetic powers. In this sense, poetry through intuition can arrive at truth by means of mysticism. This conception informed the literary theory of the Romantic period—especially that of Schelling, Novalis, and later, in England, of Carlyle—until Emerson could boast that the poet alone knows anatomy, chemistry, vegetation, and animation.[3]

According to the foregoing conception, as science fulfills the prophecy uttered by the poet, poetry pushes on ahead, along the pathway which science is to follow. How much of science already formulated it picks up on the way is a question which might well be asked. Or does it entirely disregard these scientific findings and report only what the senses reveal to it? Indeed will such a theory bear careful scrutiny? The poet is a human being, living in a world in which the fruits of science are daily manifest and in which scientific speculation is rife in popularized treatises, in essays, in novels, in plays, in the pulpit—everywhere where men are gathered together. Could he remain entirely unconscious of these influences? Will they not, in some degree, affect his mental background, even in spite of himself?

Quite another objection is offered, however, by those who oppose the contention that science is putting poetry to flight. They grant that, in so far as poetry concerns itself only with myths, science is sweeping aside these myths and may truly be said to be usurping the place of poetry. But is not something to be said, they demand, for the contention of Wordsworth, that poetry is not merely "the first" but also the "last of all knowledge"; that it is "the breath and finer spirit of all knowledge"?[4] Likewise Schiller, reinterpreting Kant, sees in poetry a means of

---

[3] "The Poet."
[4] Preface to the *Lyrical Ballads*.

"knitting together thought and feeling."[5] The artist, then, no less than the scientist, is seeking to give expression to abstract ideas. That is what Shelley felt, when he declared that poetry "comprehends all science, and is that to which all science must be referred";[6] and that which he strove to put into practice when he sought new myths to embody the latest scientific knowledge.

It was Matthew Arnold, however, who gave this conception its most classic expression:

But for poetry the idea is everything. . . . Poetry attaches emotion to the idea; the idea is the fact. . . . We have to turn to poetry to interpret life for us, to console us, to sustain us. Without poetry our science will appear incomplete.[7]

In brief, according to this conception, poetry will be needed to interpret science for us in terms of human life. It has a close relation, then, to philosophy—a philosophy which takes careful account of scientific truth.

A later version which stresses the emotional element a little more than Matthew Arnold did, is that of Santayana: "Art is the response to the demand for entertainment, for the stimulation of our senses and imagination, and truth enters it only as it subserves these ends,"[8] an idea which conforms to that of Professor Richards with which we opened this discussion.

We have now examined briefly some of the views which are held concerning the relations of science and poetry. It is my contention that not all science and poetry are mutually exclusive or even inimical, that not all poetry is merely a naïve expression of an embryonic philosophy, but that poetry has very frequently concerned itself, perfectly legitimately, with scientific questions and with the implications involved, and that theoretically at least there is no reason why it cannot pass a

[5] *Aesthetical Letters*, 28 and 29.
[6] *A Defence of Poetry*.
[7] "The Study of Poetry."
[8] *Sense and Beauty*, p. 22.

sane and healthful judgment upon the dictums of the more mature science.

Before pursuing our inquiry further, however, it is essential at the outset to understand clearly what is implied in the terms "scientific thought" and "poetry." Even the most superficial consideration reveals the fact that both of these terms have, throughout the course of their history, undergone a series of changes in meaning.

What is meant by the term "Scientific Thought"? In its most elementary form science may be defined as the earliest attempts of man to understand his environment in any way whatsoever. In this sense, then, the terms of deductive and inductive natural philosophy may be said to lie far back in prehistoric times. The myths which were then formulated were both science and religion in embryo. In the rhythmic dance and song that frequently accompanied the tribal activities were also the germs of the fine arts—especially music, poetry, and the drama as well as the dance. Along with the development of the myths, moreover, went an ever increasing body of both theoretical and practical knowledge; for any effort accompanied by a desired result was naïvely taken as the immediate cause of that result. Hence rose magical practices and astrology, until in the Pythagorean school there was an attempt to conceive every thing in the terms of numbers. Among the more practical problems to be solved were, of course, the making of weapons, of shelter, temples, ships, pyramids, aqueducts, et cetera. Thus through a promiscuous outgrowth of accident, superstition and the methods of trial and error, resulted a great array of facts—some of great worth, others of very doubtful value. The more critical scientific temper which could evaluate them was still lacking.

Something of this critical temper was supplied by the Greeks, who with their dialectic (i.e., the method of talking a thing through) brought a certain degree of detachment, or an objective attitude of mind to bear upon their rational and empirical activities. With the perfection of the syllogism a powerful instrument was furnished for logical analysis. In addition, some of the Greeks, Aristotle and his followers in particular, had an idea of empirical science, by which animals and plants were classified in a systematic manner. By this method the generalization was built up from those particulars which were furnished through observation. Indeed, here was a promising beginning of that critical and scientific spirit which the modern scientist exemplifies.

For various causes, however, in Alexandrian, Roman, and early medieval times, this aspect of the scientific temper suffered a severe setback, and the interest shifted from external matters of nature to the more specific concerns of the individual himself, his welfare, his salvation, his place in the general scheme of things. The systems of Epicureanism, Stoicism, and Christianity all tended to center attention upon man rather than upon external nature. The earliest objective interpretations were for the most part embalmed in Pliny's *Natural History*, in Ptolemy's *Astronomy,* and in Galen's *Medicine and Anatomy.*

This subordination of science and philosophy to the voice of authority, as this proceeded from "divine science" or theology, colored very materially the thought of the majority of mankind. Except for a few isolated examples little progress was made throughout the medieval period toward a scientific study of nature. Those few individuals, however, who declined to accept the voice of authority, succeeded through their efforts in paving the way for the freeing of science from the bonds that had been holding it in thrall throughout the medieval period, and in ushering in the new age of the Renaissance.

It was in Italy, where the Renaissance first got under way, that the position of authority was most seriously challenged. With the further revival of the pagan spirit and the ideal of self-culture which rapidly sprang up and which placed such a reliance upon personal experience, there was a tendency to let down the bars of an overtight logical organization, and to revive something of the Platonic, or Neoplatonic spirit, with its proneness to speculate and to seek a hidden motive behind all phenomena. Note the work of Copernicus and Leonardo da Vinci. The latter was skeptical about alchemy and astrology and brought to his speculations careful observations and research, especially in anatomy. In thus uniting speculation, criticism, and empirical evidence, he typified some of the most characteristic features in the advance of the scientific temper.

Such a hopeful manifestation was soon followed, however, by a setback; for with the growth of humanism, despite the recovery of the ancient texts which tended to strengthen man's faith in his intellectual endeavors, his attention was directed, in the main, away from scientific activity into theological channels. In spite of this tendency and the hold that medieval tradition had upon the minds and education of men, the spirit of free inquiry continued to advance. The boundaries of man's horizon were further extended by the geographical explorations and discoveries at the end of the fifteenth and the early part of the sixteenth centuries. Further advance was indicated in the latter century by Telesio's proposal to inquire into the data presented by the senses and by his conclusion that all knowledge is derived from sensation. Paracelsus advocated going to nature as the source of all true knowledge; Vesalius, in 1543, published his work on human anatomy which aimed to reduce all bodily processes to terms of physiological mechanism. A little later, Michael Servetus gave a crude description of the lesser circulation of the blood. Others were active in gathering and classifying botanical and zoölogical data.

In the early part of the seventeenth century something of the true critical spirit of the scientist was given definite expression by both Bacon and Descartes. The French philosopher pointed out that truth could be obtained only by rigorously discarding tradition and by accepting those things which the clear light of reason revealed; and as an instrument of true measurement he offered mathematics. Francis Bacon who also desired to free man's mind from all predispositions, prejudices, and desires, sought, on the other hand, to build up all true knowledge inductively. The reason was always to be held in check by the facts of experience; and these facts were to be classified, so that man could utilize them in securing dominion over the forces of nature.

Both these ideals were combined in Newton who so successfully applied the mathematical principles to the problems of nature that he convinced, at length, the most scientific astronomers that the Copernican hypothesis was the true one. Furthermore —and a very big contribution, too, to the growth of the scientific temper—he succeeded in drawing to a focus those gropings of the scientist for a true demonstration of a mechanical explanation of nature. Henceforth, the scientist was to strive for a mathematical and mechanical interpretation.

Thus, in the seventeenth century the goal of the new science was made manifest. The thought that moved steadily towards that goal could truly be called "scientific thought." This type of thinking was evident not only in the realm of the physical sciences, but also by analogy it was extended to explain all social and mental phenomena as well. It was John Locke, who pointed out the significance of this for the human mind, by making our ideas result mechanically from our experiences writing upon the blank tablet of the mind. Indeed, in only one field was there a reluctance to accept the principles of mechanism, and that was, of course, in religion. But even here the Deistic movement was an attempt to reconcile a mechanized nature with the older theology, and it compromised with the conception of God starting the world going, and then letting the whole process work out according to His own unalterable laws.

The Newtonian ideal of mechanism was worked out most completely, of course, by the French philosophes in the eighteenth century. The whole Encyclopedic movement was the expression of the optimistic faith that through science the Utopian Age was to be ushered in, and that this might be accomplished almost as soon as mankind could be induced to subscribe to that belief, and would seek to perfect the environment and the education of the child. The factor of time, therefore, had rather an insignificant rôle in that ideal.

But without the factor of time, the sciences of geology, botany, and zoölogy found themselves handicapped. There was a crying need for a readjustment of views which should allow very materially for a temporal factor. Gradually the idea of change and of growth entered more prominently into the conceptions of philosophy and science. Kant had suggested in 1755[9] that the universe had evolved gradually. Laplace, towards the end of the century, had suggested the nebular hypothesis as a possible explanation of the process. From the studies of the structures of plants and animals, made by Boerhaave, Bonnet, Buffon, and Linnaeus, the conviction grew that there had been a gradual development in both plant and animal life. The studies in comparative anatomy made by the Hunter brothers (John and William) and by Cuvier tended to show that anatomically, at least, there was no sharp dividing line between the lower and the higher animals. In the latter years of the century Lamarck, Erasmus Darwin, and Goethe were working out a theory that all living organisms have descended from a very few simple, primitive forms, or possibly from a single form.

Furthermore, fossils had long been receiving attention. In 1740, Lazzaro Moro advanced the view that the earth's crust consists of strata superimposed upon one another. In 1788, James Hutton announced in his *Theory of the Earth* the important doctrine of uniformitarianism, which states that it is reasonable to suppose that these strata were formed by the same forces at work in the past as in the present. Towards the end

[9] *General Natural History of the Heavens.*

of the century there was much discussion current as to how the fossils of sea-animals were found in the strata on mountain tops; whether by floods (the Neptunists) or by volcanic action (as the Vulcanists held).

The factor of time thus assumed, in many scientific explanations, in the latter half of the eighteenth century, a place of marked significance. Gradually there was a shifting of interest from the concept of nature working like a machine to the very different concept of nature proceeding like an organism, by growing and developing.

Along with this conception, however, went also a new and different evaluation of science itself. The scientific temper became less optimistic and very much more practical. From David Hume's account, man had little to hope for if he trusted implicitly in Reason and Science, for since man cannot, by the very limitations of his mind, know reality itself, science and reason can bring him only to an apparently insurmountable wall. Indeed, there appeared to be three pathways open to him: (1) to view the wall, with Bishop Berkeley, as only an illusion of the mind; (2) to forsake with Rousseau the pathway of Reason and Science and resort to the road of Feeling and Conscience as the main throughfare to Truth; (3) to acknowledge frankly, with Immanuel Kant, the limitations of the human mind, but to retain one's dignity through asserting the primacy of the will, in its power to accept those truths which are most necessary to mental health and happiness. In effect this was to make the Will and the Imagination the source of a higher kind of truth than that which is derived logically through the intellect alone. And this was the pathway most frequently trod by philosophical and poetical thinkers through at least the first half of the nineteenth century.

Though the prestige of science suffered somewhat by this new evaluation, it continued to grow more popular and its effects more manifest. An increasing industrial and commercial civilization demanded new machinery, new inventions, new processes—to which practical matters science now addressed itself. Theorists in the scientific field were still true to the mathematico-mechanical ideal of Newton and sought steadily, especially in physics and chemistry, to reduce everything to more exact mathematical expression. Even in biology there was an increasing tendency in the direction of exact measurements. The spectacular elements in electricity and magnetism were subordinated to technical considerations. If science could no longer occupy the lofty heights, with the full-flung banner of the Encyclopedists before it, it was well-content with its democratic rôle, among the practical interests of mankind, and with its method more clearly defined than ever before.

In its new rôle the scientific spirit continued to advance ever more triumphantly and in its more theoretical aspects to wage war with the then somewhat hazy doctrine of evolution. All through the first half of the nineteenth century the Nature philosophers continued to theorize about the unity of nature, and how man is linked, in some more or less mysterious way, with the lower animals and with plants. But even while the Newtonian science was repudiating much of the loose thinking, and the non-mathematical and non-mechanical basis of much that went on under the name of biology, it was absorbing gradually something of the general conception of growth and development.

At length a philosopher, August Comte, attempted to make philosophy itself more scientific (1830-42) by employing only positive data. Another, Herbert Spencer, began his prodigious task of attempting to explain everything in terms of evolution. Then came the master stroke of Charles Darwin, uniting these branches of Nature philosophy and the Newtonian science in *The Origin of Species* (1859), offering an explanation of evolution which was worthy to attract the serious attention of the scientists most devoted to the Newtonian school. After a long period of controversy, in which the best scientific minds of the century shared, the principle of natural selection triumphed, and evolution had won its place as an important element in the scientific attitude of mind.

It is evident, then, that the term "scientific thought" has meant something a little different from age to age. Even in the same period, or very nearly the same, it has sometimes been interpreted differently, as witness Plato regarding it as mere speculation or as a branch of philosophy, and Aristotle but a few years later holding that its material was data derived solely from observation and experience. Obviously "science" to Thomas Aquinas, in the thirteenth century, who made it subject to the voice of authority, meant something very different from what it did to Francis Bacon in the sixteenth century, who made it depend entirely upon generalizations drawn from experience. The methods employed by Galileo and Newton differed widely from those advocated by Bacon, and the gradual extension of their method to so many fields of human endeavor undoubtedly gave the impression that to regard anything "scientifically" was to explain it in terms of a mechanical principle. Then, a little later, the injection of the idea of development or growth into scientific thought served to complicate matters to such an extent that the whole issue of what really constituted the scientific attitude was very much confused. The relationship between science and philosophy, for example, was no longer so clear cut; but the scientific method or technique, on the other hand, seemed very definitely fixed.

Note a fairly recent expression of what scientific procedure should be, in J. Arthur Thompson's *The Outline of Science,* which finds the scientific method marked by:

(1) A passion for facts which includes a high standard of accuracy and detachment from personal wishes; (2) a cautious thoroughness in coming to a conclusion, which implies a persistent skepticism and self-elimination in judgment; (3) a quality of clearness, which includes a dislike for obscurities, ambiguities, and loose ends; and (4) a less readily definable sense of the inter-relation of things, an in-

sight which discerns that apparently isolated phenomena are integral parts of a system.

Obviously the first three characteristics constitute a technique and discipline which is distinct from the fourth characteristic; and it is those first three characteristics which best describe the ideal of mathematico-mechanical science. These characteristics differentiate science from all forms of "looser" thinking. Indeed the fourth characteristic seems a better description of that "looser" or "freer" attitude of mind which is commonly associated with the artist or poet. The significant point to note, however, is that this characteristic is, in the opinion of the author, essential to the equipment of a twentieth century scientist. And this view is a good illustration of the change in attitude upon the part of many modern scientists. The material basis of science is no longer regarded as fundamental, and scientists are no longer unanimous in maintaining that the scientific ideal is the mechanistic interpretation of life. This attitude is reflected in Dr. Scott Buchanan's interesting little book *Poetry and Mathematics*,[10] in which the author says:

> For the poet facts, like words, are symbols, and the knowledge consists in the insight into the symbolic relation. . . . For the mathematician and the scientist facts are to be referred to principles and causes. The allegorical correspondence of his ideas with the facts is the truth. . . . An algebraic equation is a complex pattern of ratios, and the corresponding poetic forms are expanded metaphors.

What then is the essential difference between the procedure of the poet and that of the scientist? In a general way it is vaguely sensed by nearly every one, at least to the extent of noting that the scientist proceeds much more cautiously, critically, and logically than does the poet. The scientist aims to weigh and measure his findings by some universal and external standard, referring them to mathematics as a final court of appeal: the poet seeks to give fitting expression to the feelings which a given set of phenomena inspires in him, appealing to

[10] N.Y., 1929, pp. 109-10.

an inner sanction, as well as an outer pattern established by tradition. Whereas the scientist proceeds by generalizing from the particular to the abstract, the poet frequently starts—but not by any means always—with an abstract idea which he desires to embody in concrete form, so that a complete illusion may be established. The scientist in pursuing his work seeks to escape from the sensuous and to enter the realm of abstract logic or mathematics; the poet aims to make his idea take on sensuous form, or, at least in the words of Professor Lowes, to make "a translation, not a transcript of reality."[11] The process of converting a truth into an image is what the poet means by "imagination."[12]

This power which some individuals possess to so much greater an extent than others, was frequently regarded in the past as a supernatural manifestation, especially when it was combined with a facile technique of melodious verse-making. The imagery and the rhythmical phrasing, which seemed to spring up so miraculously out of a great void, filled the possesser, as well as his charmed audience, with a reverent wonder.

Now that the new psychology has assured us that this can be readily accounted for by other than supernatural means—such as revery, a flashing forth into the clear focus of consciousness from out of the vast field of the "unconscious" where experiences from the individual's past, or perhaps from the past of the race, have assumed various shapes and patterns, through the processes of dissociation, of attention, and of a recombination of elements—we still wonder at these extraordinary powers of the human mind manifesting themselves in such an exaggerated form in certain gifted individuals. The poetic impulse lies, according o this new conception, in the poet's desires, wishes, and aspirations. Hence, "the function of poetry is to represent the imaginary fulfillment of our ungratified wishes and desires."[13]

[11] *Convention and Revolt in Poetry*, N.Y., 1919, p. 33.
[12] John Dewey, *Psychology*, N.Y., 1891, p. 192.
[13] F. C. Prescott, *The Poetic Mind*, N.Y., 1922, p. 127.

Yet, after all due allowances have been made for these irrational elements in poetry, may not the highest type of poetry also have a strong element of the rational in it? And furthermore, does not the advance of science itself depend somewhat upon a corresponding irrational element for the motive power which drives the scientist to research and experimentation? Indeed, may not the imagination of the scientist be nearly as creative as the imagination of the artist? Is not the main difference, if any, one of degree, the poet having greater freedom of movement than the scientist? And furthermore, may not the imagination be stirred both by our ungratified wishes or desires as well as by our philosophy and science?

There is a tendency today to shift from the position of Walter Pater, when he declared: "In science we have a literal domain where the imagination may be thought to be always an intruder";[14] to the position of Havelock Ellis: "Einstein . . . and many apostles of physical science today insist on the aesthetic, imaginative, and other 'art' qualities of science."[15] The imagination of the poet may spring into action more quickly than that of the scientist; and once coming into existence it is freer to proceed according to its own caprice, bound only by traditions of technique (conventions, versifications, vocabulary, imagery, et cetera), which may, nevertheless, occupy the attention and the efforts of the poet for many long years, as Gray's *Elegy* for example, and Tennyson's *In Memoriam*. The imagination of the scientist, on the other hand, may not manifest itself until after a long period of patient observation and experimentation, laborious tabulation and careful generalization; or it may leap into action in a moment of diversion. In any case, its imagery is apt to be less sensuous; it may be a mathematical formula or a colorless abstraction. Or it may image the practical results of applying an abstract scientific principle, such as a huge suspension bridge.

[14] T. W. Hunt. *Literary Principles and Problems*, N.Y., 1906, p. 57.
[15] Havelock Ellis. *Dance of Life*.

SCIENCE AND POETRY

When such an image first comes into existence it must be followed by further experimentation and verification, more tabulating and patient generalizations. It must, in fact, be checked up time and time again by referring the testimony of the senses to an external standard which must approximate the exactitude of mathematics. Hence, the goal of the scientist may be said to be a mathematical formula, whereas the goal of the poet is a series of mental images which seek to satisfy no outward standard so much as to gain an inner sanction to the process of welding sound and sense into a perfect unity.

The initial impulse of both the scientist and the poet may therefore be hidden in obscurity, or as is frequently said, it may flash forth from out of the "unconscious." Although both aim at truth, it is a truth arrived at by somewhat different processes. The scientist examines the hypothesis, however it may be derived, by the light of a highly intellectualized experience. The poet seeks a truth compounded, not from strict logic, but from "the world within and the world without, [and] a tertium quid that interprets both."[16] Although it is a world of illusion, a play world, in which the imagination is freer, it is not a lawless world. The poet seeks to reveal truth primarily in the light of emotional experience and thus to bring some kind of satisfaction to the wishes, desires, and aspirations of mankind.

If the foregoing is in any sense a correct picture of the procedure of the scientist and the poet at work, each in his own way, even though the procedure of the one differs in many details from that of the other, there need be nothing in the relationship that is mutually exclusive, permanently antithetical, or that threatens the destruction of poetry through the advance of science. Indeed the main distinction seems to be, that science must become part of the emotional experience before it can become poetry.

What is meant by the term "Poetry"? That, like the term

[16] J. L. Lowes. *Convention and Revolt in Poetry*, N.Y., 1919, p. 14.

"scientific thought," has also undergone several changes in meaning.

The two streams, to which Professor Richards refers, the "intellectual" and the "emotional," have historically always vied with each other more or less in poetry. When he refers to the intellectual stream as the minor one and of lesser importance, he is giving his own personal judgment, with which perhaps most poets and critics of his own time would agree. But throughout the history of the art of poetry there has been no such general agreement.

Indeed, some of the most significant moments in that history have been occasioned by a shifting of emphasis from the emotional to the rational, and vice versa.

In the primitive state, prior to the time of written records, or shortly thereafter, a period very probably existed when there was no conscious distinction, in the minds of the people, between philosophy, religion, poetry, and an embryonic state of science. The medium of social expression was probably through the dance and through rhythmic utterance recited or chanted. By these means, it was believed, food was got, evil averted, health sustained, the race propagated, the youth educated, and salvation won. As the process of rationalization proceeded, an embryonic philosophy came prominently to the fore, largely in the form of the myth—a naïve attempt to account for the phenomena of the universe. It contained also a rudimentary form of science, still lacking the orderly and inter-relational arrangements, deficient in a standard of accuracy and in methods of criticism.

In the dancing, however, and in the accompanying rhythmic utterance there was doubtless a certain intrinsic satisfaction in the activities themselves. They thus, not only served a useful purpose, but they were also pleasing to a rudimentary aesthetic sense. With the further rationalization of the rhythmic utterance, the myth frequently came to have a meaning which was

SCIENCE AND POETRY 19

entirely apart from the literal sense. It was then plainly recognized as an expression of an illusion and accepted as such. Myths of this kind were incorporated gradually into the rituals and the heroic legends, which also fulfilled the useful function of preserving the precious culture of the tribe or race. Naturally, there were certain individuals who could give more pleasing expression to these than other men could, and so there slowly grew up a professional class of saga singers, minnesingers, scops and minstrels. More and more these vied among themselves for beautiful and artistic forms of description, seeking always, however, to move the feelings of the audience, be it the patron, such as the ruler, the court, or the whole mass of the people. But obviously the audience addressed would affect the poet's treatment of his theme, would serve to render of varying importance the two streams: the intellectual and the emotional.

By Greek times these two diverse streams were evidently widely recognized. Plato, deploring the fact that they are so completely severed and that a tradition has grown up which sanctions in the poet a quality of "divine madness," would bring a solution to this ancient quarrel between the philosophers and the poets by banishing the poets from the state.[17] If only their compositions could be based upon truth (i.e., upon clearness of ideas), he says, in effect, they would be worthy of the name of philosophers. It seemed to Plato that the emotional stream was receiving undue emphasis in poetry.

To Aristotle, on the other hand, it appeared right that poetry should aim first of all to give emotional delight. Indeed, it must be something more than a metrical version of the facts of medicine, natural science or history.[18] But in emphasizing the importance of the emotional element in poetry, Aristotle would not at all neglect the intellectual side. This function he would exercise to the full in his method of imitating nature—not realisti-

[17] *Phaedo* 245 A; *Republic* III, 398 A.
[18] *Poetics* i, ii, IX, 1-2.

cally, not reporting scientifically, but ideally in the sense of imitating "things as they ought to be."[19]

This opinion of Aristotle was evidently not very effective in his own time, but it was destined to exert a tremendous influence at a later period. Throughout the Alexandrian and the Roman periods, however, and also during the early Middle Ages, literary criticism seemed to derive its canon, in the main, from the Platonic tradition. At any rate, the idea that poetry ought not to get too far away from philosophy, that it should contain a moral lesson, and that the intellectual stream is not in any sense a minor one, seemed to be the prevailing conception. Horace sums it up in his *Ars Poetica:*
> Aut prodesse volunt aut delectare poetae,
> Aut simul et jucunda et idonea dicere vitea.

Similarily, Plutarch held that all poetry of real excellence must be grounded in morals, the poetry serving as a sauce, a disguise for making attractive important truths which otherwise would fail to interest the young. This was also the feeling of Lucretius.

Under Scholasticism the didactic type of poetry was naturally encouraged, as the best works in art and literature were employed to express philosophical and theological conceptions. In this way the intellectual stream continued to be regarded as the more important. Nevertheless, in the twelfth and thirteenth centuries, there were not lacking signs of a revolt from this conception in the Provençal poetry with its emphasis upon the love lyric and its regard for the emotional effect that external nature and the season of the year have upon the poet; and again, more significantly in the poetry of Dante, on the threshold of the Italian Renaissance, before pseudo-classicism became the vogue —a period of much interest and importance to later science and poetry, but the consideration of which I am obliged to forego in this study, in order to give space to those later periods in

[19] *Poet,* XXV, 1.

SCIENCE AND POETRY 21

which the progress of science was so much greater than in the medieval period. The emergence of the emotional stream was further strengthened, theoretically at least, by the pseudo-classic theories of art which were fostered by Aristotle's POETICS, with its insistence that it is the function of poetry to give pleasure rather than to address the intellect primarily. Implicit in this pseudo-classicism, moreover, is the idea that the new facts of science have little or no binding power upon the poet, whose duty it is to imitate the classics and to adopt a poetic language which will distinguish it from prose.[20]

Nevertheless, whether scientific facts had any binding power upon poetry or not, it is a notable fact that a little later in France, in the early part of the seventeenth century, one ideal of poetic expression curiously coincided with one of the dominant characteristics of scientific expression—that which declared, that the language of poetry should seek for clarity, lucidity and regularity.[21]

In emphasizing correctness and purity of style, many of the former distinctions tended to break down. In so far as literary style was striving for succinctness and precision it was in harmony with the new scientific spirit in the seventeenth century, which was also searching for a medium of expression which should be clear, lucid, and precise. If verse and prose did not completely become interchangeable forms—and of course, they did not—there was, at any rate, a decided leaning in that direction. The feeling that both poetry and prose might deal with the same subjects, providing certain time-honored laws or rules were observed in utilizing them in poetry, was strengthened in Boileau's *Art Poétique* (1674), which definitely codified the "rules" derived from ancient precept and example and brought them into relation with the common sense point of view (i.e., with the perception of the average man).

[20] Du Bellay. *Deffense et illustration de la langue françoyse,* 1549.
[21] Spingarn's discussion of Malherbe's principles, pp. 236-41.

Another indication that the progress of the scientific spirit in the seventeenth century affected the idea of poetry is seen in the famous quarrel of the ancients and the moderns. As a result of this the poet felt more justified in looking to contemporary themes for his material, until in some quarters he began, in the eighteenth century, to champion the encyclopedists and their scientific ideals.

This compromise between Reason and Authority was upset first in Italy, in the seventeenth century, by Marini and his followers, in their tireless search for ingenious conceits and novelties. As a reaction from the artificialities which came with such a deluge of extravagant metaphors and antitheses there arrived at the end of the century the Arcadian movement, which went to the other extreme, and ended in an effeminency just as artificial and as far removed from the dictates of reason.

In the eighteenth century, however, the progress of thought itself began to run counter to the compromise between Reason and Authority. Gradually man's faith in the efficacy of science and reason as final arbiters of his destiny began to weaken, and the emotions and an element of mysticism were celebrated in poetry. We find the intellectual stream shrinking in its proportions and the emotional branch swelling inordinately.

This movement tended, of course, to separate poetry from science, for the poet now riding on the crest of that wave sought to stir the emotions of mankind rather than present clear images to the mind. The terms "imagination" and "fancy" were frequently on the lips of the poets of romanticism. From that time to our own, we have been inclined, on the whole, to regard the essence of poetry as something which exalts us, and expresses our inner desires, wishes, and aspirations.

That does not imply, however, that science and poetry are mutually exclusive, or entirely inimical, or that poetry is merely intuition. On the contrary, throughout the whole period, along with the other theories, the idea has also persisted that poetry

SCIENCE AND POETRY

has a very serious mission to perform, in uniting the rational and the emotional. This is, in one sense, of course, the Aristotelian principle of ideal imitation. But Kant phrased it anew in his insistence that art seeks to bring an object into harmony with the understanding. It is also what Goethe meant when he declared that beauty is an adequate realization of a hidden law of nature. It is implied furthermore in Matthew Arnold's dictum that "poetry is a criticism of life." It is what Santayana means, in part, when he writes: "Intellectual values are utilitarian in their origin but aesthetic in their form."[22] Indeed, as we shall note in a later connection, there has been a tendency in some quarters of late for poetry to strive consciously to embody the scientific spirit.

It might be well for us to bear in mind, as we proceed, that this attempt to infuse something of the scientific point of view into poetry is shared also with the other arts. In fact, it is probably nowhere more in evidence than in recent painting.

As a reaction from the impressionistic school, we note a movement there, especially at the close of the nineteenth century and the beginning of the twentieth, to bring more of the intellectual element into art. Thus, the Symbolists aim to express ideas; Fauvism seeks an expression for more abstract truth; Cubism, proceeding even farther, rejects realism entirely in expressing abstract forms; Futurism, adopting a very scientific attitude, seeks to express everything in terms of energy; while Vorticism addresses itself primarily to an industrial civilization.

This movement is still too recent for us to estimate its true significance in the history of painting; and the same may be said of kindred movements in all the fine arts. But one thing stands out very prominently, that the final word about the relationship of poetry and science has not yet been spoken and probably cannot be spoken for many years to come. It does not seem at all likely, at any rate, that this word will be spoken

[22] *Sense of Beauty*, p. 209.

by Croce, to mention only one of the most outstanding of modern philosophers who deals with aesthetic questions, and one who just now is being popularly acclaimed. In asserting that poetry is merely a certain form of expression, and in deriving this from the vital feature in his philosophy which denies the reality of the physical world, he cannot ultimately satisfy those who do not accept his philosophy of subjective idealism, but who do believe in the existence of a physical world—albeit in form different from what our senses reveal—and that poetry may conceivably continue to have definite relations with the maturest scientific formulations about that world.

In this study I am confining myself for the most part to some of those poets who have felt the effect of the "new science"—the science which took as its fundamental basis the Newtonian concept. I am letting Lucretius stand as the sole representative of science in poetry prior to the seventeenth century. A host of names might have been included, such as Dante, Fracastorius with his poem on Syphilus, Pontano and many others; but such a consideration would add nothing materially to our discussion. After a brief consideration of Lucretius and his reactions to the science of his time, a chapter is given to some of the seventeenth-century poets in England by way of noting how they react in general to the scientific thought which prevailed just prior to, and at the time of, Newton. I am more particularly concerned, however, with the poets of the eighteenth and nineteenth centuries in their reactions to the mechanism of Newton and to the concept of metamorphosis and development as these are reflected in Goethe and Darwin. Although I shall have occasion to refer to many writers in passing, I shall concentrate for the most part upon Voltaire, André Chénier, Erasmus Darwin, Goethe, Tennyson, George Meredith, and John Davidson.

Chapter II

PRE-NEWTONIAN SCIENCE IN POETRY

LUCRETIUS

From time to time poets have definitely championed the cause of science. This was especially true during the ancient and medieval periods, when poetry was sometimes regarded as having a very intimate relation to religion and to philosophy.

Occasionally verse has been used entirely as a vehicle for natural philosophy or for science, and it has often been debated whether such verse should be dignified by the title of poetry. The verse of the Greek Xenophanes, Parmenides, and even that of Empedocles comes under this category; and Aristotle, it will be recalled, objected to classifying this type of work as poetry.[1] There are certain other verses, however, of a later genesis in which the poets were all very much conscious of a distinction between natural philosophy or science, on the one hand, and poetry on the other, and who tried to express the former in terms satisfactory to the latter. In brief, they have aimed to present scientific truth (as they conceived it), so that it would appeal in some degree at least, to the emotions of the reader through the medium of rhythmic utterance. As an example of this relationship one poet is especially well adapted. I refer to the Roman, Lucretius.

Lucretius employed science, not primarily to teach its truths, as so many poets before him, both Greek and Alexandrian, had used verse to expound science and philosophy, but to establish a code of conduct, championed by reason and freed from super-

[1] *Poetics*, 1.

stition and fear. He declared that "this terror and darkness of the mind must be dispelled not by the rays of the sun and glittering shafts of day, but by the aspect and law of nature."[2] Indeed his manner of pursuing his inquiries shows something of the scientific method, together with a firm grasp of speculative ideas and the knowledge of how to apply these to the interpretation of human life and nature.

Knowledge will in the first place, he declares, bring understanding that nature craves no more than freedom from pain, and that she enjoys in mind a feeling of pleasure exempt from care and fear.[3]

This thesis, that one should regulate his life by the laws of nature, necessarily leads to a certain amount of exposition of this so-called law, or series of laws, which it is the purpose of science to discover, formulate, and apply. Therefore, Lucretius constructed in Latin hexameter verse a clear, full, and consecutive argument concerning the reign of law in nature. He was not content, however, to make merely an argument; he desired also to make a work of art. But he experienced difficulty putting in Latin verses the dark discoveries of the Greeks, especially as many points must be dealt with in new terms on account of the poverty of the language and the novelty of the questions.[4]

[2] hunc igitur terroren animi tenebrasque necessest
non radil solis neque lucida tela die;
discutiant, sed naturae species ratioque.
De Rerum Natura, 11, 59 f.

[3] ... nonne uidere
nil aliud sibi naturam latrare, nisi utqui
corpore seiunctus dolor absit, mente fruatur
incundo sensu cura semota metuque.
Ibid., 11, 17 f.

[4] nec me animi fallit Graiorum obscura reperta
difficile inlustrare Latinis uersibus esse,
multa nouis uerbis praesertim cum sit agendum
propter egestatem linguae et rerum nouitatem ...
Ibid., 1, 136 f.

Nevertheless,

> ... sed acri
> percussit thyrso laudis spes magna meum cor
> et simul incussit suauem mi in pectus amorem
> musarum, quo nunc instinctus mente uigenti
> auia Pieridum peragro loca nullius ante
> trita solo, iuuat integros accedere fontis
> atque haurire, iuuatque nouos decerpere flores
> insignemque meo capiti petere inde coronam
> unde prius nulli uelarint tempora musae.[5]

He defended his purpose on the ground that in giving an exposition of the reign of law in nature, he could, by employing the muses' charm, make these truths much more palatable.[6] He compares his procedure with that of a physician administering an unpleasant medicine by mixing it with honey and so rendering it pleasant to the taste.[7] By means of sweet verses he hopes to engage the minds of his auditors until they clearly perceive the whole nature of things, their shape and frame.[8]

According to his conception, then, poetry should teach something in a pleasing manner. He did not believe with Plato that "whilst a man retains any portion of the thing called reason, he is utterly incompetent to produce poetry."[9] Whereas Plato was emphasizing the mythological character of poetry, Lucretius, in

---

[5] ... but the great hope of praise has smitten my heart with sharp thyrsus, and at the same time has struck into my breast sweet love of the muses, with which now inspired, I traverse in blooming thought the pathless haunts of the Pierides never yet trodden by sole of man. I love to approach the untasted springs and to quaff, I love to cull fresh flowers and gather for my head a distinguished crown from spots whence the muses have yet veiled the brows of none.
  Trans. by H. A. J. Munro. *Ibid.*, 1, 922 f.

[6] deinde quod obscura de re tam lucida pango
  carmina, musaeo contingens cuncta lepore.
  Ibid., 1, 933-4.

[7] *Ibid.*, 1, 936 f.
[8] *Ibid.*, 1, 945 f.
[9] *Ion* 543, Shelley's trans.

attempting to unite philosophy and poetry, was minimizing that element.

His philosophical speculations were derived principally from Epicurus, whose praise he sings many times during the course of the poem. He was acquainted also with the philosophy of Democritus, Anaxagoras, Heraclitus, Plato, the Stoics, and Empedocles. In spite of his interest in philosophy, he is not a philosopher primarily. With his deep insight into the nature of things, his power of observation, and his steadfast belief that the life of external nature and the life of man are very closely related, if not identical, he felt as profoundly stirred in the depths of his being as ever a poet did before an ecstatic vision. It was natural, then, that he should attempt to transform science into poetry.

He had before him for examples, *The Works and Days* of Hesiod, the philosophical poems of Parmenides, Xenophanes, and especially Empedocles, whose verses, he declares, "cry with a loud voice and set forth in such wise his glorious discoveries that he hardly seems born of mortal stock."[10] These poets had utilized the epic hexameter in giving expression to philosophical and scientific speculation. From Empedocles especially he derived his model.

This poem by Empedocles of which only about four hundred lines out of five thousand are now extant, also had nature for its theme. In it is expounded the theory of the four elements (fire, air, water, earth) which combine through the powers of love and hatred, as well as a theory of animal development, which in some respects, anticipates the "survival of the fittest" theory. There were evidences also in the poem, the criticism of Aristotle notwithstanding, that the author was attempting, not merely to present an exposition in verse, but also to give a poetic setting to certain philosophical ideas.

In addition, Lucretius had for example the Alexandrian writers, such as the fragments of Callimachus, the "Hermes" of

[10] I, 730.

Eratosthenes, a poem on "Appearances and Phenomena" by Aratus, and a discusssion in verse of the nature of venomous animals[11] and of poisons and antidotes[12] by Nicander. These writers, like their predecessors, some of whom we have mentioned, looked upon poetry more or less as a vehicle for exposition; yet they were faithful also to the traditional poetry which gave a very important rôle to poetic diction, ornamentation, and mythology.

Lucretius was undoubtedly influenced by that tradition too; but in part he reacted from it: he did not wish to utilize poetry primarily as a storehouse for facts; he sought to avoid the artificial language, the diction, and the mythology. He thought much less about the manner of expressing himself, and much more about his message. He excelled in moral earnestness and sincerity. He had, in brief, all the courage of a modern scientist in facing the facts and all the enthusiasm of a true poet before a transforming vision.

The vision which beguiled him was that held out by the Epicurean philosophy: man in a happy and contented state of mind, freed from fear and superstition. This state of bliss, however, was impossible except in a world regulated by law and order. As long as man depended for his happiness upon the will of a capricious God, he could never hope to attain to that desired state; but if events in the world occurred according to a fixed and invariable law, then those things, such as earthquakes, tornadoes, floods, and all kinds of catastrophes, over which the human will had no power, must be accepted with fortitude and a ready acquiescence. In brief, man can control his mental attitude, so that he will accept nature's laws with resignation and cheerfulness. He can put himself in harmony with them, for they, he declares, are the forces which control all aspects of nature and mankind. True this view may dwarf man's importance in his own sight, but, declared the poet in effect, there is no real

---
[11] "Theriaca."
[12] "Aleximpharmaca."

and lasting happiness possible in illusion. Man must accept the facts and live according to them.

To know what these facts are one must turn to science and philosophy. In the first book of his poem, therefore, he aims to arrive at the fundamental facts, which are at the root of all things. He finds that there are three such classes of facts: (1) invisible primordial bodies (called atoms) which are eternally in motion; (2) a void, which allows for the movement of the atoms; and (3) an infinity of space, in which these atoms and the void have their being. All the things which our senses experience are composed of combinations of these invisible atoms, which are infinite in number, but limited in their varieties. Continuing the argument in the Second Book, he characterizes the atomic motions and shows how the various combinations take place, not according to any pre-arranged plan, but simply through chance impacts, which create and also destroy objects; but the atoms being indestructible, are constantly combining, disintegrating, and recombining ad infinitum.

Having established these facts logically, in theory at least, he is ready now to argue that the "soul" differs not at all from other objects, except in the fineness of its texture. Therefore, it too disintegrates at death; and hence it is folly to fear the extinction of life. The "mind," likewise, is no exception to this atomic law, for our knowledge of truth has come to us through the senses. Our knowledge of any object is due to the fact that from its surface little films peel off and fly through the air. Some of these may take possession of the eyes and provoke vision. Others however, being finer in texture "enter through the porous parts of the body and stir the fine nature of the mind within and provoke sensation."[13]

---

[13] ... quippe etenim multo magis haec sunt tenuia textu
quam quae percipiunt oculos uisumque lacessunt,
corporis haec quoniam penetrant per rara cientque
tenuem animi naturam intus sensumque lacessunt.

IV, 728-31.

LUCRETIUS

> ... Centauros itaque et Scyllarum membra uidemus
> Cerbereasque canum facies simulacraque eorum
> quorum morte obita tellus amplectitur ossa.[14]

These combinations, being due to chance encounters of atoms, moving according to the law of their nature and not according to any fixed plan or arrangement, indicate a universe formed in harmony with mechanical principles. Indeed, Lucretius preaches a philosophy of mechanism just as ardently as Descartes or Newton. Even love, which has been the theme of so many poets from the time of Euripides and through the Alexandrian age, is now shown to be the result of mechanical processes. Life first came upon the earth in a thoroughly automatic way:

> hoc ubi quaeque loci regio oportuna dabatur
> crescebant uteri terram radicibus apti;
> quos ubi tempore maturo patefecerat aestus
> infantum fugiens umorem aurasque petessens,
> Conuertebat ibi natura foramina terrae
> et sucum uenis cogebat fundere apertis
> consimilem lactis ...[15]

When he comes to account for the fact, however, that certain species of animals have died out upon the earth, while others have persisted, he resorts to an explanation which is indeed prophetic of the Darwinian theory of the survival of the fittest, "For time changes the nature of the whole world and all things must pass on from one condition to another."[16]

> ... Multaque tum interiisse animantum saecla necessest
> nec potuisse propagando procudere prolem.

---

[14] IV, 732-34.

[15] Wherever a suitable spot offered, wombs would grow attached to the earth by roots; and when the warmth of the infants, flying the wet and craving the air, had opened these in the fullness of time, nature would turn to that spot the pores of the earth and constrain it to yield from its opened veins a liquid most like to milk. ...

V, 807-13.

[16] "... sic igitur mundi naturam totius aetas
mutat et ex alio terram status excipot alter"

V, 834-35.

> nam qualcumque uides uesci uitalibus auris,
> aut dolus aut virtus aut denique mobilitas est
> ex ineunte aeuo genus id tutata reservans.
> ... multaque sunt, nobis ex utilitate sua quae
> commendata manent, tutelae tradita nostrae.[17]

Perhaps unconscious upon his part, but, nevertheless very prophetic of the course that the scientific temper was to take many centuries later, is his appeal to another principle than that of a mechanism, when he traced the growth of civilization. Men at first lived after a roving fashion of wild beasts; then they began to soften and live in huts, wear skins and employ fire. Leagues of friendships were formed, a language grew up, riches and gold were accumulated, laws and codes had to be devised, and religious practices came into being.[18] Man did not start in a golden age from which he later fell. Society developed or grew according to this conception; and if it does not mark a steady progress from the simple to the complex, yet the theory intimates vaguely something of that sort.

Man ought not to be afraid, therefore, he says in effect, because all things work according to natural laws, perfectly indifferent to man's welfare, his desires, or his wishes. Even Nature in her terrible aspects—in thunder and lightning, waterspouts, earthquakes, volcanoes, in floods, and pestilences,—should not make one believe in the supernatural, nor render the conditions of mankind more wretched.[19]

In the course of his argument, as we have noted, Lucretius resorted from time to time to physics, astronomy, botany, bi-

---

[17] And many races of living things must then have died out and been unable to beget and continue their breed. For in the case of all things which you see breathing the breath of life, either craft or courage or else speed has from the beginning of its existence protected and preserved each particular race. And there are many things, which, recommended to us by their useful services continue to exist consigned to our protection.
V, 855-62.

[18] Book V.
[19] Book VI.

ology, and a crude form of psychology. These sciences he summoned to help him with his argument. The problem of putting them into poetry, however, merges into the greater problem of expressing a highly rationalized philosophy in the language of emotion. He is well aware of the difficulty of thus making poetry the handmaiden of philosophy and science.

This problem at once becomes apparent when we reflect how difficult it is to embody in concrete language such an abstraction as infinity, for example, or that the invisible bodies (or atoms) are in constant motion, or that these atoms, habitually move downward, and that they have a diversity of shapes, and that they unite to form all the visible bodies, et cetera. And yet this is precisely the problem with which Lucretius wrestled.

Note, for example, how he turns the abstraction of infinity into concrete imagery:

> praeterea si iam finitum constituatur
> omne quod est spatium, siquis procurrat ad oras
> ultimus extremas iaciatque uolatile telum,
> id ualidis ultrum contortum uribus ire
> quo fuerit missum mauis longeque uolare,
> an prohibere aliquid censes obstareque posse?
> . . . alterutrum fatearis enim sumasque necessest.
> quorum utrumque tibi effugium praecludit et omne
> cogit ut exempta concedas fine patere.[20]

Again, observe the illustration he employs to demonstrate how the invisible atoms move about:

> Contemplator enim, quom solis lumina seque
> inserti fundunt radii per opaca domorum:

---

[20] If for the moment all existing space be held to be bounded, supposing a man runs forward to the outside borders and stands on the utmost verge and there throws a winged javelin, do you choose that when hurled with vigorous force it shall advance to the point to which it has been sent and fly to a distance, or do you decide that something can get in its way and stop it? for you must admit and adopt one of the two suppositions; either of which shuts you out from all escape and compels you to grant that the universe stretches without end.   1, 968-76.

> multa minuta modis multis per inane uidebis
> corpora misceri radiorum lumine in ipso
> et uelut aeterno certamine proelia pugnas
> edere turmatim certantia nec dare pausam,
> conciliis et discidiis exercita crebris;
> conicere ut possis ex hoc, primordia rerum
> quale sit magno iactari semper inani.
> ... dumtaxat rerum magnarum parua potest res
> exemplare dare et uestigia notitiai.[21]

To give an idea of the velocity with which these atoms move he compares them, in a charming picture, with the speed of the sunlight:

> primorum aurora nouo spargit lumine terras
> et uariae uolucres nemora auia peruolitantes
> aera per tenerum liquidis loca uocibus opplent,
> quam subito soleat sol ortus tempore tali
> conuestire sua perfundens omni luce,
> omnibus in promptu manifestumque esse uidemus.[22]

His general method of procedure may be very well illustrated from the Second Book (which aims to establish the character of the atomic motions, their form, and their combinations). These first two books seem to have received more attention from their author than the later ones, and therefore probably represent

---

[21] Observe whenever the rays are let in and pour the sunlight through the dark chambers of houses: you will see many minute bodies in many ways through the apparent void mingle in the midst of the light of the rays, and as in never-ending conflict skirmish and give battle combating in troops and never halting, driven about in frequent meetings and partings; so that you may guess from this, what it is for first-beginnings of things to be ever tossing about in the great void. So far as it goes, a small thing may give an illustration of great things and put you on the track of knowledge.
11, 114-24.

[22] When morning first sprinkles the earth with fresh light and the different birds flitting about the pathless woods through the buxom air fill all places with their notes, we see it to be plain and evident to all how suddenly the sun after rising is wont at such a time to overspread all things and clothe them with his light ...
11, 144-49.

more nearly his mature conception of how science may be utilized in poetry.

He frequently begins by stating an abstract fact:
>Nunc locus est, ut opinor, in his illud quoque rebus
>confirmare tibi, nullam rem posse sua ui
>corpoream sursum ferri sursumque meare;[23]

After having made such a general statement, he then gives a particular instance:
>ne tibi dent in eo flammarum corpora fraudem
>sursus enim uersus gignuntur et augmina sumsunt
>et sursum nitidae fruges arbustaque crescunt,
>pondera, quantum in se est, cum deorsum cuncta ferantur.[24]

This is followed by a concrete example which gives a picture:
>nec cum subsiliunt ignes ad tecta domorum
>et celeri flamma degustant tigna trabesque,
>sponte sua facere id sine ui subiecta putandum est.
>... quod genus e nostro cum missus corpore sanguis
>emicat exultans alte spargitque cruorem.[25]

Again, in illustrating the power of will manifesting itself in the motion of the atoms, he employs the following simile:
>... nonne uides etiam patefactis tempore puncto
>carceribus non posse tamen prorumpere equorum
>uim cupidam tam de subito quam mens auet ipsa?
>omnis enim totum per corpus materiai

---

[23] Now methinks is the place, herein to prove this point also that no bodily thing can by its own power be borne upwards and travel upwards.
11, 184-86.

[24] The bodies of flames may not in this manner lead you into error. For they are begotten with an upward tendency and in the same direction receive increase, and goodly crops and trees grow upward, though their weights, so far as in them is, all tend downwards.
11, 187-90.

[25] And when fires, leap to the roofs of houses and with swift flame lick up rafters and beams, we are not to suppose that they do so spontaneously without a force pushing them up. Even thus blood discharged from our body spirts out and springs up on high and scatters gore about.
11, 191-95.

copia conciri debet, concita par artus
omnis ut studium mentis conexa sequatur;[26]

Sometimes he will sketch two pictures to illustrate a statement of fact. For example, to explain the truth that although all the atoms are in motion, yet the sum total appears to stand still, he employs first the following:

> ... nam saepe in colli tondentes pabula laeta
> lanigerae reptant pecundes quo quam (que) uocantes
> inuitant herbae gemmantes rore recenti,
> et satiati agni ludunt blandeque coruscant,
> omnia quae nobis longe confusa uidentur
> et ueluti in uiridi candor consistere colli.[27]

Then follows a second illustration:

> ... praeterea magnae legiones cum loca cursu
> camporum complent belli simulacra cientes,
> fulgor ibi ad caelum se tollit totaque circum
> aere renidescit tellus subterque uirum ui
> excitur pedibus sonitus clamoresque montes
> icti reiectant uoces ad sidera mundi
> et circumuolitant equites mediosque repente
> tramittunt ualido quatientes impete campos.
> ... et tamen est quidam locus altis montibus (unde)
> stare uidentur et in campis consistere fulgor.[28]

---

[26] See you not too, when the barriers are thrown open at a given moment, that yet the eager powers of the horses cannot start forward so instantaneously as the mind itself desires? the whole store of matter through the whole body must be sought out, in order that stirred up through all the frame it may follow with undivided effort the bent of the mind.
11, 263-68.

[27] Thus often do wooly flocks as they crop the glad pastures on a hill, creep on whither the grass jewelled with fresh dew summons and invites each, and the lambs fed to the full gambol and playfully butt; all which objects appear to us from a distance to be blended together and to rest like a white spot on a green hill.
11, 317-22.

[28] Again when mighty legions fill with their movements all parts of the plains waging the mimicry of war, the glitter then lifts itself up to the sky and the whole earth round gleams with brass and beneath a noise is raised by the mighty trampling of men and the mountains stricken by the shouting reëcho the voices to the stars of heaven, and horsemen fly about and suddenly wheeling scour across the middle of the plains, shaking them with

Having illustrated the fact that although objects may seem to stand still even while the atoms which compose them are constantly in motion, he proceeds to make clear next the truth that just as in the natural world every living creature differs from every other, so the atoms differ among themselves as regard their shapes. The remainder of the Second Book is taken up with the characteristics of the atoms, and the argument is developed by precisely the same methods.

Not until he comes to the Fifth Book does he describe how the universe was formed: by the atoms mingling together, chaotically giving battle, clashing, cohering for a time, then several parts flying asunder and rejoining like with like, and so the world was marked out and its parts arranged.[29]

> Quippe etenim primum terrai corpora quaeque,
> propterea quod erant grauia et perplexa, coibant
> in medio atque imas capiebant omnia sedes;
> quae quanto magis inter se perplexa coibant,
> tam magis expressere ea quae mare sidera solem
> lunamque efficierent et magni moenia mundi.[30]
> . . . .
> V, 449-453.
>
> Ideo per rara foramina terrae
> partibus erumpens primus se sustulit aether
> ignifer et multos secum levis abstulit ignis.[31]
> . . . .
> V, 457-59.

---

the vehemence of their charge. And yet there is some spot on the high hills, seen from which they appear to stand still and to rest on the plains as a bright spot. 11, 323-32.

[29] V, 419-48.

[30] First the several bodies of earth, being heavier and closely entangled, met together in the middle and took up all of them the lowest positions. And the more they got entangled and the closer their union, the more they squeezed out those particles which were to make up sea, stars, sun, and moon, and the walls of the great world.

[31] Therefore the fire-laden ether first burst forth from the different parts of the earth through all the porous openings and lightly bore off with itself many fires.

> Hunc exordia sunt solis lunaeque secuta
> interutrasque globi quorum uertuntur in auris;[32]
>
> V, 471-72.

Then the earth sank in places, the poet tells us, and these hollows filling up with water formed the ocean.[33]

> Sic igitur terrae concreto corpore pondus
> constitit atque omnis mundi quasi limus in imum
> confluxit grauis et subsedit funditus et faex;
> inde mare inde aer inde aether ignifer ipse
> corporibus liquidis sunt omnia pura relicta,
> et leviora aliis alia, et liquidissimus aether
> atque leuissimus aerias super influit auras,
> nec liquidum corpus turbantibus aeris auris
> commiscit; sinit haec uolentis omnia uerti
> turbinibus, sinit incertis turbare procellis,
> ipse suos ignis certo fert impete labens,
> (nam modice fluere atque uno posse aethera nisu
> significat ponti mare certo quod fluit aestu
> unum labendi conseruans usque tenorem.)[34]

It must be clear from the consideration of these examples, that Lucretius possessed a keen eye for picturesque effect. He aimed, whenever possible, to illustrate philosophic and scientific truth by pictures rather than by diagrams. His word pictures are

[32] After it followed the rudiments of sun and moon, whose spheres turn round in air midway between earth and ether.

[33] See V, 480.

[34] Thus then the ponderous mass of earth was formed with close-cohering body and all the slime of the world so to speak slid down by its weight to the lowest point and settled to the bottom like dregs. Then the sea, then the air, then fire-laden ether itself, all are left unmixed with their clear bodies; and some are lighter than others, and clearest and lightest of all ether floats upon the airy currents, and blends not its clear body with the troubled airs; it suffers all these things below to be upset with furious hurricanes, suffers them to be troubled with wayward storms, while it carries along its own fires gliding with a changeless onward sweep. For, that ether may stream on gently and with one uniform effort the Pontus shews, a sea which streams with a changeless current, ever preserving one uniform gliding course.

V, 495-508.

not in any sense hackneyed, and his style is comparatively free from the conceits which abounded in the Alexandrianism of his day.[35] He eschewed for the most part the convention of mythology. It is true he began his poem with an address to Venus:

Aeneadum genetrix, hominum diuomque uoluptas,
Alma Venus, caeli subter labentia signa
quae mare nauigerum, quae terras frugiferentis
concelebras; —per te quoniam genus omne animantum
concipitur uisitque exortum lumina solis:[36]

Later in his argument, however, he is to urge the abandonment of the gods and a substitution of a reverence for natural law in the place of the ancient religion. But this is not as inconsistent as it seems, for Venus in his mind is the personification of the principle permeating and invigorating all life. For that principle he has the profoundest respect, but he sees nothing supernatural in it, nothing but what can be explained rationally.

Lucretius is, indeed, unique among the poets we are considering, because he bends all his efforts towards making a mechanical conception of the universe acceptable to his readers, on the ground that such an explanation frees man from fear and superstition and makes him master of the forces of the universe, for through the power of his mind he can control his will. The problem of determinism vs. free will does not trouble him. Indeed it is doubtful if anything analogous to such a wholesale appeal in poetry for the acceptance of science and its implications can be found before the eighteenth or nineteenth centuries, and then with no such deep conviction and calm assurance that happiness for mankind lies only in that direction.

[35] M. S. Slaughter. *Roman Portraits.* New Haven, 1925, p. 22.

[36] Mother of the Aeneadae, darling of men and gods, increase-giving Venus, who beneath the gliding signs of heaven fillest with they presence the ship-carrying sea, the corn-bearing lands, since through thee every kind of living thing is conceived, rises up and beholds the light of the sun. . . .

1, 1-5.

Chapter III

POETRY AND THE NEW SCIENCE

One of the essential differences between the old science, in which the emphasis had been mainly upon deductive reasoning, and the new science, in which the main emphasis was upon inductive processes, was pointed out clearly in the early years of the seventeenth century.

One of the first effects that we note in this change of emphasis among seventeenth-century writers in England is to be seen in the controverisal state of mind which prevailed in the first quarter of that century. This is to be noted in the contrasting views of Sir John Davies, Samuel Daniel, Francis Bacon, and Fulke Greville.

To Sir John the only knowledge is that which is related to God and to self, for it was "the desire to know first made men fools, and did corrupt the root of all mankind",[1] and he asks, if we, "their wretched off-spring

> Do we not still taste of that fruit forbid
> Whiles with fond fruitlesse curiositie
> In bookes profane we seek for knowledge hid.[2]

The trouble with the inquiring attitude of mind is, he argues, that we seek to know

> ... all things without,
> But that whereby we reason, live and bee
> Within ourselves, we strangers are thereto.
> We seek to know the moving of each sphere,
> And the strange cause of the ebs and flouds of Nile;

---
[1] *Nosce Teipsum.*
[2] *Ibid.*

> But of that clocke within our breast we bear,
> The subtle motions we forget the while.³

Here we have a direct criticism of the new scientific attitude: it is all too prone to put its trust in outward things as our senses reveal them to us, thereby forsaking the counsels of the inner consciousness and the highest reason which is expressed in theology.

Samuel Daniel, on the other hand, in the person of Musophilos, calls learning a "sacred art," which "never takes [its] ways by Reason, but by Imitation."

> Soul of the world, Knowledge, without thee,
> What hath the Earth, that truly glorious is?⁴

This knowledge, however, which seems to him to be the very soul of the world, is based entirely upon authority, not the authority of theology, but of the classical writers. It does not include the new science which builds from experimental evidence.

Bacon, quite to the contrary, argued that there was no true knowledge apart from that gained by experience and experiment, and that by regarding the fruits of these, the natural reason can discover unaided the "summary law of nature."⁵

In this he was opposed by Fulke Greville, who began by writing sonnets like Sir Philip Sidney, but later tended to draw many of his images from real life and from the natural sciences, and finally used characters to illustrate philosophical concepts. He contended that what Bacon lacked was a metaphysical ground for his science.⁶

It is evident, then, that by the beginning of the seventeenth century English poetry had definitely met the new science and was trying to evaluate it. Indeed, seventeenth-century England offers an excellent field in which to study the effect of the growth of the scientific spirit on poetry, because there poetry was freer

³ *Nosce Teipsum.*
⁴ *Ibid.,* 199.
⁵ *Advancement of Knowledge.*
⁶ *A Treatie of Humane Learning.*

than in France where the ideals of classicism hampered its movement somewhat, and it was in closer touch with the inductive process of scientific thought than in Italy or Germany, for in England the people seemed more naturally responsive to empirical arguments and less inclined to accept those based merely upon authority or abstract reason.

One of the poets who was especially aware of many of the implications in the new science was John Donne.[7] His reaction on the whole was one of resistance to the new thought, because it seemed to imply that man's dignity suffered as a consequence.

> The new philosophy calls all in doubt;
> The element of fire is quite put out;
> The sun is lost, and th' earth, and no man's wit
> Can well direct him where to look for it.
> And freely men confess that this world's spent,
> When in the planets, and the firmament
> They seek so many new: they see that this
> Is crumbled out again to his anatomies,
> 'Tis all in pieces, all coherence gone,
> All just supply, and all relation.[8]

Being well grounded in scholasticism, Donne missed in the new science much of its definiteness, its encyclopedic character, and its systematic arrangement of knowledge. Many of the ideas fostered by the new thought gave him the unpleasant feeling that the old reliable foundations were being swept away. So he complains:

> We think the heavens enjoy their spherical,
> Their round proportion, embracing all;
> But yet their various and perplexed course,
> Observed in divers ages, doth enforce
> Men to find out so many eccentric parts,
> Such diverse downright lines, such overthwarts,
> As disproportion that pure form.[9]

---

[7] 1573-1631.
[8] "First Anniversary," l. 205 f.
[9] *Ibid.*, l. 251 f.

POETRY AND THE NEW SCIENCE

There is furthermore, he feels, a disconcerting lack of uniformity, as for example, in the case of the sun, for,

> . . . where he rose today
> He comes no more, but with a cozening line,
> Steals by that point, and so is serpentine.
> . . . .
> So if the stars which boast that they do run
> In circle still, none ends where he begun,
> All their proportions lame, it sinks, it swells;
> For of meridians and parallels
> Man hath weaved out a net, and this net thrown
> Upon the heavens, and now they are his own.[10]

Moreover, this disfiguring of the world's proportion and uniformity affects morality itself, in

> That those two legs whereon it doth rely,
> Reward and punishment, are bent awry.[11]

Furthermore, now

> Wicked is not much worse than indiscreet.[12]

Man can no longer be sure of the meaning of things:

> Th' air shows such meteors as none can see,
> Not only what they mean, but what they be.[13]

All this new thought, he says in effect, is directing man's attention too much to outward things, and hence is preventing him from really knowing himself. He must "shake off this pedantry of being taught by sense and fantasy." These but exhibit fallacies to him; he must put his trust in reason and logic.

Between the ideal of relying upon sense experience and that of trusting to reason and logic, Donne felt himself torn throughout his life. Trained to an appreciation of the high importance of logic in Trinity College, Cambridge, he continued to let logic play with all the subtlety of a Scholastic over all his speculations in both prose and verse. Indeed, his appeal was always to

[10] *Ibid.*, l. 271.
[11] *Ibid.*, l. 303 f.
[12] *Ibid.*, l. 338.
[13] *Ibid.*, l. 387.

the intellect before the emotions. Yet in his youth, for several years he gave himself up with heart and soul to all kinds of emotional experiences, as eager apparently to experience through sensuous means as though he had been wedded to the empiric method of investigation. Over these perceptions a logic, enlivened by a fertile and ingenious fancy, played impishly and boldly. And although he grew ashamed of many of these lyrical expressions in his later life, especially in the dignity which attached to the deanship of St. Paul's, still much of the empirical quality remained. If, in his intellect, he despised the pedantry of being taught by sense and fantasy, much of both his poetry and his prose continues to bear evidence of the fruits of this teaching.

Rebelling against the classical ideal of poetry, especially the pseudo-classic concept of slavish imitation, he was desirous of making poetry more vital. He wanted it to express the life of his own day. But trained to look at life from an analytical and logical point of view with everything fixed and ordered according to a scholastic hierarchy, he felt troubled by a discrepancy of which he was painfully aware between the new thought and the medieval ideal. So intellectually he rebelled against these new ideas which were tending unmistakably towards the scientific attitude of today. But his naturally alert and inquiring mind, strengthened by this new point of view, even while he intellectually condemned it, made him speculate concerning it, play with some of the ideas, and take over much of the imagery which the new science supplied. Therefore, in his attempt to revitalize the stream of poetry he welcomed this new source which served to yield abundant material to his subtle fancy.

When he declared, however, that "witchcraft's charms bring not now their old fears, nor their old harms,"[14] he exhibited a scepticism that was more in harmony with the true scientific spirit, a scepticism, moreover, that was finding a frequent ex-

[14] Satire II, l. 17.

POETRY AND THE NEW SCIENCE

pression in the poetry of his time, such as Ben Jonson exhibited when he said of the alchemist:

> If all you boast of your great art be true;
> Sure, willing poverty has most in you.[15]

It was akin to the temper displayed later in the century by George Wither,

> But now, I think, it may a question be
> Whether the sun, the moon, and the stars be free;
> For sometimes false predictions they impart
> Or are belied by abused art.[16]

And again by Thomas Randolph, when, after a prediction that his Aunt Lane would give birth to a son, a daughter was born instead, the poet playfully demanded:

> Is Friar Bacon, nothing but a name?
> Or is all witchcraft brained with Dr. Lambe?
> Does none the learned Bungies soul inherit?
> Has Madame Danvers dispossest her spirit?[17]

And also by William Habington, when he declared,

> All these fond human misteries
are
> As the deceitful and unwise
> Distempers of our braine.[18]

Donne was very much more interested, however, in the new field of imagery which science opened up. Though perfectly well aware of the controversy that was then being waged between the Ptolemaic and the Copernican systems in the field of astronomy, he offers no apologies for employing the Ptolemaic when that suited his purpose best. Thus, desiring to illustrate that love is from its very nature changeable, he writes:

> If, as in water stir'd more circles bee
> Produced by one, love such additions take,

---
[15] "Epigrams," No. 6.
[16] "Of the Inconstancy and Weakness of Man." Satire I.
[17] "An Apology for his false Prediction."
[18] "Cupio Dissolvist," 6.

> Those like so many spheres, but one heaven make
> For they are all concentrique unto thee.[19]

Again, in arguing for variety in love, he draws upon astronomy for his imagery:

> The heavens rejoice in motions, why should I
> Abjure my so much lov'd variety
> And not with many youth and love divide.[20]

From mathematics he takes the image of the compass, when bidding his wife farewell.

> If they be two, they are so
> As stiffe twin compasses are two
> Thy soule the fix't foot, makes me slow
> To move, but doth, if the other doe.[21]

With geography in mind, he writes:

> The nose (like the first Meridian) runs
> Not 'twixt an East and West, but twixt two suns:
> It leaves a cheek, a rosie Hemisphere.[22]

From anatomy and physiology, he draws such images as nerves are sinew threads which "my brain lets fall through every part"[23] and

> When I am dead, and Doctors know not why
> And my friends curiositie
> Will have me cut up to survay each part;
> When they shall find your picture in my heart . . .[24]

and

> But as in cutting up a man that's dead,
> The body will not last out, to have read
> On every part, and therefore men direct
> Their speech to parts that are of most effect;
> So the world's carcase would not last, if I
> Were punctual in this anatomy;

---

[19] "Love's Growth," 1, 21.
[20] Elegy 17.
[21] "A Valediction: Forbidding Mourning." 1, 25.
[22] Elegy 18, "Love's Progress." 1, 47.
[23] "The Funerall." 1, 9.
[24] "The Dampe."

POETRY AND THE NEW SCIENCE 47

Nor smells it well to hearers, if one tell
Them their disease, who fain would think they're well.[25]

It is to be noted that Donne does not champion the new science, nor can it be said that his many ingenious images were drawn primarily from that source. The influence that science had upon him can best be seen, I believe, in his questioning attitude of mind, and in his tendency to experiment with poetic imagery. Much of his imagery was drawn from scientific analogies, and he pointed the way in this respect to many other English poets of his time. Thus, Richard Corbet speaks of contemporary political events in terms of astronomical imagery.[26] Phineas Fletcher, in his allegorical description of the human body, "The Purple Island," refers to veins, arteries, and nerves as a "thousand brooks in azure channels glide in silver sand." Here we have the converse of Donne's method—the facts of science are given a more literary connotation.

> Their serpent windings, and deceiving crooks
> Circling about, and wat'ring all the plain,
> Empty themselves into th' all-drinking main;
> And creeping forward slide, but ne'er return again.[27]

The skin
> ... is that round spreading fence
> Which like a sea, girts the Isle in every part.[28]

And the teeth are "twice sixteen porters, standing at the cave's mouth."[29]

Andrew Marvel is very fond of drawing his images from mathematics, as in the "Definition of Love."

> As lines, so loves, oblique may well
> Themselves in every angle greet:
> But our so truly parallel
> Though infinite, can never meet.

These few examples serve to illustrate the new source of imagery which the science of the seventeenth century was furnishing to

---

[25] "First Anniversary," p. 435.
[26] "A Letter to Sir Thomas Ailesbury," 1618.
[27] Canto II, st. 9.   [28] II, 16.   [29] II, st. 30.

poetry. Examples may be found in the work of nearly every poet after the time of Donne, until Waller, Denham, and Dryden (in the latter part of his life) reacted against the extravagant conceits which this method tended to encourage.

Donne did more, however, than merely show a sceptical attitude and draw some of his imagery from the new science. For while refusing to accept this as a revealer of the highest truth, he occasionally speculated along the pathway that biological science was to take. Note, for example, the purpose and intent of the "Progress of the Soul," in which he sought to represent through a metapsychosis the history of a soul in its ascent from the vegetable plane of existence, through the animal stage, and finally to the human plane. The underlying idea is that of a steady progress from a lower to a higher. Many of the ideas of his time, in so far as they tend to destroy a neat, orderly philosophical system, really annoyed him. He could not find anything amusing in the situation, as Samuel Butler (1612-80), did later in the century. Butler also refused to accept the new science as a revealer of the highest truth, but to him the whole scientific method and outlook furnished abundant material for his satirical pen. He satirized not only the superstitions of the past and the pseudo-science which he saw practiced about him, but also the experimental science, which he failed to distinguish from the pseudo-science. Of Hudibras, he says:

> In Mathematics he was greater
> Than Tycho Brahe, or Erra Pater:
> For he by Geometrie scale,
> Could take the size of Pots of ale;
> Resolve by Signs and Tangents, streight
> If bread and butter wanted weight;
> And wisely tell what hour of the day
> The clocks doth strike by Algebra.

He ridicules those who would evolve an explanation from their own natural reason. Thus, Ralph, the Squire of Hudibras

> Knew many an amulet and charm
> That would do neither good nor harm.

POETRY AND THE NEW SCIENCE

> . . . .
> He could fortell what's ever was
> By consequences to come to pass.
> As Death of Great Men, Alterations,
> Diseases, Battels, Inundations.
> All this without the eclipse of Sun,
> Or dreadful comet, he hath done
> By inward light, a way as good,
> And easie to be understood.
> But with more lucky hit than those
> That use to make the stars depose
> . . . . . .
> They'l feel the Pulses of the Stars
> To find out Agues, Coughs, Catarrhs.

Hudibras goes to visit the learned Sidrophel:

> He had been long t'wards Mathematicks
> Optick, Philosophy, and Staticks,
> Magic, Horoscopy, Astrology
> And was old Dog at Physiology.

It is quite evident that in the poet's mind all these stood more or less upon an equal footing. Mathematics and Physiology are just about on the same level as astrology. And yet after the Knight has seen Sidrophel, the poet through the Knight pours out some harsh invective upon the superstitions of the day.[30]

> Some (soothsayers) calculate the hidden fates,
> Of Monkeys, Puppy-dogs, and Cats
> . . . .
> Some take a measure of the lives
> Of fathers, mothers, husbands, wives.
> . . . .
> As if the Planete's first aspect
> The tender infant did infect
> In Soul and Body, and instill
> All future good, and future ill.
> . . . . . .
> Are not these fine commodities
> To be imported from the skies?
> And vended here among the Rabble,
> For staple goods and unwarantable?

---
[30] Pt. II, Canto III.

The scientists, however, come in for their full share of ridicule in "The Elephant in the Moon," a satire upon the Royal Society itself. The poet relates how the members look through a telescope at the moon and discover the inhabitants engaged in warfare. Then one member espies a mighty elephant broken loose. They see the elephant advance,

> And from the west side of the Moon
> To th' east was in a moment gone.

One of the wisest of their number then accounts for this strange phenomenon by the following ingenious explanation:

> ... As the earth and moon
> Do both move contrary upon
> Their axes, the rapidity
> Of both their motions cannot be
> But so prodigiously fast,
> That vaster spaces may be past
> In less time than the beast has gone,
> Though h' had no motion of his own,
> Which we can take no measure of
> As you have clear'd by learned proof.

From this data, the wise scientist proceeds to establish the hypothesis of the motion of the earth. Soon after this learned exposition, however, it was discovered that

> A mouse was gotten in
> The hollow tube, and shut between
> The two glass windows in restraint
> Was swell'd into an Elephant.

But some of the learned group, who had already written up and signed the account swore:

> That they never would recant
> One syllable of the Elephant.

And what of the war in the moon? When the tube is let down, they discover at the end, "prodigious swarms of flies and gnats, like men in arms." The constant occupation of the scientist is

> To measure wind, and weigh the air,
> And turn a circle to a square;

POETRY AND THE NEW SCIENCE

> To make a powder of the sun,
> By which all doctors should b' undone;
> To find the northwest passage out,
> Although the farthest way about;
> If chemists from a rose's ashes
> Can raise the rose itself in glasses?[31]

Obviously Samuel Butler was not indifferent to the scientific movement. The mere fact that he takes account of the theories of Hobbes, Gassendi, and Descartes bears this out, to say nothing of his attention to the doings of the Royal Society. But his point of view, in the main, is that of the Schoolman who is laughing at the efforts of science and philosophy striving for an existence independent of theology. That such a point of view can scarcely adjust itself to a true comprehension of what the new science is trying to do scarcely needs elucidation. John Donne, on the other hand, felt no such sense of security in the old scale of values. Before Milton, Cowley, and Henry More voiced their fears, he felt himself beset by the same doubts.

It will be recalled how this attitude is reflected in the second half of the century in *Paradise Lost* when the Tempter addresses the Tree of Knowledge:[32]

> Oh Sacred, Wise, and Wisdom-giving Plant,
> Mothers of Science, now I feel thy Power
> Within me cleere, not only to discerne
> Things in their causes, but to trace the wages
> Of highest agents, deemed however wise.

It was of the fruit of this tree that Eve tasted and tempted Adam, whereby occurred the fall of man. It was not merely that man disobeyed, but also because he sought to pry into divine or hidden knowledge:

> But apt the Mind or Fancie is to roave
> Uncheckt, and of her roaving is no end,
> Til warn'd, or by experience taught, she learne,
> That not to know at large of things remote

---

[31] "A Satire upon the Royal Society." Fragment.
[32] IX, 1, 679.

> From use obscure and suttle, but to know
> That which before us lies in daily life,
> Is the prime Wisdom, what is more, is fume,
> Or emptiness or fond impertinence.[33]

A similar note of warning is sounded by Abraham Cowley in "The Tree of Knowledge," and he points out in addition that Divine Truth must be assisted by Reason, for

> . . . in seas,
> So vast and dangerous as these,
> Our course by stars above we cannot know
> Without the compass too below."

By "Reason" he means, like Henry More and many others, the kind of reason which Plato championed, which is not primarily the result of empirical evidence built up by inductive processes, but that which is received by contemplation and by deductive means. Thus More in "A Platonic Song of the Soul" insists that

> Those things are true
> That utterly opunge our outward sense.
> Then are you forced to sense to bid adieu
> Not what your sense gainsayes to holden untrue."

The tendency to build up our truths from sense experience, as the Baconian philosophy advocated, would, thinks John Pomfret,[34] in process of time, "bind the soul in chains, and lord it o'er the mind."

> For now, who truth from falsehood would discern,
> Must first disrobe the mind, and all unlearn.

It is not surprising then that the Copernican hypothesis, still one of the most novel scientific formulations of the age, should receive slow acceptance at the hands of the seventeenth-century poets, especially when the theory was yet disputed in the ranks of the scientists themselves. Thus Milton describes the system in his *Paradise Lost* and compares it with the Ptolemaic, but

---

[33] VIII, 190 f.
[34] 1667-1702.

POETRY AND THE NEW SCIENCE 53

naturally he retains the Ptolemaic in his great epic. In the first place, it suited the conditions of the poem much better; secondly, it was in harmony with the poetic tradition of Dante's great poem; and thirdly, his own attitude towards the controversy might well, for all the evidence we have to the contrary, be expressed in the angel Raphael's reply to Adam's question concerning the motions of the heavenly bodies.[35]

> From Man or Angel the great Architect
> Did wisely to conceal, and not divulge
> His secrets to be scann'd by them who ought
> Rather admire; or if they list to try
> Conjecture, he his Fabric of the Heav'ns
> Hath left to their disputes, perhaps to move
> His laughter at their quaint Opinions wide
> Hereafter when they come to model Heav'n
> And calculate the Starrs, how they will weild
> The mightie frame, how build, unbuild, contrive
> To save appearances, how gird the Sphear
> With centric and Eccentric scribbl'd o're,
> Cycle and Epicycle, Orb in orb.

Then, turning more specifically to a consideration of the Copernican theory, the angel Raphael continues:

> God to remove his wayes from human sense,
> Plac'd Heav'n from Earth so farr, that earthly sight,
> If it presume, might ere in things too high,
> And no advantage gaine. What if the Sun
> Be center to the World, and other Starrs
> By his attractive vertue and their own
> Incited, dance about him various rounds?
> Their wandring course, now high, now low, then hid,
> Progressive, retrograde, or standing still,
> In six thou seest, and what if sev'nth to these
> The Planet Earth, so steadfast though she seem,
> Insensibly three different Motions move?
> . . . .
> Whether the Sun predominant in Heav'n
> Rise on the Earth, or Earth rise on the Sun,

---
[35] Book VIII, 72 f.

54 POETRY AND THE NEW SCIENCE

> Hee from the East his flaming rode begin,
> Or Shee from West her silent course advance
> With inoffensive pace that spinning sleeps
> On her soft Axle, while she paces Eev'n.
> And bears thee soft with the smooth Air along,
> Sollicit not thy thoughts with matters hid,
> Leave them to God above, him serve and feare;[36]

In brief, the purpose of knowledge, and its only excuse for being, is "to magnifie" the works of God.[37]

Henry More, however, finds himself confronted with something of a paradox when he considers the Copernican hypothesis as an expression of the new science. According to the revelation of his senses the Ptolemaic system is preferable, while the arguments for the Copernican hypothesis are based upon more abstract and generalized considerations. Therefore, in referring to the Soul he asks:

> Flies she to sense? sense pleads for Ptolemee.
> Flies she to her low phansie? that's so swayed
> By sense, and fore-imprest astronomie.
> By botch'd, incalcate paradigmes made
> By senses dictate, that they'll both persuade
> That Philolaus and wise Heraclide
> Be frantick both, Copernicus twice mad,
> She cannot then this question well decide,
> By ought but her own forms that in herself reside.[38]

Indeed, because sense seemed to favor the Ptolemaic system was a strong reason for accepting the Copernican hypothesis. He believes that Reason, in time, will fully sanction it. To the more ethically-minded poets, however, the acceptance of the Copernican hypothesis is fraught with dire disaster. Sir William Davenant speculates as to whether the sense of inferiority which such an acceptance must bring with it might not be salutary to man's overweening pride.

[36] Book VIII, 119f.
[37] Book VII, 95.
[38] "A Platonick Song of the Soul." Book III, Canto 2.

POETRY AND THE NEW SCIENCE

> Man's pride (grown to religion) he abates
>   By moving our Lov'd Earth; which we think fix'd;
> Think all to it, and it to none relates;
>   With others motions scorn to have it mix'd;
>
> As if 'twere great and stately to stand still
>   Whilst other Orbes dance on; or else think all
> Those vaste bright Globes (to show God's needless skill)
>   Were made but to attend our little Ball.[39]

Another effect of the Copernican theory upon the poets was to extend their notion of space. The universe of Dante was more compact and definite than the wider and vaguer Ptolemaic universe of Milton. William Drummond (1585-1649) especially appeared obsessed with the idea of "unbounded," "vast," and "far-extended" space. Note, when he is searching for a simile to express the greatness of God:

> As far beyond the starry walls of heaven,
> As is the loftiest of the planets seven
>
> . . . .
> Thou, all-sufficient, omnipotent,
> Thou ever-glorious, most excellent,
> God various in names, in essence one,
> High art installed on a goldern throne,
> Outreaching heaven's wide vasts, the bounds of nought,
> Transcending all the circles of our thought;
> With diamantine sceptre in thy hand.[40]

Also,

> What bands enclusterʼd near to these abide,
> Which into vast infinity them hide;
> Infinity that neither doth admit
> Place, time, nor number to encroach on it?[41]

Along with the growth of science in the seventeenth century went an increasing tendency to question many values which had been merely accepted before. About the middle of the century Robert Herrick declared:

---

[39] "Gondibert," Book II, Canto V, st. 19.
[40] "A Hymn to the Fairest Fair," l. 17 f.
[41] *Ibid.*, ll. 91-94. Note also ll. 153-58.

> Putrefaction is the end
> Of all that Nature doth entend.[42]

William Habington, at nearly the same time asked:
> Where sleeps the north-wind when the south inspires
> Life in the spring, and gathers into quires
> The scatter'd nightingales; whose subtle ears
> Heard first th' harmonious language of the spheares?
> Whence has the stone magneticke force t' allure
> Th' enamoured iron? From a seed impure
> Or natural did first the mandrake grow?
> What powre i' the ocean makes it ebbe and flow? . . .[43]

Sir Thomas Browne could write: "Let thy studies be free as thy thoughts and contemplations: but fly not only upon the wings of imagination. Join sense unto reason, and experiment unto speculation, and so give life unto embryonic truths, and verities yet in their chaos";[44] yet in his *Vulgar Errors* he bore witness to the fact that he was a prey to superstition and had very little real understanding of the meaning of the scientific attitude of mind. Although he was "a man of active scientific curiosity and philosophic imagination . . . over all his thinking is the pale cast of the medieval mind."[45] This is characteristic of much of the thinking of the period in which scepticism and credulity is strangly intermingled.

This spirit of inquiry and scepticism found very much fuller expression after the Restoration. The naturalism of Thomas Hobbes, who was in his seventies in 1660, along with his rationalistic temper and his principles derived entirely from nature, promulgating the far-reaching ethical doctrine that human nature at its basis is essentially selfish, was constantly growing in popularity. The generation which was just maturing at that time, and during the two decades which followed, tended to regard human nature from that standpoint. Rochester's[46] poem,

---

[42] "Putrefaction."
[43] "To Castara" (Of the Knowledge of Love).
[44] *Christian Morals*, part II, section V.
[45] William P. Dunn. *Sir Thomas Browne.* Columbia Dissertation.
[46] John Wilmot, 1647-80.

POETRY AND THE NEW SCIENCE

"A Satyr against Mankind" is an example. The poet declares that he would prefer to be a dog, a monkey, a bear

> Or anything, but that vain animal,
> Who is so proud of being rational.
> The senses are too gross, and he'll contrive
> A Sixth, to contradict the other five;
> And, before certain instinct will prefer
> Reason, which fifty times for one does err
> Reason, an ignis fatuus of the mind,
> Which leaves the light of nature, sense, behind.

He then pictures the "pathless dangerous wandering ways" that reason takes and makes "the misguided follower climb with pain mountains of whimsies, heapt in his own brain," who

> Stumbling from thought to thought, falls headlong down
> Into Doubt's boundless sea, where like to drown
> Books bear him up for a while, and make him try
> To swim with bladders of philosophy.

Finally, "After a search so painful and so long," he understands, "That all his life, he has been in the wrong." The poem concludes with the statement:

> Man differs more from men, than man from beast.

Mulgrave,[47] another of the rebel poets of the age, openely praised the naturalistic point of view,

> Our appetites are Nature's laws, and giv'n
> Under the broad authentic seal of Heav'n.[48]

To Hobbes he gives credit for this emancipation:

> While in dark ignorance we lay afraid
> Of fancies, ghosts, and every empty shade
> Great Hobbes appeared, and by plain Reason's light
> Put such fantastic forms to shameful flight.[49]

These sentiments, it is to be noted, are thoroughly in harmony with facts derived from experience rather than from authority, and these poets are no longer afraid of the new science, or its

---

[47] John Sheffield, 1649-1721.
[48] "The Rapture," l. 89.
[49] *Ibid.*

implications and applications, but are actually engaged in singing its praises.

If the spirit of the age tended to make some of the poets more analytical, they desired nevertheless to bring a certain order out of chaos. Note William Walsh's questioning analysis of love:

> Love is a medley of endearments, jars,
> Suspicions, quarrels, reconcilements, wars;
> Then peace again, Oh, would it not be best
> To chace the fatal poison from our breast?

And his conclusion,

> But since so few can live from passion free,
> Happy the man, and only happy he
> Who with such lucky stars begins his love,
> That his cool judgment does the choice approve.[50]

It was indeed a time when interest in science was gaining great momentum. In 1661 Robert Boyle published his *Sceptical Chemist;* in 1662 the Royal Society was officially founded. Charles II himself and many of his courtiers were interested in chemical experiments, and an ever increasing number found themselves intrigued by the mysteries of magnetism and the demonstrations of anatomy and medicine. "The principal men and women [of the court of Charles II]," declares Masson in his *Life of Milton,* "spoke and thought among themselves in the language of the shambles and the dissecting room." Thus science and pseudo-science were gaining the attention of an ever increasing audience, and they were stirring the imagination of more men and women than at any previous time in modern history. It is not surprising therefore, that there should be a change in the attitude of the poet towards science. Hence, Waller, at the age of fifty-eight, addressed some verses to Dr. George Rogers, on his taking the Degree of Doctor of Physics at Padua, 1664. Sir William Davenant in "Gondibert" described the course of scientific procedure in the house of Astragon. Cowley

---

[50] "To His Book."

wrote an "Ode upon Dr. Harvey," in which he fantastically compared Nature to Daphne and Harvey to Apollo, who pursues his beloved into the heart of man.

> Thus Harvey fought for truth in Truth's own book,
> The Creatures, which by God himself was writ;
>   And wisely thought 'twas fit
>   Not to read comments only upon it
> But on th' Original itself to look.[51]

In his lines "To the Royal Society," the poet says that philosophy has been kept in Nonage "till of late," because the Guardians and the Tutors,

> Some negligent, and some ambitious Men
> Would ne'er consent to set him free
> Or his own Natural Powers to let him see;
> Lest that should put an end to their Authority.

He then pictures authority as a creature having a body of condensed air which stalks about "like some old Giant's more Gigantic Ghost," and praises Bacon who slew this abnormality.

Cowley, it appears, grows very enthusiastic over the achievements of the new science. In his tract, "A Proposition for the Advancement of Experimental Philosophy," he says:

We want good Poets (I mean we have but few) who have purposely treated of solid and learned, that is, Natural Matters (the most part indulging in the Weakness of the World, and feeding it either with Follies of Love, or with the Fables of Gods and Heros) we conceive that one Booke ought to be compiled of all scatter'd little Parcels among the ancient Poets, that might serve for the Advancement of Natural Science.

He sought in his own person to advance natural science in verse by means of his Latin poem, "Plantarum Libri duo" (1662). He writes of herbs, flowers and trees, and he sees no reason why these should not be fit subjects for poetry, but the fact that the great poets have so rarely treated of them may be due to the fact that they were "discouraged by the greatness and almost

---

[51] St. 4.

inexplicable Variety of the Matter."[52] John Dryden declared: "A man should be learned in several sciences, and should have a reasonable, philosophical, and in some measure, a mathematical head to be a complete and excellent poet; and besides this, should have experience in all sorts of humors and manners of men."[53] One critic of Dryden has pointed out however, that although he was a member of the Royal Society still "he took a good deal of stock in astrology."[54]

In our own brief survey of how the new science which grew up in the seventeenth century affected the view point of some of the English poets, we have observed upon the part of a certain number a sense of uneasiness, of uncertainty, and occasionally a little resentment. Nevertheless, as the century advances, we find a tendency to question certain values of life, the validity of which had previously been assumed. A few poets celebrate in their verse certain scientific achievements. We have noted also upon the part of some an attitude which is no longer intolerant of experimental science, nor opposed to introducing the subject matter of science into poetry. Poetry, in fact, seems to be working towards a new synthesis, and in this respect is redolent of the eighteenth-century spirit. Yet the age is building up a sharp distinction between prose and poetry. Poetry is conceived as being more elevated than prose; it is regarded as a neat and epigramatic way of expressing a general truth. It has more regard for the practice and precepts of the classical writers, hence a high regard for tradition, which is not shared by the prose of the period. Poetry may treat, in the main, the same subjects as prose—philosophical, theological, and scientific—as long as the "rules" prescribing a definite decorum are painstakingly observed.

[52] Author's Preface to first two books.
[53] *Notes and Observations on the Empress of Morocco.* 1674.
[54] Mark Van Doren, *The Poetry of John Dryden.* N.Y., 1920.

CHAPTER IV

POETRY SOLEMNLY SURVEYS THE NEWTONIAN WORLD MACHINE

In 1687 Newton's *Principia Mathematica* was published, and thus was opened for the whole field of human thought the mathematical ideal of science. Its underlying philosophy is that the universe is a vast machine and that the goal of science is to discover the mathematical relations which hold in every part of that great mechanism. This is to be accomplished mainly through reasoning deductively from mathematical principles already discovered, but also by making facts derived empirically fit under some mathematical law, perhaps still undiscovered.[1] Thus was strengthened the position of Descartes, taken over forty years before, that man himself had been formed by mechanical means, though always under the governing power of God, and that he acts and reacts according to a complicated system of springs. Less than a quarter of a century after Descartes, Spinoza was attempting, in his *Ethics,* to deal with man's passions and motives, as if they were part of a geometric system. The idea that man was furnished with a sure guide in his conscience (i.e., a source of revelation of the divine will) was rudely shattered in 1690 with the publication of Locke's *Essay Concerning Human Understanding,* which denied the doctrine of innate ideas, and which made sensation the only source of knowledge. This knowledge was gained mechanically, inasmuch as man's mind was considered a blank tablet upon which experience wrote. Thus the new science and the philosophy which under-

[1] Preface to *Principia Mathematica.*

lay it offered a challenge to the conception of man as a free moral agent.

It would appear that such a doctrine of mechanism must tend to crowd out everything mysterious, supernatural, or divine. Logically it would do so, except for the fact that there must have been a Master Mechanic to build the Mechanism and to start it going. Newton argued that the world machine was not quite perfect and that it was constantly requiring regulation. The most classical expression of the argument from design came over a hundred years afterwards, in William Paley's *Natural Theology* (1802), in which he argued that the forms which organized bodies bear prove the necessity of an intellectual designer. This Deistic movement which aimed to preserve the ancient religion by making it rational, believed, in the main, that by taking out of religion the mysterious element, or nearly all of it, the reason, through scientific knowledge of how Nature works, would establish logically the existence of God. It attempted, in brief, a synthesis between orthodox religion and the new science. In England Deism continued to mark the most liberal religious thought until the last quarter of the eighteenth century, when we find the views of Hume and those of Gibbon, Tom Paine, and William Godwin coming to the fore. In France, however, as we shall note in the next chapter, a more atheistic point of view gained ground with greater rapidity.

Our purpose here is to note how English poetry in certain of the more outstanding instances reacted to these changes in philosophical and religious thought, in so far as this was itself acted upon by the new science. Poetry, as we have noted, has been sensitive at least in some of its aspects, to the philosophical and religious thought of the time. That eighteenth-century poetry was sensitive, in part at least, to these changing factors is evidenced by comparing Bernard de Mandeville's "Grumbling of the Hive" (1705),[2] with Pope's *Essay on Man* (1732-34).

[2] Rep't 1714 as "Fable of the Bees."

Mandeville upheld the idea of Hobbes, which we noted was current among some poets in the latter part of the seventeenth century, that selfishness and not the moral sense, is the sole principle by which man should be governed. Nay more, Nature herself is relentless, subjecting all her creatures to the vagaries of a ruthless chance. But in Pope's poem we have a versified exposition of the deistic position, as Pope[3] understood it from Bolingbroke. Here nature is conceived in a very different light from that which prompted those seventeenth-century poets and Mandeville himself. Although Nature is a "mighty maze," it is "not without a plan."[4] Like Milton, he is going to attempt to "vindicate the ways of God to Man."[5] Since man can see only a part and not the whole, he cannot know God's plan.[6] Man's time is a moment and his space is only a point.[7] The universe in all its parts works harmoniously and keeps a fixed order, which only the "madness, pride, impiety," of "a vile worm" could expect to have changed for his special benefit.[8] Therefore, "whatever is, is right."[9] Man should not presume to scan God, but "the proper study of Mankind is Man."[10] Then follows a section in which the poet endeavored to fit the physical sciences into his scheme of values,[11] and in which he concludes that this knowledge is of little worth to the individual himself. Of the two principles of man, Self-love and Reason, both are equally necessary, but it is the office of Reason to distinguish between the good and the bad. "The state of Nature was the reign of God."[12] Reason teaches that man serves himself best

[3] 1688-1744.
[4] *Essay on Man,* I, 6.
[5] I, 16.
[6] I, 60.
[7] I, 72.
[8] I, 256-57.
[9] I, 294.
[10] II, 1-2.
[11] II, 19-51.
[12] III, 147.

who serves the welfare of society. The Universal cause acts by general laws, and happiness subsists not in one but in all.[13] "Order is Heav'n's first law."[14] Faith, Law, Morals, all end in Love of God and Love of Man.[15] Self-love wakes the virtuous mind to action,[16] extending to friend, parent, neighbor, country, and finally the whole human race.

Pope is content to rest upon the assurance which his reason gives him that there is a "Great First Cause" about which he can know little, and beside which he feels very insignificant and blind, but which, because of the law and order that he finds in the world, he "knows" to be right and good.[17]

This act of "faith," as we must term it in contradiction to "knowledge," seems to contain nothing contradictory so far as the poet is aware. But can we blame the poet, when so many philosophers and theologians of his time were falling into the same fallacy of arguing from design? Or, ought we to term this a "rationalization," in the sense that James Harvey Robinson defines the term, as "the spontaneous and loyal support of our preconceptions"?[18] At any rate, Hume had not yet pointed out the fallacy in this argument. Whether it is to the credit of the poets that they have steadfastly refused to accept the mechanical explanation as the final one, is a question that will naturally be answered according to one's scientific creed or one's philosophy. It is a fact, however, that Pope consistently declined to endorse this principle in its entirety. So sure is he that there is a divine plan of some kind towards which everything is working, and also because the thoroughly scientific attitude in its implications at least refuses to take account of this, the poet condemns what he considers the presumptions of science. He who mounts

[13] IV, 37.
[14] IV, 49.
[15] IV, 340.
[16] IV, 363.
[17] "The Universal Prayer," Globe Edition of Pope, p. 227.
[18] "On Various Kinds of Thinking," in *The Mind in the Making*.

"where Science guides," and measures earth, weighs airs, and states the tides, et cetera, is like him who attempts to "Teach Eternal Wisdom how to rule."[19]

> Superior beings, when of late they saw
> A mortal Man unfold all Nature's law,
> Admir'd such wisdom in an earthly shape,
> And shew'd a Newton as we shew an Ape.[20]

He warns the Scientist that he must be modest. If we would see what Science really is,

> First strip off all her equipage of Pride;
> Deduct what is but Vanity, or Dress,
> Or Learning's Luxury, or Idleness;
> Or tricks to shew the stretch of human brain,
> Mere curious pleasure, or ingenious pain;
> Expunge the whole, or lop th' excrescent parts
> Of all our Vices have created Arts;
> Then see how little the remaining sum,
> Which serv'd the past, and must the time to come![21]

The tendency of modern science to rely too much upon the testimony of the senses is apt to promote false pride in us, because,

> To observations which ourselves we make
> We grow more partial for th' Observer's sake;
> To written Wisdom, as another's less:
> Maxims are drawn from Notions, those from Guess.[22]

Furthermore,

> How little, mark! that portion of the ball,
> Where faint at best, the beams of Science fall.[23]

Indeed, many of the scientists whom he has observed, or conjured up in his imagination, deserve, he thinks, to be classified among the dunces, and Science itself is pictured as groaning beneath the footstool of the Goddess of Dullness. These dull ones,

---

[19] *Essay on Man,* II, 19-30.
[20] *Ibid.,* II, 31-34.
[21] Epistle II, 43-52.
[22] *Moral Essays,* Epistle I. "To Sir Richard Temple," Globe Edition, p. 229.
[23] *Dunciad,* III, ll. 83-4.

> Full in the midst of Euclid dip at once,
> And petrify a Genius to a Dunce:
> Or set on Metaphysic ground to prance,
> Show all his paces, not a step advance.[24]

A gloomy clerk, "whose pious hope aspires to see the day when Moral Evidences shall quite decay," dogmatizes upon the meaning of contemporary science thus:

> Let others creep by timid steps, and slow,
> On plain Experience lay foundations low,
> By common sense to common knowledge bred,
> And last, to Nature's cause thro' Nature led,
> All-seeing in thy mists, we want no guide,
> Mother of Arrogance, and Source of Pride!
> We nobly take the high Priori Road
> And reason downward, till we doubt of God;
> Make Nature still encroach upon his plan;
> And shove him off as far as e'er we can:
> Thrust some Mechanic cause into his place;
> Or bind in Matter, or diffuse in Space.[25]

Is not the poet here deploring that characteristic which he feels is lying implicit, at least in eighteenth-century science, "Of naught so doubtful as of Soul and Will," and which is tending to see God as Lucretius saw him, a God,

> Wrapt up in Self, a God without a Thought,
> Regardless of our merit or default.[26]

Many other poets and writers in the eighteenth century felt that the scientists were presumptuous and filled with overweening pride. Swift's ridicule of the philosophers and the scientists in Gulliver's voyage to Laputa is a case in point. Dr. Arbuthnot, likewise, while finding much to praise in mathematics, nevertheless, ridicules the abuses of learning and pedantry in his contribution to the Scriblerus Club (1713-14).

Mark Akenside, however, composed a "Hymn to Science"[27]

[24] *Ibid.*, III, l. 264.
[25] *Ibid.*, IV, l. 465 f.
[26] *Ibid.*, IV, p. 484.
[27] Published in *Gentleman's Magazine*, Oct. 1739.

in which he bade Science descend and "illumine each bewildered thought" and "bless" his "laboring mind," disperse phantoms, scholasts' learning, sophists' cant, visionary bigot's rant, monk's philosophy.
> Let thy powerful charms impart
> The patient head, the candid heart,
> Devoted to thy sway.

But he also prays that he may proceed cautiously
> And from the dead, corporeal mass,
> Through each progressive order, pass
> To Instinct, Reason, God.

Science is warned, moreover, against soaring "too high, in that divine abyss," and admonished to be content to lend "thy beams" to faith and
> Make me the judge of my desires,
> The master of my heart.

Akenside showed a discrimination in his handling of the problem, that appeared all too rare. He pointed out that there were three classes of truth: "matter of fact, experimental, or scientific truth; which last is either metaphysical or geometrical, either purely intellectual or perfectly abstracted."[28]

Among the poets who championed science, James Thomson (1700-48) is worthy of an important place, not because he wrote one of the many poems on Newton, but because of the knowledge of science he displayed in that poem, and the attitude which he manifested. The poet, writing just after Newton's death in 1727, who speaks of himself as aspiring like the "ethereal flames . . . in Nature's general symphony to join,"[29] does not, as Cowley did, depict Newton Apollo-like chasing Daphne into the secret heart of man, but as one who,
> . . . from motion's simple laws
> Could trace the secret hand of Providence
> Wide-working through the universal frame.[30]

---
[28] "Pleasures of Imagination," 1765, Book II.
[29] "To the Memory of Sir Isaac Newton." I, 10-11.
[30] *Ibid.*, I, 14 f.

He "sat not down and dreamed Romantic schemes,"[31] but

> ... with heroic patience years on years
> Deep-searching, saw at last the system dawn,
> And shine, of all his race, on him alone.[32]

The poet then enumerates more specifically what Newton contributed to science: the principle of gravitation,[33] a declaration concerning the influence of the moon upon the tides,[34] the fact that the stars are all suns, subject to the laws of gravitation as our own solar system,[35] that the comet pursues a long elliptic curve, that sound proceeds by waves,[36] that a ray of sunlight can be broken up into its component parts by passing it through a prism,[37] and innumerable other things.[38] Thomson asks:

> Did ever poet imagine aught so fair,
> Dreaming in whispering groves by the hoarse brook?[39]

Another virtue displayed by the scientist is the order-bringing characteristic of his work, restoring "whirling vortices and circling spheres to their first great simplicity."[40] Surely such a great man, the poet says in effect, must be more than a "finer breath of spirits dancing through the tubes awhile, and then forever lost in vacant air."[41] Indeed, in the case of this renowned scientist, the poet boasts, "his devotion swelled responsive to his knowledge":

> For could he
> Whose piercing mental eye diffusive saw

---

[31] Ibid., I, 24-25.
[32] Ibid., I, 28 f.
[33] Ibid., I, 41.
[34] Ibid., I, 52.
[35] Ibid., I, 59-68.
[36] Ibid., I, 91-92.
[37] Ibid., I, 96 f.
[38] Ibid., I, 132 f.
[39] Ibid., I, 118 f.
[40] Ibid., I, 83-84.
[41] Ibid., I, 168 f.

> The finished university of things
> In all its order, magnitude and parts
> Forbear incessant to adore that Power
> Who fills, sustains, and actuates the whole?[42]

The poet can eulogize the scientist because the scientist recognizes something more than mere mechanism. The issue between a world-machine and a loving personal God is not at all clearly drawn; but we feel, if it were, the poet would be upon the side of religion.

About seventeen years after Thomson penned his lines, and about a decade after Pope's *Essay on Man,* another poet was turning the same problems over in his mind. Edward Young (1683-1765) wrote *The Complaint, or Night Thoughts,* in 1742-44, the occasion of some of these gloomy thoughts being the deaths of his wife and his step-daughter. Although he often mused conventionally, as shown in the following lines,

> Not deeply to discern, not much to know
> Mankind was born to wonder, and adore,[43]

yet during the course of his thinking he found himself beset with many doubts. In the first place, the great sense of space which the new science has revealed rather terrifies him:

> What involution! what extent! what swarms
> Of worlds, that laugh at earth? immensely great!
> Immensely distant from each other's spheres
> What, then, the wondrous space thro' which they roll?
> At once it quite engulf's all human thought;
> 'Tis comprehension's absolute defeat.[44]

and furthermore,

> The boundless space, thro' which these rovers take
> Their restless roam, suggests the sister thought
> Of boundless time.[45]

---

[42] *Ibid.,* I, 137 f.
[43] *The Complaint,* Night IX, p. 325.
[44] *Ibid.,* IX, p. 298.
[45] *Ibid.,* IX, p. 301.

On the other hand, however, the conception of the world as a machine seems a comfort:

> Nor think thou seest a wild disorder here;
> Through this illustrious chaos to the sight,
> Arrangement neat, and chastest order reign.
> The path prescrib'd inviolably kept,
> Upbraids the lawless sallies of mankind.[46]

There seems to be then, a great plan in nature:

> We rave, we wrestle, with great nature's plan:
> We thwart the Deity; and 'tis decreed,
> Who thwarts his will, shall contradict their own.
> Hence our unnatural quarrels with ourselves;
> Our thoughts at enmity, our bosom broils . . .[47]

In that case the cure for all this melancholy and doubt is to "read Nature" which "bids dead matter aid us in our creed."[48]

So many scientists, he complains, fail to read the moral truth which lies in nature:

> And dive in science for distinguisht names,
> Dishonest fomentation of your pride;
> Sinking in virtue, as you rise in fame.
> Your learning, like the lunar beams, affords
> Light, but not heat; it leaves you undevout,
> Frozen at heart, while speculation shines.[49]

And anyway, there is something in the scientific temper of his time that appears more curious than devout,

> More fond to fix the place of heaven, or hell,
> Than studious this to shun, or that secure.[50]

But, from his religion comes the thought that:

> Humble love,
> And not proud reason, keeps the door of heaven;
> Love finds admission, where proud science fails.

---

[46] *Ibid.*, IX, p. 298.
[47] *Ibid.*, II, p. 25.
[48] *Ibid.*, IV, p. 86.
[49] *Ibid.*, V, p. 116.
[50] *Ibid.*, IX, p. 324.

POETRY AND NEWTONIAN SCIENCE

> Man's science is the culture of his heart;
> And not to lose his plummet in the depths
> Of nature, or the more profound of God.[51]

Indeed,

> Take God from nature, nothing is left;
> Man's mind is in a pit, and nothing sees.[52]

The poet finds comfort that in the wondrous motions of the heavenly bodies a design is to be seen. He cannot bear the thought that the world is simply a vast machine. The planets, cast off from the sun, feel something of the great central love.

> By sweet attraction, no less strongly drawn;
> Aw'd, and yet raptur'd; raptur'd, yet serene:[53]

The forces which the scientist labels as mechanical are thus personified by Young in terms of an egocentric world. In his thinking he has not even yet sensed the deep significance of the Newtonian physics. He has, perhaps, a premonition of what it may mean, but against the logical implication of the idea he rebels. And with reason, I think it must be admitted, because according to the classical tradition, the poet should seek to express beauty. It is true, as Thomson pointed out, that the scientist may also express beauty; but as Lucretius found, it is difficult to make a mechanical idea of life appear beautiful to people who have been nourished upon the other conception. The scientist has to close his eyes and heart to most of his natural inclinations and desires; he is a scientist, primarily through great mental discipline. The poet, on the other hand, at least according to the traditions he has inherited, must address man's feelings as well as his intellect. The relative proportions of feeling and intellect which have gone into poetry, have of course, varied from time to time, and to a certain extent, with man and man within any given period. In the main, however, one period demands more of one element than the other. In this sense, at

[51] *Ibid.*, IX, p. 324.
[52] *Ibid.*, IX, p. 308.
[53] *Ibid.*, IX, p. 324.

least, the eighteenth century, especially the first half, tended to exact more of the intellectual element in poetry than the element of feeling. The poets in the main, however, in England—and this appears to be a very vital fact in our discussion—could not bring themselves to sing whole-heartedly about a mechanical world. It remains for us, then, to consider to what extent the traditional elements in poetry can account for this fact.

It will be recalled that for Aristotle poetry was an ideal imitation of truth and that its aim was aesthetic pleasure. While this theory, to be sure, did not attract a great deal of attention in either the ancient or the medieval periods, it became very prominent in Italy during the sixteenth century, spread to France in the seventeenth, and was reflected in English criticism during the first half of the eighteenth. This pseudo-classicism came to have implications which the original theory never intended. These principles were regarded in the light of laws formulated by the ancients, but which had all the force of the scientific laws of a Newton. Indeed, they were regarded in much the same light.

> Those Rules of old discover'd, not devis'd,
> Are Nature still, but Nature methodiz'd.[54]

Therefore,

> Learn hence for ancient rules a just esteem
> To copy Nature is to copy them.[55]

The poet owed little or nothing to that very intangible thing known as "inspiration." Poetry was an art, the rules of which had been supplied by the Ancients. One could become a poet almost mechanically, then, by following the precepts and examples of these legislators.

If there was something rather machine-like in that idea of poetry, there was at the same time, something which marked a difference in attitude between the poet and the scientist. Thus,

---

[54] Pope's "Essay on Criticism." I, 88.
[55] *Ibid.*, I, 139.

while the true poet must look backward for his guide and counsel, the scientist (when he was most worthy of that name) was looking forward to new formulations and discoveries in the future. This difference in outlook tended naturally to keep the work of the scientist and the poet apart, even though both might be equally rational. Poetry in looking back, was fostering respect for a traditional past; science, on the other hand, was shaking off the shackles of that same past. No wonder, then, that poetry should feel itself more in harmony with theological and traditional philosophy than with science. Hence, the poet Thomson pictures poetry as

>   Tutored by Philosophy and informing the page
>   With music, image, sentiment, and thought,
>   Never to die; the treasure of mankind,
>   Their highest honour, and their truest joy![56]

One of the best expositions of the pseudo-classicism in England was that given by Samuel Johnson, after the full force of the movement had already spent itself. He, it will be recalled maintained that the function of art was to express the typical rather than the particular and that only the best examples should be exhibited.[57] It is necessary to imitate only those parts of nature "which are proper for imitation."[58] The theory which primarily keeps science and poetry apart, however, is the fact that

Poetry cannot dwell upon the minute distinctions, by which one species differs from another, without departing from that simplicity of grandeur which fills the imagination; nor dissect the latent qualities of things without losing its general power of gratifying every mind, by recalling its conceptions.[59]

Johnson, however, was not a slave to rules. "Whatever part of an art," he writes in one connection, "can be executed or criticized by rules, that part is no longer the work of genius, which

---

[56] "Summer," 1, 1753 f.
[57] *The Rambler*, No. 4.
[58] *Ibid.*
[59] *The Rambler*, No. 36, "The Reasons that Pastorals Delight," p. 178.

implies excellence out of the reach of rules."[60] Indeed, his allowance for genius, for enthusiasm,[61] for novelty,[62] may not be orthodox pseudo-classicism, but it does not tend to bring science and poetry any nearer. On the contrary, it is looking in the direction of a further revolt.

Are we justified in concluding then, that the English poet's respect for tradition in the first half of the eighteenth century is a sufficient explanation of the fact that he does not whole-heartedly praise the conception of a mechanical world? Or are we to assume with William Blake, considerably later, that imagination and reason are really inimical, though perhaps not necessarily irreconcilable?

Believing that his poems, or at least large portions of them, were truly the products of supernaturalism, William Blake (1757-1827) very naturally could not rest content with ideas built entirely upon human experience.[63] It is true, as some critics have pointed out, that many of his poems have received careful and painstaking revision at his hands, yet believing in inspiration as he did, he condemned what he considered the mocking spirit of Voltaire and Rousseau against religion:

> The Atoms of Democritus
> And Newton's Particles of Light
> Are sands upon the Red Sea Shore,
> Where Israel's tents do shine so bright.[64]

Yet, it is hardly fair to Blake to attribute his antagonism to science entirely to religion, for with him it went very much deeper than any creed. He was concerned very much more with the limitations of the reasoning power itself:

[60] *The Adventurer*, No. 76.
[61] *Ibid.*, No. 79.
[62] *Ibid.*, No. 82.
[63] He testifies that many passages of his poems were dictated to him directly by spirits. See Diary, Reminiscences, and Correspondence of Henry Crabbe Robinson. Boston. 1880, Vol. 2, pp. 34, 38-39.
[64] "Mock on, mock on, Voltaire, Rousseau." Ll. 9-12.

POETRY AND NEWTONIAN SCIENCE

> The Reasoning Power in Man . . . is a false Body,
> an Incrustation over my Immortal Spirit, a selfhood
> which must be put off and annihilated alway.[65]

He is, moreover, attacking a particular power of the mind—that of drawing generalizations from sense data and regarding these as sufficient explanations of final causes. And right there, it seems to me, lies Blake's special significance for this study. He definitely connected that attitude of mind with the Baconian and Newtonian philosophy in a time when such a clear understanding of the matter, particularly upon the part of a poet, was all too rare.

> For Bacon and Newton, sheath'd in dismal steel, their
> terrors hang
> Like iron scourges over Albion, Reasoning like vast
> Serpents
> Enfold around my limbs, bruising my minute articulations.[66]

Furthermore, he states definitely that he is opposed to a "Philosophy of Five Senses . . . complete," which was given "into the hands of Newton and Locke."[67] Note, in addition, how he characterizes the machine-age:

> I turn my eyes to the Schools and Universities of Europe,
> And there behold the Loom of Locke, whose Woof rages
> dire,
> Wash'd by the Water-wheels of Newton: black the cloth
> In heavy wreaths folds over every Nation: cruel works
> Of many Wheels I view, wheel without wheel, with cogs
> tyrannic,
> Moving by compulsion each other; not as those in Eden,
> which,
> Wheel within wheel, in freedom revolve, in harmony
> and peace.[68]

Whatever we may feel about Blake's visionary propensities, it is indeed clear that he understood the character of the New-

---

[65] "Milton," f. 42, ll. 34-36.
[66] A Vision of Albion,—from "Jerusalem," f. 15, ll. 11-12.
[67] The Song of Los, ll. 47-48.
[68] "Jerusalem," f. 15, ll. 14-20.

tonian science and its implications better than the other poets we have been considering in this chapter, and better, I believe, than any English poet contemporary with him. The issue that the acceptance of the mechanical conception of the universe also implied logically the rejection of all forms of supernaturalism was clearly perceived by him:

> But the spectre, like hoar-frost and a mildew, rose over Albion,
> Saying, 'I am God, O Sons of Men! I am your Rational Power
> Am I not Bacon and Newton and Locke, who teach humility to Man,
> Who teach Doubt and Experiment? and my two wings, Voltaire, Rousseau?
> Where is that Friend of Sinners, that Rebel against my Laws,
> Who teaches Belief to the Nations, and an unknown Eternal Life?
> Come hither into the desert and turn these stones to bread!
> Vain, foolish Man wilt thou believe without Experiment,
> And build a World of Phantasy upon my great Abyss,
> A World of Shapes in craving lust and devouring appetite?"[69]

The consequences of such a philosophy are very apparent to him, for if our knowledge is to be limited to only what our five senses reveal to us and these generalizations are to be taken as the final words then "the Philosophic and Experimental would soon be at the Ratio of all things; and stand still, unable to do other than repeat the same dull round over again."[70] But from this, we are saved, he declares, by the "Poetic or Prophetic Character."[71] Indeed, the real world is the world of Imagination, of which "this Vegetable Universe is but the faint shadow."[72]

This explains, in part, at least, his opposition to classicism, for the "Grecian is Mathematic Form: Gothic is Living Form.

[69] "Jerusalem," f. 54, ll. 15-24.
[70] Oxford Edition of Blake's *Poetical Works*, p. 426.
[71] *Ibid.*
[72] "Jerusalem," f. 77.

POETRY AND NEWTONIAN SCIENCE

Mathematic Form is eternal in the Reasoning Memory: Living Form is Eternal Existence."[73] "We do not want either Greek or Roman models if we are but just and true to our Imaginations."[74] He does not mean to imply, however, that the ancient writers were not inspired. In the new age "those grand works of the more ancient and consciously and professedly inspired men will hold their proper rank and the Daughters of Memory shall become the Daughters of Inspiration."[75] In brief, poetry is not to be regarded as the handmaid of science or philosophy. Instead, "let the Philosopher always be the servant and scholar of Inspiration."[76]

Even though Blake's attitude appears at first to be one that definitely places poetry and science in opposition, he does not, it will be noted, state that the poet should eschew science. Rather, his own concern for, and his discussions of, space, time, and infinity, and the limitations of the scientific attitude of mind would belie any such conclusion had he made it.[77] His main quarrel with the scientific point of view is, as we have already seen, that it is all too content to rest upon the assumption that the dictums derived from sense experience and from experimentation constitute the one and only truth. He steadfastly refuses, for example, to accept the idea of mechanism as being the whole explanation of human existence. Instead, this higher truth, he believes, is revealed through poetry, which pierces beyond the veil of semblance and discovers the true essence beyond.

But how is poetry to reveal this truth which transcends human experience? That was Blake's problem, to which he addressed himself assiduously. Poetry, of course, must express beauty. The poet, therefore, must strive to render this trans-

---

[73] "On Virgil"—"Poems," p. 431.
[74] "Milton," from the Preface.
[75] *Ibid.*
[76] From, *Descriptive Catalogue,* see "Poems," p. 439.
[77] "Poems," pp. 372, 373, 378, 387.

cendent truth in sensuous form, to translate his conception into an image which shall serve as a key or a symbol, just as the luminous eye of the tiger symbolizes the whole tiger in a dark jungle,

> Tiger! Tiger burning bright
> In the forests of the night.[78]

He tried, in brief,

> To see a World in a grain of sand,
> And a Heaven in a wild flower.[79]

It scarcely needs to be pointed out that this is a dangerous pathway to tread, because it so easily leads into the morass of visions imperfectly realized and of obscurities which are apparently meaningless, and this was the fate which overtook many of the so-called prophetic books of Blake in the latter part of his life.

In these prophetic books he sought myths to express, not the latest philosophical truths, but the truth which is itself the source of philosophy—the immediate revelation of which poets and prophets partake. Since these works cover a comparatively long period of time, his mythological characters, symbolizing the higher truth, undergo many modifications in the course of his labors; but in the main it is fairly clear, thanks to some recent researches,[80] what Blake was attempting to accomplish. When, for example, he wished to symbolize the "Eternal Essence," he sometimes referred to it as "Jesus" and sometimes as the "Four Zoas," of which he says:

> What are the Natures of those Living Creatures the
>   Heavenly Father only
> Knoweth! No individual Knoweth, nor Can Know in all
>   Eternity.[81]

---

[78] *Ibid.*, "The Tiger," p. 85.

[79] *Ibid.*, "Auguries of Innocence," p. 171.

[80] *The Prophetic Writings of William Blake*, by D. J. Sloss and J. P. R. Wallis, in two volumes, published by the Clarendon Press, Oxford, in 1926, is a work that is especially illuminating on this point.

[81] "Four Zoas," I, 7-8.

POETRY AND NEWTONIAN SCIENCE 79

From this Eternal Essence, he represents the creator of men (symbolized as Urizen) separating himself and existing in time. So Time (symbolized by Los) came to have a separate existence from the Eternal Essence; and Space (personified as Enitharmon), by seceding from Time, is still further removed from Eternal Truth. Thus, the assertion of selfhood tends to take one further away from the initial Truth, and this fact he represents symbolically by the Fall of Man.

Whatever we may feel about Blake's success in accomplishing what he set out to do, we must acknowledge that his attempt was at least significant, because obviously he was trying to make poetry perform a very difficult task: to present not merely abstract truths in sensuous imagery, but also mystical, intuitive perceptions, and

... to open the immortal Eyes
Of Man inwards into the Worlds of Thought, into Eternity
Ever expanding in the Bosom of God, the Human Imagination.[82]

If our conclusion is that Blake did not succeed entirely in his purpose, that decision does not, of course, imply that the task is impossible. With that question we are not here immediately concerned. But with his objections to representing the mechanical conception in poetry and in insisting that true poetry must deal with sensuous images and not abstractions, he is running counter to much of the poetic theory of the eighteenth century. Nor is his insistence that poetry and science are essentially different due to his respect for poetic tradition, or entirely to religious scruples, but rather to his steadfast belief that the poetic power transcends the powers of the human mind.

Are we to accept his declaration that the poet presents a truer picture of reality than the scientist? And are we to conclude that his objection to the mechanical ideal which eighteenth-century science had set for itself, along with the protestations of the other poets we have been considering, is valid? Before

[82] Blake, *Jerusalem*, 5, ll. 18-21.

attempting to come to a conclusion in regard to these questions, let us see how some of the eighteenth-century poets in France applied more logically and consistently the philosophy of mechanism.

Chapter V

POETRY ADVANCES A STEP TOWARDS THE CONCEPTION OF THE WORLD MACHINE: VOLTAIRE AND ANDRÉ CHÉNIER

1. The Age of Voltaire

We have remarked that in eighteenth-century France the philosophy of mechanism was worked out more logically and more completely than in England. If we accept as our major premise that the universe is a vast machine and if we specifically include man, then it is illogical to make any exceptions when difficulties in philosophy and religion assert themselves; we should proceed boldly to the inevitable conclusion. Just in so far as we can do this, we may be said to possess the scientific attitude of mind. We have noted the difficulty that English thinkers encountered when they took the conception of mechanism as their major premise, and we have noted the aversion of the poets towards such a conception. In what respects, then, were the French in the eighteenth century more logically consistent than the English?

The notion of the world as a machine had certainly been voiced in Descartes' system of thought, but he had made an exception of God and of the soul. Pierre Bayle (1647-1706) was a precursor of the more thoroughgoing sceptical spirit in France, in so far as[1] he emphasized the opposition between reason and revelation. In such a conflict, however, he declares, it is reason that must give way. This was about as far as radical thought

---

[1] In "Thoughts on the Comet," 1682.

had proceeded in France before Voltaire made his eventful journey to England (1726-29), where he learned much of English empiricism, as it was exemplified in the work of Newton, Locke, and the Deists in general. It seemed to Voltaire that the Newtonian physics gave to man the necessary assurance that the law of cause and effect held throughout the universe; it appealed to him as sounder than the poetized Cartesianism of Fontenelle, who had been popularizing the physics of Descartes in the salons of Paris. So upon his return to France in 1729, he proceeded to expound the Newtonian physics and to insist, with all the fire of his personality and the wit of his rapier-like tongue, that ecclesiasticism and superstition were holding mankind from knowing their true heritage. He wanted man to realize his limitations and his possibilities, but not have him close his mind to facts as they existed. Perfectly content to adopt the agnostic attitude about many things, he did not feel that atheism was necessarily the outcome. Some power or force had obviously started things moving; he believed that there were evidences of a great Intelligence at work behind these. He wanted, however, in so far as it was possible, to deal with objects which his senses revealed to him, with tangible things rather than with abstract or imaginary concepts. He had very much the scientific attitude in this respect. He had faith in the dictums of science, and if reason and authority conflicted, it was authority that must give way to reason. That he faced resolutely and unflinchingly. In that regard he embodied the spirit of the philosophes and the makers of the great Encyclopedia (1752-72), who were attempting to extend logically and completely the principles of mechanical science into the various fields of human thinking. Voltaire must have viewed with a certain amount of satisfaction the activities of such men as La Mettrie, Condillac, Helvetius, and D'Holbach.

La Mettrie gave greater impetus to the mechanical idea towards the middle of the century by his two books, *Histoire naturelle de l'âme,* and *L'Homme Machine.* Condillac "worked out the epistemological and psychological basis of the French Enlightenment Philosophy."[2] In *De l'Esprit* (1755), Helvetius argued that it is interest alone which dictates all our judgments, and that the virtues or vices of the people depend on the goodness or badness of legislation. Hence, by wise legislation and education, selfishness and all the evil passions can be eradicated, and so philosophy through the Utopian Age can be ushered in. Baron d'Holbach's *La Systeme de la Nature* (1770), marked the furthermost development of the ideas of the Encyclopedists, in denying the existence of God, and in maintaining that there is nothing in the universe save matter in spontaneous movement.

Voltaire, however, could not accept this extreme view. His position was somewhere between the English thinkers and D'Holbach. Nevertheless he gave a great impetus to the whole movement. In fact, the effect of the science which had bloomed in England in the seventeenth century found its fullest cultivation and extension in France in the second half of the eighteenth century. Not only as a prime mover in this Enlightenment Philosophy does Voltaire deserve a prominent place in our account, but also because he was one of the leading literary figures of the period. But the movement of thought which he championed in philosophy, and in fact, upon general principles as well, encountered an obstacle in his theory and practice of literature.

As a youth he had written verses, trifles for the most part, very much in the poetic style of the period—a period which still cherished the teachings of Malherbe and the examples of Boileau in Horatian satire, the Vers de Société of Voiture, the bacchanalian songs of Saint-Amant, the fables of La Fontaine; but an age which was growing fonder of epigrammatic expres-

---

[2] Höffding: *History of Modern Philosophy,* Vol. I, p. 466.

sions, and which was seeking to express its poetry, for the most part, in lyric quatrains or in the form of pindaric odes.

After his experience in England, however, life presented a somewhat more serious aspect to him. At any rate, he bent a great part of his energy towards establishing among his countrymen the Newtonian hypothesis and many of its far-reaching implications. He did this in his prose treatises, in his prose romances, and in verse. When Cardinal de Polignac, for example, reacted against the mechanical conception of nature in his "Anti-Lucretius" (1745), and attempted to establish the dualistic system sanctioned by the Cartesians, Voltaire attacked his position, first directly in prose, and then indirectly by singing the praises of Newton and of the mechanical philosophy in verse.

He declared, in his attack upon the "Anti-Lucretius," that the Newtonian philosophy should not be discussed in verse; that since it is founded wholly on geometry, it eludes the grasp of a true poet. Poetry might, he agrees, embellish the outside of the system, but those who mean to dive into the truths it contains must have recourse to calculations, and not to verse.

A few years before he made that attack, he addressed some verses to the Marquise du Châtelet on the philosophy of Newton, which contained the following:

Tranquille au haut des cieux que Newton s'est soumis,
Il ignore en effect s'il a des ennemis:
Je ne les connais plus. Déjà de la carrière
L'auguste Vérité vient m'ouvrir la barrière;
. . . .
Etait enseveli dans une nuit obscure:
Le compas de Newton, mesurant l'univers,
Lève enfin ce grand voile, et les cieux font ouverts.
. . . .
Comètes que l'on craint a l'égal du tonnerre,
Cessez d'épouvanter les peuples de la terre:
Dans une ellipse immense achevez votre cours;
Remontez, descendez près de l'astre des jours;

> Lancez, vos feux, volez, et revenant sans cesse,
> Des mondes épuisés ranimez la vieillesse.
> Et toi, soeur du soleil, astre qui dans les cieux,
> Des sages, éblouis trompais les faibles yeux,
> Newton de ta carriere a marqué les limites;
> Marche, éclaire les nuits, tes bornes sont prescrites,
> Terre, change de forme . . .[3]

The poem draws to a close with the supplication that he may with Emilia (Madame Du Châtelet)
> Puissé-je auprès de vous, dans ce temple écarté,
> Aux regards des Français montrer la vérité!

It is quite evident from the perusal of this poem that Voltaire is quite content to embellish merely the outside of the Newtonian system in his verses. While he is very willing to stop writing plays, as he declares in another section of this poem, and follow "divine philosophy's all powerful-charms," he is not at all sure that science can find a suitable expression in poetry.

In so far as science, in any of its manifestations, sought to extend the bounds of knowledge without flinching, in the face of cherished traditions, unreasoned superstitions, and organized

---

[3] Wrapt in his heaven, great Newton scarcely knows
Amongst the sons of men that he has foes;
Of mine I think not, to my ravished eyes,
Truth shows how I may to that heaven rise;
. . . .
The spring of nature, but dark ignorance night
Concealed, had long lain hid from mortal sight:
Newton the compass takes, he lifts its veil,
He makes truth's light o'er ignorance prevail:
. . . .
Comets which men as much as thunder fear,
To terrify the world at length forbear;
In an ellipse immense your wanderings end.
Rise near the star of day and never descend;
Your fiery tresses shake, returning strive,
Exhausted, drooping nature to revive.

ecclesiasticism, Voltaire found himself heartily in sympathy with it. He was as quick to ridicule the spirit of intolerance or a dogmatic assertion upon the part of a scientist or a philosopher, as upon the part of an ecclesiastic. He could not follow the philosophes to their extreme positions, such as Baron d'Holbach and Diderot represented, because he felt that their enthusiasm was blinding their rational habits. Yet in his perverse nature there was something which would not allow his will to be crossed with impunity. When Frederick of Prussia, for example, compared him with a squeezed orange,[4] Voltaire awaited his opportunity for vengeance. It was the products of science which he desired, and not the discipline of mind which it enacted from its devotees.

Perhaps it was this trait, in part, that made Clairault inform Voltaire that the science of number and quantity was not his true vocation. For when Voltaire settled at Cirey with the Marquise Du Châtelet, he fitted up an expensive laboratory and proceeded to devote himself to study and physical research. Indeed, "he was very near," declares Henry Lord Brougham, "to discovering both the nature of oxygen and the process of oxydation, which last he had in general terms described."[5] He narrowly missed discovering the true theory of fluidity and latent heat a quarter of a century before Black.[6] His interest in sci-

---

Sister of Phoebus, star which in the skies,
Long time deceived the inquirer's erring eyes:
Newton has fixed the bounds of thy career,
Move on, and rule the day, the month and year:
Earth change thy form. . . .

Œuvres completes de Voltaire. Tome 13, Paris 1785. A Madame La Marquise Du Châtelet, 1738. Translation, from Works of Voltaire—William F. Fleming, 22 Vols. Lond., 1901, Vol. X, p. 94.

[4] Tallentyre, 226-30.

[5] "Lives of Men of Letters and Science who Flourished in the Time of George III," essay on Voltaire.

[6] *Ibid.*

ence, then, was scarcely that of a dilettante, if it was not that of a professional scientist. At any rate, much of the theoretical side of physics was understood by him and much of the procedure and technique of laboratory methods; he had great faith in science and realized its importance in advancing truth, especially in overthrowing dogmas, authority, and traditional beliefs.

If he was limited in his scientific outlook, it was in the direction of biology, as well as in mathematics. He did not, for example, have even a glimmering of the idea of development in the biological sense, such as La Mettrie gave expression to when he declared that the impelling force which made animals develop from lower to higher forms was desire or want; or such as Diderot sponsored when he declared that all "the living molecules of primitive chaos have given rise to all the forms of life, vegetable, and animal, from the lowest to the most highly organized[7]; or such as his contemporary Buffon, who wrote in 1749, that "we can descend by almost imperceptible degrees from the most perfect creature to the most formless matter—from the most highly organized animal to the most entirely inorganic substance."[8] Of that movement in contemporary thought Voltaire apparently took very little notice. And yet in his *"Essai sur les Mœurs,"* he was very much interested in tracing the development of culture; and he was one of the pioneers in evolving a philosophy of history. He certainly had fixed in his mind the conception of progress, whether he understood the implications of that idea or not.

The conception of progress had been making headway in France from 1690 to 1740.[9] It was taken up in the Encyclopedic movement and readily accommodated itself to a subordinate position under the lead of science. By knowledge of, and by

[7] R. L. Cru. *Diderot as a Disciple of English Thought*, p. 210 f.
[8] *Histoire Naturelle*, 1749.
[9] J. B. Bury. *Idea of Progress*.

applying, scientific laws mankind could achieve the goal it desired.

Naturally all this was not without its effect upon men's opinions about literature, and especially poetry. We have already noted the conventional element in Voltaire's early verse. How did he justify this tendency to look to authority for example and precept in poetry, when in his philosophy and his science he was well content to throw precedent overboard?

In the first place we must remember how this domination of the past in the arts was viewed in France in the eighteenth century. From the preceding age was inherited the strict code of literary decorum and the compromise between authority and reason which had conveniently made these one and the same thing. Towards the end of the seventeenth century however, it grew apparent that the wisdom of the ancients was obsolete—especially in their conclusions about the phenomena of nature which now appeared so different, owing to the tools man had invented, such as the microscope and the telescope. If our knowledge concerning the ancients had to be supplemented and modified, might not their precepts and beliefs about art also? This was the issue which underlay the famous quarrel of the ancients and the moderns. Towards the later part of the century (in 1687) Charles Perrault wondered if it might not be true[10] that, since in philosophy Plato is becoming tedious and since the telescope and the microscope have entirely depreciated the science of Aristotle, the inimitable Homer himself would not have written better had he lived in an age of refinement and taste, like that of Louis XIV. Since we know more, through our science than the ancients did, the "Modern authors ought to be better than the Ancients, on the ground of opportunity, if no other."[11]

[10] *Siècle de Louis le Grand.*
[11] *Parallels des Anciens et des Modernes.*

In the eighteenth century, this superiority was defended further on the grounds that the moderns cannot appreciate the beauties of expression in a dead language as well as they can in their own. Now that classicism had been attacked at its very foundations, what was to be the result upon literary practice? As a matter of fact there was very little immediate effect. Poems continued to be written in many quarters strictly according to the "rules"; and, especially, the idea of "good taste" which had been established continued, as it had for nearly a century, to exert something of a healthful influence upon the art of poetry, in keeping it from too great encroachments on the part of rationalism. It tended to keep the older works before the minds of both poets and readers, for these furnished the criterion of good taste. As the classics were reread and rediscovered, the scientific poems of Empedocles and Lucretius were called to mind, as well as the praise of country life in Virgil's *Georgics* and the satires of Horace, Juvenal, and Martial. In this way secure patterns were offered for the expression in verse of current scientific and philosophic interests.

Voices were still raised in protest at the merest suggestion that the fields of mechanical science and poetry were not as disparate as ever. L'Abbé Dubos was one of these. Scientific-minded as he was in reality, he held nevertheless that literary tradition should be regarded as something quite apart from scientific development. Philosophic schemes can be revised or rejected, he argued, because they establish themselves by the voice of authority and are submitted to the proof of new discoveries. The reputation of the works of art, on the other hand, establishes itself by the "voice of sentiment" and is founded on the general experience of pleasure which they give.[12] The writers of the

[12] F. Vial, and L. Denise, *Idées et Doctrines Littéraires Du XVIIIe Siecle,* p. 42.

Encyclopedia, while they did not in the main regard art and scientific development as entirely separate, decided that the ancients are nearer to nature, and though the present age is more learned, yet the ancients have as much and perhaps more, taste and genius.[13] Turgot, in this same connection, assigned indefinite progress to the sciences, but denied it to the arts. The height of perfection in the arts was attained by the ancients.

The new scientific spirit, it ought to be noted, however, had a distinct tendency now to break down the rigorous classifications of the genres which pseudo-classicism had prescribed. In the ode, for example, which was regarded as the true field of the sublime and the pathetic, the critics warned the poets against excessive enthusiasm,[14] declaring that reason should be the guide. Likewise, we note a change in the conception of the elegy. The earlier view that it ought to be pictorial and express a tender, delicate, and faithful love, gives way to the simpler form of a more truthful picture lightly embellished, and also to a more reflective type which seeks to express in pastoral form all the sentiments of the human heart. There was as well, in the second half of the century, another interesting modification of the pastoral and the elegy into the genre known as "descriptive poetry." Some critics assailed this practice and called the product monotonous and cold. Its defenders, such as Saint-Lambert, Delille, et cetera, agreed, however, that descriptive poetry ought to be varied by episodes and not limited entirely to its own kind.

Other critics, taking their cue from current philosophical and scientific procedure, advocated a greater conformity to the methods of science. Thus, Abbé De Pons declared that La Motte, in refusing to bow before Homer, did for literature what Descartes did for philosophy.[15] Similarily, L'Abbé Terrasson in-

[13] *Ibid.*, p. 69 f.
[14] *Ibid.*, p. 69 f.
[15] Lettre sur l' "Illiade" de La Motte (1714).

sisted that "it is necessary to carry into the appreciation of literary works the same rationalistic spirit as in philosophic and scientific studies."[16] With the progress of the human understanding, he pointed out, has gone also a progress in art. Late in the century, after the idea of development had gained headway, Condorcet made the statement: "The arts are susceptible to an infinite progress, not only because knowledge, philosophy, technique do not cease to perfect themselves, but also because physical and moral faculties of the human species transmissible by heredity, are indefinitely perfectible."[17]

Other theorists felt even more strongly upon this subject and sought to minimize still further the claims of poetry as a fine art. Such writers for example, as Fontenelle, De Bons, and La Motte were inclined to look upon the poetry of the past and much contemporary work as a harmonious extravagance, a kind of delirium.[18] Some of them maintained that rhythm, rhyme, and the "rules," are not the essentials of poetry, and that one can be a poet while writing in prose. Versification is only a useless constraint. Prose is superior to verse, because it says plainly what it wishes to express.[19]

Fontenelle perhaps illustrated this tendency best of all. He asked what was to be gained by using a sublime style for something which in itself is not at all sublime. What is to be gained by referring to Neptune and his trident when picturing a storm at sea? "Je le défie de lever les eaux plus qu'elles ne l'ont été, de repandre plus d'horreur dans ce malheureux vaisseau, et ainsi de tout le reste; la réalité seule a tout epuisé.[20] He fears that few authors are capable of producing pure philosophical poetry

[16] F. Vial, and L. Denise, *op. cit.*, p. 31.
[17] *Ibid.*, p. 31 f.
[18] *Ibid.*
[19] *Ibid.*
[20] *Ibid.*, p. 94.

and that few readers are capable of tasting it. Nevertheless, he believes that poetry may ascend to these heights. "The great difficulty is that these images find expression in a barbarous language of which poetry cannot avail itself without too much offending the ear, that sovereign and delicate mistress."

Voltaire was not one of these radicals, though champion of science he certainly was. While he doubtless believed his own times were wiser than the ancients, yet "taste" and "genius" he thought depended not on extent of knowledge. He implied, at least, that there was a universal beauty, an absolute, which should serve as a guide in all the fine arts. He, along with many others, found much to admire in the practice of the English poets. Indeed, Voltaire at thirty-nine could find a great deal to satirize in contemporary French poetry.[21] While living at Cirey he could write the following lines in praise of novelty:

> Peut-être je gâte â la fois
> La poësie et la physique.
> Mais cette nouveauté, me pique;
> Et du vieux code poëtique
> Je commence à braver les lois.
> Qu'un autre, dans ses vers lyriques,
> Depuis deux mille ans répétes,
> Brode encor des fables antiqués,
> Je veux de neuves vérités.
> . . . . .
> Trop d'art me révolte en m'ennuie,
> J'aime mieux ces vastes forêts;
> La nature libre et hardie,
> Irrégulière dans ses traits,
> S'accorde avec ma fantaisié.
> Mais dans ce discours familier
> En vain je crois-étudier
> Cette nature simple et belle;

---

[21] "Temple du goût."

> Je me sens plus irrégulier,
> Et beaucoup moins aimable qu'elle.[22]

Even in his poetic work where he professed to follow the "rules" and be guided by "good taste," the desire to experiment is sometimes to be noted. He refused, for example, to follow the unities too closely in his plays; he appears frequently to have been influenced by Shakespeare even more than he would admit.

Later in his life, however, he tended to react against the English influence and to stress antiquity somewhat more and especially the French poets of the seventeenth century—the heyday of French classicism. He could not, like Diderot, hold that the eloquence and poetry of his day might be superior to those of the ancients, just as his day surpassed them in physics, astronomy, mechanics, et cetera. Diderot criticized the tragedy of the preceding century as untrue to life and throughly artificial in tone, and advocated an illusion of reality and a simple style. More specifically, he recommended a "genre sérieux," which should be taken from life and from truth, but which should, however, respect the three unities and be written in prose.

If we turn from discussions about poetry to an examination of the actual practice of French poets in the time of Voltaire, we find something of the same conservatism that we have noted upon the part of that outstanding figure of the age. While a great body of poetry praises nature and lauds the scientists and scientific achievements, it is discovered that these poems do not depart to any marked extent from tradition, or at least from the English practice. Let us glance at some of these verses before considering those others which are more directly concerned with the new philosophic spirit of the age.

Saint-Lambert was one of the poets who set out to praise nature in *Les Saisons,* a poem which owed much of course, to the

---

[22] Épître XLVII. "Au Prince Royal De Prusse." 1738, p. 103.

English *Seasons* of Thomson. In his preface he upheld the theory that details of nature and country life are fit material for poetry, and he cited as his authorities Ovid, Virgil, Lucretius, and Horace; and among the English poets, Thomson and Philips. He maintained, however, that the facts should be taken from nature first hand and not from the descriptions of other writers. It is necessary, furthermore, to enlarge and embellish these, in order to make them interesting to the reader.

Vincent Campenon, recalling Virgil's handling of the joys of country life attempts to do something similar in "La Maison des Champs,"[23] which contains the exclamation:

> Ah! ce bonheur que je peints, dans mes chants,
> Il appartient à l'homme vraiment sage
> Qui, sous l'abre de sa maison des champs,
> Cultive en paix son modeste héritage;
> Dans ses jardins, dans ses vergers en fleurs,
> Va de ses fruits épier les primeurs,
> Sème ses blés, recueille ses fermages,
> Et du ciel redoute les orages.

Similarly, François Bernis, in his "Discours Sur la Poesie," advocated a study of Homer and Virgil, but he also likened the poet to the painter. "Toute poëte qui n'est pas peintre n'est qu'un versificateur." In theory at least, he would not have the poets copy the works of the ancients. "La nature entiere est l'object de la poesie. Les poetes ignorans sont toujours de foibles copisies.—Steriles dans les tableaux de la vie champête, ils ne décrivent jamais que les fleurs des prairies, le murmure des ruisseaux, les pleurs de l'aurore, et le badinage des zephyrs. In his "Epître sur le Goût," he advocates a return to nature in poetry, by which he apparently means a return to simplicity. For there is a tendency, he believes, to strive after too much ingenuity and refinement of expression. In his two poems, "Les

[23] Paris, 1844, p. 49.

Quatre Parties Du Jour" and "Les Quatre Saisons," we do note a simpler style, but very little freshness of observation or spontaneity of expression. Likewise, Delille, a very popular poet of the time, pleads in his poem on gardens, for natural beauty, instead of the artificial variety as exemplified in the gardens of Versailles.[24]

> Des ornements de l'art l'œil bientôt se fatigue;
> Mais les bois, mais les-eaux, mais les ombrages frais,
> Tout ce luxe innocent ne fatigue jamais.
> Aimez donc des jardins la beauté naturelle;
> Dieu lui-même aux mortels en traça le modéle.

There is little evidence, however, throughout the entire poem of any first hand observation. At times it resembles a mere catalogue of superficial details.

While in theory many of these poets were ready to break away from the conventional type of poetry, or poetry based too closely upon the classics, and to report what they really found in nature, yet in actual practice we find few signs of any original or careful observation. Much of the poetry continued, despite protestations to the contrary, to be either imitative or derivative. When the scientific virtues of careful and painstaking perception manifested themselves in French literature, as they did towards the end of the eighteenth century, it was in prose rather than in verse, in the works of Chateaubriand, Saint-Pierre, and others.

Those French poets who directed some of their efforts, at least, to praising the scientists and the scientific achievements of their age, approached a little nearer perhaps to the scientific spirit of the time. Many verses of course are centered about Newton, such as that of Dorat:

> L'épaisse nuit regnoit sur le monde encor brut;
> Dieu dit: que Newton soit, sondain le jour parut,

---

[24] "Les Jardins," Chant I, p. 59.

> Pour second Créateur, tout l'univers le nomme.
> Interrogez le Ciel, la Nature et le Tems:
> C'est un Dieu, diront-ils, qui ne craint rien des ans;
> Hélas! Ce marbre seul atteste qu'il fut homme.

And again that of Roucher, who pictures nature as being for a long time without voice and without an oracle. "But as soon as Newton, that audacious eagle, had looked . . . man broke the fetters of antique ignorance."

> Mais sitôt que Newton, cet aigle audacieux,
> En face eût regardé le roi brûtant des cieux,
> L'homme brisa les fers de l'ignorance antique:
> L'homme fut possesseur des secrets de l'optique
> Dans les angles d'un verre en prisme façonné
> Il vit que du soleil un rayon émané
> Déployait ses couleurs de nature première:
> Il reconnut enfin que ce traits de lumière.
> Ou seuls, on combinés en différens accords,
> D'une teinte céleste empreignaient tous les corps.[25]

Buffon also comes in for praise:

> Buffon, laisse gronder l'envie;
>
> . . . . . .
>
> L'Olympe, qu'assiege un orage,
> Dedaigne l'imprussante rage
> Les acquilons tumultueux;
> Tandis que la noire tempête
> Gronde à ses pieds, sa noble tête
> Garde un calme majestueux . . .[26]

But it is to be noted that in these verses the praise is all of a very general type, nothing that indicates a penetrating or clear understanding of the scientific principles involved, nothing quite as lucid and definite, as those observed previously in Thomson's lines in praise of Newton.

There are a number of poets who, while attempting to cele-

---

[25] "Les Mois," II, Avril, p. 43.
[26] Lebrun. "Ode à M. de Buffon sur ses détracteurs."

brate the new philosophy in their verses, find it difficult to adjust the rival claims of the poetic tradition with the Encyclopedic spirit. Such a rebel in theory as Fontenelle, when he turns to writing poetry, employs the artificial pastoral form. Bernis, while declaring that French poetry has always been related to philosophy and metaphysics, finds, however, that the system of Spinoza is so monstrous in its principles, so horrible in its consequences, that it seems to lend itself but indifferently well to French poetry.[27] Saint-Lambert comments upon this in his preface to "Les Saisons":

Les progrès des sciences comprises sous the nom de physique, l'astronomie, la chimie, la botanique, etc., ont fait connâitee le palais du monde et les hommes qui l'habitent. . . . Des philosophes éloquens ont rendu la physique une science agréable; ils en ont répandu les idées; elles sont devenues populaires. Le language de la philosophie, reçu dans le monde, a pu l'être dans la poésie: ou a pu entreprendre des poëmes qui demandent une connoissance váriée de la nature, et leurs auteurs ont pu espérer des lecteurs. . . . Il faut faire pour la nature physique, que nous avons sous nos yeux, ce qu' Homère, le Tasse, nos poëtes dramatiques, ont fait pour la nature morale; il faut l'agrandir, l'embellir, la rendre intéressante.

Such a poet as Houdar de La Motte (1672-1731), however, delights in that fact that:

> J'ose Célébrer ce Parnasse
> Que tes soins ont fait refleurir.
> J'y vois l'adroite Mécanique;
> Ingenieuse, elle s'applique
> A mille prodiges nouveaux;
> Elle force tous les obstacles.
> Et fait servir à ses miracles,
> L' Air, le Feu, les Vents, et les Eaux.
> . . . .
> La Gèomètrie est le guide
> Qui sans cesse e'clairant leurs pas,

---

[27] *Discours sur la Poésie.*

Leur prête, les secours solide
De sa Régle et de son Compas.
. . . .
Mieux qu'elle encor l'exacte Algébre,
Ce grand art aux magiques traits,
Aussi négligé que célébre.

He takes up in turn the contributions of anatomy "en ses emplois,"

Du corps, où notre amie est captive,
Examine toutes les loix
Elle suit ce secret Méandre
Que la Nature y sçut repandre.

He touches upon "la Botanique secourable" and Chemistry, which

De la Nature trop cachée,
Seule elle sçait ouvrir le sein:
Voit par quels secrets assemblages.
Elle à varie ses ouvrages,
Animaux, Plantes, Mineraux;
Et scait en mille expériences,
Faire à son gré les alliances
Et les divorces des Mataux.[28]

The Encyclopedic spirit found even fuller expression, moreover, in a group of poems which sought definitely to make poetry the handmaid of science. Poinsinet has a poem on Inoculation; Marquis de Fontaines on astronomy; Pierre Louis Castel on "Les Plantes"; Luce de Lancival on geography; Charles de Chenedollé on the genus man; Lemierre on the origin of chemistry. The primary aim of these poems, is of course, to teach some scientific truth or to glorify the new scientific method.

The Encyclopedic character of such a poem as Delille's "Les Trois Règnes de la Nature" is very evident. Combined with the comprehensiveness is a wealth of material which modern science has unearthed. It treats of light, fire, air, water, and earth, be-

[28] "L' Académie des Sciences Ode à Monsieur l'Abbé Bignon." Works. Paris 1754, Vol. I.

VOLTAIRE AND CHÉNIER 99

fore it turns to a consideration of the three kingdoms—mineral, vegetable, and animal. In the canto on the air, for example, the poet pays homage to Pascal and comments upon electricity and its effects. Again when he treats of water, he enumerates its various properties and analyzes its different effects in the works and scenes of nature. Similarly, in the canto "La Terre," there is a discussion of chemistry and volcanic action; and in his treatment of the vegetable kingdom there is an elegy to Linnaeus, a discussion of the habits of plants, how they love, et cetera.

Delille, however, is not willing, in theory at least, for poetry to be merely the handmaid of science:

Evitons cet ecueil: laissons de ses entraves
L'esprit systématique enchâiner ses esclaves
La seule expérience est un guide pour moi;
Instruire est son devoir, et peindre est mon emploi.[29]

Indeed, this idea of the poet making a word picture by way of describing some scientific fact—and more especially when such a fact is derived through experience or by experimental means—is in many instances the beau ideal of the poet. But he is not content merely to imitate a classical model, it is to be observed; he desires rather to follow, with something akin to the scientific temper, the findings of experience.

It is not fair, Delille implies, in another poem,[30] for us to assume that poetry has a monopoly of the imagination. For while it is a fact that the works of nature, the sea, the mountains, and the sky, all affect the imagination, yet—and this appears to be an important factor in his implication—some of the sciences themselves, such as geometry, the mechanical arts, astronomy, printing, navigation, are also under the influence of the imagination.

We find a similar attempt to express scientific facts by means

[29] "L'Imagination."
[30] "Les Arts."

of word pictures in the botanical discussion of Campenon, in which he dwells fantastically upon the love of the plants, in a way resembling Delille and Erasmus Darwin. Again in the poem "La Navigation" by J. Esménard, we have a series of word pictures embodying the history of the art of nagivation from its unknown origin, through the time when the Egyptians first applied astronomy to the art; and the Phoenicians, the Greeks, and the Romans improved it; and tracing the gains at the hands of the Venetians, the important discovery of the mariner's compass, the explorations and the making of maps, and finally how maritime supremacy passed in turn from Holland to Spain and thence to England.

This tendency to use verse to do the work of the Encyclopedia did not, of course, meet with universal approval upon the part of the poets. Thus, for example, we find that attitude rather satirized humorously in the poem, "La Gastronomie,"[31]

> Je ne suis point jaloux du poète lyrique
> Qui semble se nourrir de fleurs de rhétorique,
> Qui, plein de son sujet, sans en être moins creux
> Parle souvent à jeun le langage des dieux.
> Qu'un rival de Virgile, amoureux des campagnes,
> Fasse a l'Homme des Champs aplanir des montagnes
> Et l'instruise dans l'art de jourer avec échecs:
> Pour mois de tels sujets sont arides et secs.
> Je me sens emparé d'une heureuse matière:
> Je chante l'Homme à Table, et dirai la manière
> D'embellir un repas; je durai le secret
> D'augmenter les plaisirs d'un aimable banquet.

He describes the cuisine of the Greeks and Romans, and finally he leads up to his own times.

> Les poètes ont trop dedaigné la cuisine
> Sans donte ils auraient cru, jusque-la s'abaissant,
> Dishonorer leur muse, avilir, leur talent;
> . . . .

---

[31] Josephe Berchoux. "La Gastronomie." Bruxelles, 1837.

> Pour moi, paisible ami des demeures agrestes,
> Je dois borner ma muse à des sujets modestes.
>
> Delille, dans ses vers nobles, harmonieux,
> A fait de la campagne un tableau précieux;
> Il peint l'homme entouré de ruisseaux, de prairies;
> Promenant dans les bois ses douces rêveries;
> Le loto, le trictrac l'attendent au retour,
> J'admire ces plaisirs d'un champêtre sejour;
> Mais je ne vois jamais l'homme des champs à table.
> Réparons, s'il se peut, cet oubli condamnable.
> Puissent tous mais lecteurs, approuvant mon project,
> Pardonner à mes vers en faveur du sujet!

He then considers painstakingly, and in great detail, the progress of a three course meal. The poem concludes:

> Que ne puis-je fermer la bouche à mes critiques!
> Ils n'approuveront pas mes conseils didactiques.
> Messieurs, je vóus entends, je sais vous diviner
> Un poème jamais ne valut un diner.

A more serious attempt to condemn this tendency to celebrate the new science in poetry was the poem on the eighteenth century by Nicholas Gilbert (1751-80), who objected on the ground of both religion and art:

> Un monstre dans Paris croit et se fortifie,
> Qui, paré du manteau de la philosophie,
> Que dis-je? de son nom faussement revêtu.
> Étouffé les talens et detruit la vertu:
> Dangereux novateur, par son cruel système,
> Il veut du ciel désert chasser l'Être-Suprême;
> Et du corps expire l'âme eprouvant le sort,
> L'homme arrive au néant par une double mort.

The effect of this, complains the poet:

> Mais de la poësie usurpant les pinceaux,
> Et du nom des vertus, sanctifiant sa prose,
> Par la pompe des mots l'éloquence en impose.

The poet makes the suggestion that if poetry is going to aim primarily at pleasing the reason, then it is poetry of an inferior order, for

> Apollon sans pinceaux n'est plus qu'un lourd pedant.[32]

The principal line of objection to the type of poem which aimed to give expression to the ideas that the Encyclopedists were upholding was, that when poetry too definitely placed itself under the tutelage of science or philosophy, it was forgetting to a great extent its traditions as a fine art. These traditions had grown up very largely, of course, with the pseudo-classicism which had been an outgrowth of the Renaissance. Neglect of poetic diction was one of the chief offenses, especially in the sense of employing a general term instead of a pictorial, concrete one; for another thing, sometimes this type of poetry would become too rationalistic at the expense of the fanciful or ornamental qualities. That poetry was distinctly an art, and not something to be swayed by the fickle winds of doctrine, or to be bound to the service of any one idea or speculation was, as we have noted, the belief and practice of Voltaire. Indeed, the shoots of pseudo-classicism and their roots, which lay much farther back than the seventeenth century, were still vibrant with life, as was manifested in the latter part of the eighteenth century, in the work of André Chénier.

2. ANDRÉ CHÉNIER (1762-94)

Chénier was only sixteen at the time of Voltaire's death. A student at that time in the Collège de Navarre in Paris, he was much interested in making verse translations from the classics. A little later his interests were widened by the cultivated circle of his mother's salon, where he met Lavoisier, Dorat, and Parny. When he visited Rome in 1784 and stopped at Naples and at the ruins of Pompeii, his taste for the antique was further in-

[32] Gilbert, Nicholas. "Le Dix-huitième Siècle," 1875.

creased. His interest in the ancients was not merely in the pseudo-classic expression of antiquity, but very much more in the writings of the Greek poets themselves—a liking which had indeed been fostered from his earliest years by his Greek mother. He possessed a lyrical power which was apparently denied to his contemporaries, for even in his earlier experimental verse, in the Idylls and Bucolics which were patterned for the most part upon Theocritus, Bion and the Greek Anthologists, he not merely employed the classical mythology, but achieved that individual and personal expression for which so many French poets before him had been striving. His verses were not in the main slavish imitations of the classical models. On the contrary, he liked to test and experiment; nor was he so lost in contemplating those models that he was not aware of the contemporary movement in scientific thought and in philosophy.

As early as 1783 he had commenced his didactic and philosophic poem, which aimed to condense the Encyclopedia into verse, just as Lucretius had attempted to put the philosophy of Epicurus into his great poem. The subject matter of this work —fragmentary, not for lack of interest in the subject, but because the Revolution intervened and the poet was guillotined in 1794—may be gleaned from his note books, in which he had recorded what the general plan was to be. He proposed giving in verse an exposition of how the world came to be as it is, utilizing always the findings of the most advanced science of his time, and not seeking to uphold any definite religious thesis or philosophical tenet. This attitude the poet here shares with the scientist. He is no longer talking vaguely of nature nor praising in general terms the scientific achievements of the age; nor is he merely content to use his verse as a handmaid to science; he is trying to make a genuine synthesis between science and the art of poetry, by being fair to the spirit of the former and also to the traditional element of the latter. He had, in brief, a definite poetic creed, tempered in no small degree by a traditionalism derived from the Greeks and from the seventeenth-century group of poets known as the Pléiade. This poetic creed finds full expression in "L'Invention," which begins:

> O fils du Mincius, je te salue, Ô toi
> Par qui le dieu des arts fut roi du peuple-roi!
> Et vous, à qui jadis, pour creer l'harmonie,
> L'Attique et l'onde Egée, et la belle Ionie,
> Donnèrent un ciel pur les plaisirs, la beauté,
> Des mœurs simples, des lois, la paix, la liberté,
> Un langage sonore, aux douceurs souveraines,
> Le plus beau qui soit ne sur des lèvres humaines.
> . . . .
> Les coutumes d'alors, les sciences, les mœurs
> Respirent dans les vers des antiques auteurs.
> Leur siècle est en dépôt dans leur nobles volumes.
> Tout a changé pour nous, mœurs, sciences, coutumes.

His high regard for ancient poetry, however, has not blinded him to the changes which time has brought, and he demands:

> Pourquoi donc nous faut-il, par un penible soin,
> Sans rien voir près de nous, voyant toujours bien loin,
> Vivant dans le passé, laissant ceux qui commencent,
> Sans penser, écrivant d'après d'autres qui pensent,
> Retraçant un tableau que nos yeux n'ont point vu,
> Dire et dire cent fois ce que nous avons lu?
> De la Grèce, heroique et naissante et sauvage
> Dans Homère à nos yeux vit la parfaite image.
> Démocrite, Platon, Epicure, Thalés,
> Ont de loin à Virgile indiqué les secrets
> D'une nature encore à leurs yeux trop voilée,
> Toricelli, Newton, Kepler et Galilée,
> Plus doctes, plus heureux dans leurs puissants efforts,
> À tout nouveau Virgile ont ouvert des trésors.
> Tous les arts sont unis: les sciences humaines
> N'ont pu de leur empire étendre les domaines,
> Sans agrandir aussi la carrière des vers.
> Quel long travail pour eux à conquis l'univers!

> Aux regards de Buffon, sans voile, sans obstacles,
> La terre ouvrant son sein, ses ressorts, ses miracles.

Here we have a definite declaration that although poetry is distinctly a fine art, its scope depends nevertheless upon the advancement of science. There is, furthermore, nothing new in this relationship: it is precisely what Virgil did and what all poets have always done. Therefore:

> Changeons en notre miel leurs plus antiques fleurs,
> Pour peindre notre idée empruntons leurs couleurs;
> Allumons nos flambeaux a leurs feux poétiques;
> Sur des pensers nouveaux faisons des vers antiques.

Later in the poem he demands:

> Oh qu'ainsi parmi nous des esprits inventeurs
> De Virgile et d'Homère atteignent les hauteurs!

But he abhors the modern tendency which "en langage des dieux fasse parler Newton!"

It is indeed unfortunate that Chénier was not permitted to give us a full exhibition of how he would reconcile the warring elements of science and poetry. He makes it clear to us that the poem is to consist of three parts. The first of these was to discuss in a general way the system of the earth and the world, the seasons, the birth of animals, and the soul; and his first canto was to end, "par une magnifique description de toutes les espéces animals et végétales naissant."

The second canto was designed to trace man's progress from the beginning of his savage state to the birth of society. It is man's chief glory, he insists, that he alone is perfectible, while the animals reach a point beyond which they cannot advance. He planned a section on the senses, which followed in the main, Condillac's treatise.

> Tous les hommes ont le même fonds de goûts, de passions, de sentiments, qui se façonnent, différement dans chacun. Ils sont donc tous assez semblables pour être la même race, assez divers pour n'être pas le même individu.

The third canto treats of human society. We have a discussion of its origin, and an exposition of the social contract from Rousseau and Hobbes. There is a long discussion of law, legislation, and politics, and the inventions of the sciences. The poem ends with a more specific account of the system of the world, and with an epilogue in which the poet testifies how dear to his heart is this poem, over which he has labored for so long. It is a very significant point, moreover, that in his exposition Chénier notes the passing of the Newtonian form of the mechanical thesis and the substitution in its place of a theory of organic development, derived, in part perhaps, from the theory of Empedocles, or perhaps from Buffon, Lamarck, or Cabanis. In his notes to his first canto he writes:

> Il faut manifiguement représenter la terre sous l'emblême métaphorique d'un grand animal qui vit, se meut, est sujet à des changements, des révolutions, des fièvres, des derangements dans la circulation de son sang.
> La terre est éternellement en mouvement. Chaque chose naît, meúrt, se dissout. Cette particule de terre a été du fumier; elle devient un trône et qui plus est un roi.

The mechanical conception is still upheld, however, along with the organic principle:

> Chaque chose a dans soi ses ressorts. Les autres choses la frappent au dehors. . . . Ces atomes de vie ces semences premières sont toujours en égale quantité sur la terre et toujours en mouvement. Ils passent de corps en corps, s'alambiquent, s'élaborent, se travaillent, fermentent, se subtilisent dans leur rapport avec le vase où ils sont actuellement contenus. Ils entrent dans un végetal, ils en sont la séve, la force, les sucs nourriciers. Ce végetal est mangé par quelque animal, alors ils se transforment en sang et en cette substance qui produirira un autre animal et qui fait vivre les espéces, ou dans un chêne ce qu'il y a de plus subtil se rassemble dans le gland. . . .

The struggle between the organic and the mechanical interpretations of nature was an issue which was only just beginning to play a very important part in philosophical thinking. By degrees, throughout the course of the century, there had been forming a counter movement in human thought, away from the universal application of the Newtonian mechanism. In the early years of the eighteenth century, Shaftesbury had pointed out that the emotional and non-reflective agencies in human conduct are of vital importance in understanding mankind. Towards the middle of the century, Hume had argued that all reasoning about matters of fact is really a species of feeling and belongs to the sensitive rather than the cogitative side of our nature.

The implications emanating from this line of thought were fraught with great danger for the Encyclopedia ideal, for Hume further showed that the ideas of cause and effect were simply correlative in our minds and merely the fruit of our experience, and that we cannot know the permanent identical thing or things which constitute reality itself. In 1749, Jean Jacques Rousseau gave to the world his *Discours sur les Arts et Sciences,* in which he argued that reason is in truth secondary to conscience and to feeling. Man, before he became rational, was essentially good —his goodness springing from his heart. The development of his intellect was necessary in the struggle which ensued between the instincts of self-preservation and his natural sympathy for his fellow-beings. But this reason was put to bad uses when man attempted to subjugate his fellow-beings by means of it and to establish his power over them. And then in his arrogance, man began to teach that through this science and this rationalization was to be obtained the highest truth. He declares that astronomy is but the child of superstition; geometry of avarice; and physics of idle curiosity. Indeed, the arts and the sciences have tended to destroy man's natural goodness of heart and thereby to corrupt his morals.

Still later in the century, Kant tried to find the way out of the dilemma which arose from the Encyclopedic implicit faith in science on the one side, the scepticism of Hume on the other, and the glorification of the feelings at the expense of the reason from the hands of Rousseau. Thus, Kant, in conceding to Hume the limitations of the human mind, in advocating a strict application of scientific mechanical principles (thereby paying homage to the Encyclopedic spirit), and in granting to Shaftesbury and Rousseau that the feelings must also have their share of recognition, sought to balance these contending forces. The concession to Rousseau found expression in the idea that although man could not know reality itself, he could,—after he had proceeded as far as science would take him in that direction —choose to make his conduct conform to the principles that seemed most desirable to him. It was desirable, for instance, that man should continue to believe in God, in immortality, and in the freedom of the will—even though these might not be proved scientifically.

This modification in the philosophic point of view received further substantiation from scientific sources, especially from the fields of geology and biology, where a theory was forming that tended to modify the Newtonian concept of a World-machine. In this hypothesis the factor of time was stressed, and gradually the idea of a growing and developing world supplemented the Newtonian outlook. This new conception seized upon the imagination of both philosopher and scientist and soon spread contagiously to other fields. We shall notice the extension of this idea in greater detail in the discussions which follow, and especially, of course, its invasion of the field of poetry.

That André Chénier was giving some attention to this line of thought seems evident from the excerpts which I have quoted from his notes on his poem, destined never to be completed. It is clear moreover, that he aimed to follow out his poetical theory as announced in "L'Invention," to imitate the ancients, but to utilize the latest scientific and philosophical ideas and to transfuse the whole with the glow of his lyrical imagination. From the fragmentary state of the poem, it is difficult to determine how completely he would have succeeded in doing that. This attempt to synthesize the classical ideal of poetry, the lyrical imagination, and the new science is very significant; for since the time Lucretius had attempted to do very much the same thing, science and men's ideas about science had, as we have observed, changed very materially. Implications were now perceived which were unknown then; the issue between science and lyrical poetry was more clearly drawn, and out of the diverse elements Chénier tried to bring harmony.

In England, almost contemporaneous with the attempt of Chénier, Erasmus Darwin was also trying to bring science and poetry nearer together, with the result to be noted in the next chapter.

Chapter VI

POETRY SMILES AT A GROWING WORLD
ERASMUS DARWIN

Erasmus Darwin (1731-1802), in attempting to bring science and poetry nearer together, felt his interest divided between the two fields of activity. More of a scientist than André Chénier and less of a literary artist, he is, nevertheless, a very notable figure for what he accomplished, no less than for what he undertook.

One of his biographers hails him as being "equally eminent as philanthropist, physician, philosopher, and poet."[1] Certainly he was philanthropical in the pursuit of his profession and also in his general interest in the welfare of humanity. His fame as a physician is said to have reached King George III, who made it evident that he would like him to become his own medical adviser, but Dr. Darwin declined this honor, doubtless because he preferred the freedom which the quiet life in the country at Lichfield afforded.

After having attended St. John's College, Cambridge, and studied medicine at Edinburgh for a year, he settled in Nottingham as a physician in 1756. Meeting with little encouragement, he moved to Lichfield the same year and there apparently he was successful in his calling from the beginning. Lichfield, indeed, became his home for a quarter of a century. In 1757 he married Mary Howard, and their entire married life of thirteen happy years was passed there. After her death in 1770, he continued there for eleven years more. In Lichfield also origi-

[1] Ernest Krause. *Erasmus Darwin,* N.Y., 1880, p. 132.

nated the celebrated botanical garden, and from the same town emanated Miss Seward's *Memoirs* which have continued to be the chief source for all subsequent biographies of Erasmus Darwin. In 1781 he married Mrs. Pool, and the same year moved to Derby and then to Breadsall Priory, where he continued to make his home, until a sudden attack of heart disease caused his death, April 18, 1802.

Outwardly, at least, his life created no apparent stir, differing little perhaps from the life of the average country doctor who has an unusual interest in plants and flowers. Inwardly, however, that life found much, in his association with his friends, in his avocations, and most of all in his reveries and speculations, to excite it and make it glow.

One of his avocations was the study of botany, a pursuit which found its fullest expression after he had fitted out his botanical garden of eight acres. Another avocation, even from his earliest days, was the writing of verses—an indulgence which he allowed himself while making his round of calls, or sitting at the bed-side of his patients. It is not surprising that these activities should later, in 1789, bear fruit in a botanical poem, "Loves of the Plants." Here we have an expression of his poetic creed, for in the first prose interlude the Bookseller asks the Poet questions which serve to develop it, and the Poet answers his interlocutor as follows:

Poetry admits of but few words expressive of very abstract ideas, whereas Prose abounds with them. The poet writes principally to the eye. . . . Science is best delivered in Prose, as its mode of reasoning is from stricter analogies than metaphors or similes. . . . The matter must be interesting from its sublimity, beauty, or novelty; this is the scientific part; and the art consists in bringing these distinctly before the eye, so as to produce the ideal presence of the object.

The poem itself illustrates this perfectly. Here the Poet is desirous of transmuting the system of Linnaeus, commonly referred to as the "sexual system," into poetry. The matter is interesting, he thinks, because the extension of the idea of sex into plant life is sufficiently novel to warrant poetic treatment. Therefore, in order to bring this notion "distinctly before the eye," he personifies the various plants and seeks to call up a series of mental images.

> First the tall Canna lifts his curled brow
> Erect to heaven, and plights his nuptial vow;
> The virtuous pair, in milder regions born,
> Dread the rude blast of Autumn's icy morn;
> Round the chill fair he folds his crimson vest,
> And clasps the timorous beauty to his breast.
>
> Two brother swains, of Collin's gentle name,
> The same their features and their forms the same,
> With rival love for fair Collina sigh,
> Knit the dark brow, and roll the unsteady eye,
> With sweet concern the pitying beauty mourns,
> And sooths with smiles the jealous pair by turns.

There is nothing new in this poetic theory. It is in complete harmony with the Horatian tradition, which seeks both to amuse and instruct. His poetry endeavors, he says in the preface to the *Temple of Nature,* "simply to amuse by bringing distinctly to the imagination the beautiful and sublime images of the operations of Nature." Earlier, in connection with *The Botanic Garden,* he is trying "to inlist Imagination under the banner of Science, and to lead her votaries from the looser analogies, which dress out the imagery of poetry, to the stricter ones, which form the ratiocination of philosophy."

Not all science, it would appear, can find poetic expression— only that which is sublime, beautiful or novel. Given a "scientific" fact which fulfills one of these attributes, it may be made to appeal to the eye by the use of metaphors and similes. There is something of a mechanical procedure in this, a following of "rules," in the sense that Pope advocated. Thus, in 1803, the year after the Doctor's death, the critic in the Edinburgh Review could write, that if Darwin's "fame be designed in anything to outlive the fluctuating fashion of the day, it is on his merit as a poet that it is likely to rest," and that "his reveries in science have no other chance of being saved from oblivion but by having been 'married to immortal verse.'" Modern criticism, with its ideas of growth and development, has been inclined to reverse this. Judged by modern standards of poetry, and especially by those which grew up in the course of the nineteenth century, most of Erasmus Darwin's attempts in the field of poetry seem merely verified science. The "reveries in science," on the other hand, strike a modern reader as being much more significant.

By his father, Robert Darwin, his attention had been early turned to science. This interest was naturally increased by his medical studies in Edinburgh and by the subsequent experiences in his professional life; and it was further widened by the rather broad scope of his reading, and by association with some important British thinkers of his day. Professor H. F. Osborne[2] finds evidence of a careful reading of at least Leibnitz, Buffon, Linnaeus; the Greeks, especially Aristotle; and of David Hume, who gave emphatic expression to the idea that Nature was under the operation of natural and not supernatural law.

His circle of "philosopher friends," as Miss Seward calls them, constitute a cosmopolitan group. Among them were Reverend Mr. Michell, who was greatly interested in astronomy, and Captain Keir of Birmingham, the leading spirit of the Lunar Club which met in Birmingham monthly for philosophical discussions, by profession a chemist, interested in geology, and for a time an assistant to Priestly in some of his experiments. Two more members of the circle were Matthew Bolton, a mechanic philosopher, and James Watt, the improver of the steam engine, who numbered among his acquaintances Joseph Black, Adam Smith and John Roebuck. Dr. Small and Dr. Darwin were often together, and after 1770, were joined by Richard Edgeworth,

[2] *From the Greeks to Darwin.* N.Y., 1894, p. 142.

greatly interested in mechanics, and the originator of many inventions. Along with Edgeworth came Thomas Day, breathing the spirit of revolt against eighteenth-century society, and endeavoring to put into practice the theory of Rousseau in regard to the natural instincts. Thomas Wedgwood, the potter, frequently visited Darwin, and of course Anna Seward, his biographer; later came Sir Brook Boothby, a devotee to botanic science, and according to Miss Seward, "a deep reasoner and clear sighted politician," and Mr. Munday, the poet. Once the Doctor met Rousseau at Wootton Hall, and they are known to have corresponded. Association with such men must have greatly augmented his scientific knowledge and whetted his inborn curiosity still further.

Naturally such a group could not fail to be affected to some degree, at least, by the current of thought that was tending to regard critically the mathematico-mechanical conception of life. We have already seen how the philosophers Shaftesbury, Rousseau, Hume, and Kant all reacted from that view. If these "philosopher friends" of Erasmus Darwin knew nothing of the romantic philosophy which was then crystallizing in German idealistic thought, and which was seeking to raise to a position of dignity,—above the mere mechanical and machine-world conception,—the aspirations, strivings and imagination of men, they were at least trying to understand something of the underlying meaning of things. As a part of the reactionary movement, there was a desire manifest upon the part of many thinkers to exclude definitely and unquestionably all mankind from the workings of the mechanical principle. If the planets, if all inanimate objects of the universe, if the chemical elements themselves, were all subject to mechanical laws, was that reason to assume that man functioned mechanically, like a machine? Could it not be established, in short, that mankind was subject to different laws than the laws which govern "things"?

Some of the sciences themselves—those which were advancing most rapidly, in the latter part of the eighteenth century and the first half of the nineteenth, such as geology, for example—tended to give some support to this contention. Thus in geology, the time element was coming to be recognized as very important in bringing about changes and differences. Obviously, according to the fossil remains, there had been changes in the forms of life upon the earth over a long period of time. But, on the other hand, if science appeared to set off mankind from inanimate objects, it was also breaking down distinctions between man and the lower animals. In anatomy and biology, the more minute study of the constitution of animal tissue, which followed the improvement of the microscope and the advance of organic chemistry, served to make it apparent that a similarity of structure existed here also, and at the same time tended to set organic nature off from inorganic. In John Hunter's studies in comparative embryology this idea received even further confirmation. Among physiologists the doubt was steadily growing as to whether all physiological processes could be entirely accounted for by chemical and mechanical agencies, such as Harvey and Descartes had believed. A kind of animism or vitalism was entering into physiological theory. The idea that organic nature might be something very different from the inorganic forms received still further corroboration, when, in botany, microscopic study revealed a similarity of structure in plants in general, and that this structure was obviously different from anything which had been observed in inorganic nature.

Gradually the theory of the world as one that is constantly changing and growing received scientific acknowledgement from the findings of geology and embryology. Hence, it was becoming more evident that the element of time was very important in all explanations of natural phenomena. This factor, combined with the dogma of the Encyclopedists that the world is definitely progressing, connected the history of mankind with the concept of advancement through growth, or a process of unfolding.

The idea of evolution or development was not by any means new. The Greek Empedocles, nearly five hundred years before the Christian era, had voiced a crude "survival of the fittest" theory to explain the origin of the various plants and animals. The atomic philosophers had sought in a theory of cosmic evolution a mechanical explanation of the formation of the various parts of the universe. Aristotle himself had noted that in organic life there was a "progressive scale of complexity determined by its final end—man."[3] These speculations, lost for the most part through the Middle Ages, had been revived again with the Renaissance. Campanella, had sought to derive the organic part of Nature out of the inorganic. And in the seventeenth century, at the time that the Newtonian conception was in greatest favor, we find hints of the development idea.

In the eighteenth century evolution received still further confirmation from Kant's *Natural History of the Heavens* (1755), which foreshadowed a theory of development of unformed planets. But this, according to Haeckel, exerted little effect before 1845. As the end of the century approached, increasingly more attention was paid to this idea. Lessing in 1780 voiced the theory of a gradual development underlying human history.[4] Likewise Herder thought of the lower stages conditioning the higher; Laplace worked out a theory of the evolution of the solar system.[5] James Hutton[6] suggested the principle of uniform growth which was finally established by Lyell's *Geology* in 1830.

Gradually it came to be accepted, that the world instead of being a mere machine, was a living, growing organism. This, in its effect, was little short of a revolution in human thinking. It implied that whatever is has developed from something which

[3] P. C. Mitchell, article "Evolution," Encyclopedia Britannica.
[4] *Die Erziehung des Menschemgeschlechts.*
[5] *Exposition du systeme du Monde.* Paris, 1796.
[6] *Theory of the Earth.* 1795.

was simpler and will, in all probability, continue to change into something that is more complex and diverse. There is indeed, in all this, an element which calls forth something more than pure logic; it encourages speculation, exalts the fancy or the imagination,—characteristics, be it noted, which Cartesianism and the Encyclopedic ideal had minimized or explained away.

The principle of growth and development was accepted, in part at least, by the physical scientists, while they tried to accommodate it to the orthodox Newtonian-mechanical conception. The biological scientists, on the other hand, were in a quandary whether to take their cue from the physical scientists or from the "nature philosophers." Since the method employed by the former group had the sanction of science and stood in good repute, the biologists continued, in the main, to search for a mechanical principle and tended to discourage the free speculations of the philosophers. These "nature philosophers" on the other hand, in letting their conjectures range more widely, gathered quantities of data, which subsequently proved valuable to many of the scientists.

Such a one was Lorenz Oken (1779-1851), who was always speculating, always attempting a unified account of biological development. Nevertheless, in 1807, he was able to announce to the world the vertebral nature of the skull.[7] Buffon, as early as 1749, had begun to speculate upon the idea that the species were not unalterable, and that the simple may have become the complex. This he derived in part from contemplation and in part from observation until he was able to declare: "We can descend by almost imperceptible degrees from the most perfect creature to the most formless matter—from the most highly organized animal to the most entirely inorganic substance."[8]

It is not surprising, then, that Erasmus Darwin found a keen

[7] He probably did not know of Goethe's earlier discovery.
[8] *Histoire Naturelle.*

excitement in his inner life, for his mind was wrestling with some of these problems, turning them over, musing upon them, and perceiving some of their implications more clearly than his friends. In touch with the scientific movement of his time, he became deeply affected by the idea of growth and development. His imagination was stirred, and like so many others among the nature philosophers he began to meditate upon the why and how. He was disposed to accept in part an explanation based upon the mechanical principle, especially for the formation of the universe and even for the spontaneous generation of life. However, when life appeared and the organism was capable of feeling a need, of willing in even a most rudimentary form, then the mechanism of the whole process did not seem to him to be at all evident. So his mind began to consider how this development or growth might have taken place. That he was aware of the conjectural character of his science is apparent from his Apology, published in the *Botanic Garden:*

It may be proper here to apologize for many of the subsequent conjectures on some articles of natural philosophy, as not being supported by accurate investigation or conclusive experiments. Extravagant theories, however, in those parts of philosophy, where our knowledge is yet imperfect, are not without their use; as they encourage the execution of laborious experiments, or the investigation of ingenious deductions, to conform or refute them. And since natural objects are allied to each other by many affinities, every kind of theoretic distribution of them adds to our knowledge by developing some of their analogies.

If his suppositions appear to us in the light of "scientific reveries," as the critic in the Edinburgh Review, for July, 1803, designated them, we would do well to remember that his mind and method were not devoid of a genuine scientific bias, for he boldly opposed the popular movement of his time, which was finding in every scientific achievement a further strengthening of the theological argument from design. The classical example of the arguments based upon design, Paley's *Natural Theology*

(1802) was, if we are to accept the statement of Samuel Butler, "written throughout at the 'Zoonomia'."[9] But Erasmus Darwin, quite to the contrary, one of his critics pointed out,

did not inquire how far this or that property of plants or animals was directly or indirectly serviceable to man, but rather whether particular properties were not useful to the organisms themselves, and whether it was conceivable that they could have acquired such properties as favored their well-being by an internal impulse and gradual improvement.

This was, indeed, a very decided approach towards the scientific attitude; but during the closing years of the eighteenth century, and far into the nineteenth, this system of speculation, as Erasmus Darwin applied it, was condemned most heartily by the physical scientists, who continued to hold as their ideal the mathematical-mechanical procedure of Newton. This procedure, it is true, gives a place to speculation too, speculation issuing in hypothesis is the method followed by both the physical scientists and the nature philosophers; but the method followed by the latter is much more free, in the sense that its goal is not necessarily a mathematical formula. The conjectures, being less rigidly restrained, result in hypotheses that frequently go far afield.

If we compare these two methods with one which is most prevalent today in science, we note that although the scientific mind is still seeking for a mechanical explanation and still trying to reduce all data to a mathematical basis of measurement, a prominent place is given, however, to the factor of speculation, through the exercise of which some of the greatest scientific hypotheses of modern times have found expression.

Erasmus Darwin had not primarily a Baconian type of mind, patiently accepting only those facts which can be derived from induction, content to plod along, until out of a vast array of particulars, a generalization can be drawn. Indeed, if he had

[9] *Evolution Old and New.* 1879.

been content with that method he never would have given his theory of development. Furthermore, if his illustrious grandson had not resorted to speculation, he never could have formulated his theory of natural selection. In brief, the method which Erasmus Darwin employed is, with certain more rigid restrictions, very much the same used by the modern scientist, a view which differs from the mathematical-mechanical ideal, in that it allows more scope for reflection and imagination.

May we not at this point ask ourselves if the most illustrious men in the history of science have not shown the possession of a creative imagination which has often been as soaring and as bold as that evinced by the greatest poets?

Erasmus Darwin, influenced somewhat more by the Nature Philosophy of his time than his grandson was two generations later, made greater assumptions than the author of the *Origin of Species* and subjected his data to a less rigid scrutiny, in his desire to embody his beliefs and findings into a perfect system. It was this longing that encouraged him to theorize boldly, where he could not definitely prove. So, when in 1775, he wrote that he was giving up poetry and preparing a medical work, he was seeking, as he later testified in the introduction to that work, the *Zoonomia*, "to reduce the facts belonging to animal life into classes, orders, genera and species, and by comparing them with each other to unravel the theory of diseases," for, he continues, "there is need of a theory in the medical profession—a theory founded upon nature, that should bind together the scattered facts of medical knowledge and converge into one point of view the laws of organic life."

Not merely was he inquisitive in his own particular field of medicine—which, naturally enough, frequently served as a starting point for his speculations—but his curiosity spread to all regions, and he wanted to connect them into a unified whole. His interest in botany found a practical outlet in the botanical garden which he had fitted up near Lichfield. Here he had a chance to observe at first hand the phenomena of plant growth in general, and to reflect in particular upon the classifications of Linnaeus. It was perfectly natural, given an interest in versifying and possessing a theory of what poetry should do, that he should attempt to give poetic expression to the fruits of his study and observation in *The Loves of the Plants* (1789).

Soon, however, speculation gains the upper hand. It is not enough to observe how plants grow and to classify them. He needs must ponder how plants came to be at all,—a thesis which leads him back to the still more fundamental question of the formation of the universe, and naturally enhances his interest in geology, and especially in the writings of Whitehurst and Dr. Hutton. The result of all this finds utterance in "The Economy of Vegetation" (1792), in which he strives to give abstract ideas further pictorial expression.

> When Love Divine, with brooding wings unfurl'd,
> Call'd from the rude abyss the living world,
> 'Let there be light!' proclaim'd the Almighty Lord,
> Astonish'd chaos heard the potent word;
> Through all his realms the kindly Ether runs,
> And the mass starts into a million suns;
> Earths round each sun with quick explosions burst,
> And second planets issue from the first.[10]

More detailed information about the birth of the earth is given in the Second Canto:[11]

> Gnomes! you bright forms, presiding at her birth,
> Cling in fond squadrons round the new-born Earth;
> When high in ether, with explosions dire,
> From the deep craters of his realms of fire,
> The Whirling Sun this ponderous planet hurl'd
> And gave the astonish'd void another world.

The rotation of the earth on its axis, he explains in a note, "was occasioned by its greater friction or adhesion to one side of the

---

[10] Canto I, l. 101 f.
[11] Line 11.

cavity from which it was ejected, and from its rotation it acquired spheroidical form." Then:
>   When its vaporous air, condensed by cold,
>   Descending torrents into oceans roll'd;
>   And fierce attraction with relentless force
>   Bent the reluctant wanderer to its course.

How did the first land appear?
>   You [the Gnomes] trod with printless step Earth's tender globe,
>   While Ocean wrapp'd it in his azure robe;
>   Beneath his waves her hardening strata spread,
>   Raised her Primeval Islands from his bed,
>   Stretched her wide lawns and sunk her winding dells,
>   And deck'd her shores with corals, pearls and shells.

The original nucleus of the earth, he goes on to explain, consisted of "the masses or mountains of granite, porphyry, et cetera. On this nucleus, thus covered by the ocean, were formed the calcareous bed of lime-stone marble, chalk, spar from the remains of marine animals. . . ." This land was then "burnt by central fires, islands and continents were raised, consisting of granite or lava in some parts, and of limestone in others."

>   [And] rose the continents and sunk the main,
>   And Earth's huge sphere exploding burst in twain.

So the moon was born,
>   Dimpled with vales, with shining hills emboss'd
>   And roll'd round Earth her airless realms of frost.

As a result of this explosion,
>   [The] Earth recoiling stagger'd from her course;
>   When, as her line in slower circles spun,
>   And her shock'd axis nodded from the sun.
>   . . . .
>   And while new tides their shouting floods unite,
>   And hail their Queen, fair Regent of the night.

"On some parts of these islands and continents were gradually produced morasses from the recrements of vegetables and land animals; and from these morasses, heated by fermentation, were produced clay, marble, sand-stone, coal, iron, et cetera."

The production of salt is then described:
> Gnomes! you then taught the transuding dews to pass
> Through time-fall'd woods, and root-unwove morass
> Age after age; and with filtration fine
> Dispart, from earth and sulphurs, the saline.

Numerous and deep fissures were formed in the elevation of the mountains, and in these fissures many of the metals are found. ... The summits of the new mountains, cracked by cold dews or snows falling upon them when red-hot, cubes and lozenges descended gradually into the valleys and were rolled together in the beds of the rivers. ... The positions above described were deranged by subsequent earthquakes and volcanoes, and hence we have the earth as it is today.

Having shown that plants behave in some respects like human beings, and having explained how they came to be at all, and how the earth itself upon which they are dependent came into existence, he is led to a consideration of man himself. Carrying forward the idea of development, which he has utilized in his theorizing about the formation of the universe, he extends it into the organic world as well.

His theory of the origin of man, and man's connection with the lower animals and with plant life is shown at first in his prose *Zoonomia* (1794-96). His primary purpose in this work was, as has already been remarked, to seek out a theory of disease which should have a scientific foundation. Therefore, it was necessary to get down as far as possible to the basic principles underlying the life of mankind. Here his professional and his philosophical interests met and coincided. He reduced nature to the two substances of spirit and matter, but his discussion was confined in the main to the phenomenon of motion, which he found to be the chief characteristic of life. After a detailed study of the various kinds of fibrous motions, he concluded that there were four kinds of these—Irritative, Sensitive, Voluntary, and Associative—and furthermore that this same classification extended down the scale to the lower animal forms and also even into the vegetable domain. In order to understand these movements it was necessary to study what stimulated them and how they functioned, and thus he concluded, that in the higher forms of animal life, ideas were a contributing cause, while in the lower forms, instincts played a similar rôle. The term "disease" then, implied a disturbance of one or more of these classes of fibrous activities, and the physician's place was to apply remedies which would restore their normal functioning.

Here we have an example of patient investigation supplemented by his ever urgent desire to develop a system. Observation and philosophic speculation were given nearly equal emphasis. In his conjectures the concept of development was always present. Having had occasion to note a certain resemblance in structure which obtained in all warm-blooded animals, he wondered if they might not have been produced from a similar living filament.

It remained for him to connect his theory of animal life with his earlier studies in plant life; and this he proceeded to do in another prose work, the *Phytologia* (1799), where the same idea of progression was further applied to plant life. There he declared that: "Vegetables are inferior animals," and that they differed by not having muscles of locomotion or organs of digestion; "they have absorbent, placental, and pulmonary vessels, arteries, glands, organs of reproduction; with muscles, nerves, and brains."

In his observation of vegetables he noted that "many changes are due to their perpetual contest for light and air above ground, and for food and moisture beneath the soil, from climate or other causes"; and with a boldness that fairly startles one in its audacity, he inquired: "Shall we conjecture that one and the same kind of living filament is and has been the cause of all organic life?" But this was not all, he had an explanation ready at hand: "From their first rudiment or primordium, to the termination of their lives, all animals undergo perpetual transformations which are in part produced by their own exertion in consequence of their desires and aversions; of their pleasures and pains; or of irritations, or associations, and many of these acquired forms or propensities are transmitted to their posterity."

This deduction is very like that offered by Lamarck in his *Philosophic Zoologique*, published in 1809, fifteen years after the *Zoonomia* of Erasmus Darwin. It is similar also to that offered by Treviranus in 1796, two years after the *Zoonomia*.

The question of Dr. Darwin's place in the history of Science is really very difficult. While it appears evident that the *Zoonomia* antedates both the *Philosophic Zoologique* of Lamarck and the *Biologie* of Treviranus, it is not at all clear that these later works owe anything to Erasmus Darwin's theory. The controversy has been waged by such men as Samuel Butler, Charles Darwin, and Professor Osborn, as well as many others. Samuel Butler declares that the theory put forth in the *Zoonomia* in 1794, was adopted almost in its entirety by Lamarck, who when he had caught the leading idea (probably through a French translation of *The Loves of the Plants* in 1800), began to elucidate it in 1801 and continued to do so up to his death in 1831.[12] Charles Darwin suggested that he must have been familiar with the *Zoonomia* and made use of it in the *Philosophic Zoologique* in 1809.[13] In this connection Professor Osborn points out that Lamarck made no reference to the *Zoonomia* and paid very scant attention to Buffon. Yet there is the strongest internal evidence that Lamarck was largely influenced by Buffon in the writings of his second period.[14] In his latest edition of the *Animaux sans vertébrés* Lamarck makes the following statement: "It is the first, so it seems to me, which has been presented, the

---

[12] Samuel Butler, *op. cit.* (Perhaps Butler meant the "Economy of Vegetation," for Erasmus Darwin did not explain this theory in the portion of the poem entitled *Loves of the Plants*.)
[13] See "Preliminary Notice" appended to Ernest Krause's work.
[14] Osborn, p. 153.

only theory, therefore, which exists, because I do not know any work which offers another theory based upon a large number of principles and considerations." "This seems satisfactory evidence," concludes Professor Osborn, "that Erasmus Darwin and Lamarck independently involved their views."[15]

Erasmus Darwin undoubtedly derived something from Buffon and Linnaeus and from the general thoughts of the nature philosophy of his time. As to what he educed specifically from Goethe there may indeed be some question. In 1786 Goethe showed the existence of the intermaxillary bone in man, the supposed absence of which had been regarded by anatomists as a character clearly separating man from animal. Also about the same time he put forth the idea of vegetable metamorphosis, and he is generally credited with the discovery of the vertebral nature of the skull in 1790. In 1794 came Darwin's *Zoonomia*. This naturally promotes the inquiry, is there a connection between the work of Darwin and Goethe? Since Goethe's views on anatomy were not published until 1820, there is, indeed, no probability that Darwin knew anything of them. On the other hand Butler declares that since the *Zoonomia* was translated into German between 1795-97, Goethe must have known of the work in 1807, when he wrote that "plants and animals in their most imperfect condition . . . can hardly be distinguished." "There is no proof," Butler concludes, "that Goethe enunciated any new principles." Ernest Krause, however, who admits a similarity in their views, says, "they both felt a need to give utterance to their conceptions in verse; but the agreement may be easily explained if we consider that both of them started from the investigation of Buffon and Linnaeus.[16]

What place, then, can we assign to Erasmus Darwin in the history of Science? It may be true, as is often claimed, that he had no definite part in the main line of advance of the evolution-

---
[15] Osborn, *op. cit.*, pp. 154-55.
[16] Ernest Krause. *op. cit.*, p. 137.

ary theory. It seems reasonable to suppose we should have had the enunciation of natural selection whether Erasmus Darwin had lived or not. It is one of those hypothetical questions which does not admit of a categorical answer. For our present purposes, moreover, the solution is not vital. It is sufficient for us to recognize that we have in this physician of Lichfield a man with a marked curiosity in natural phenomena, a keen observer, one thoroughly alive to the philosophical movement of his time, with its aim to explain things in terms of growth and development, and one who sought to utilize the material revealed to him by his senses in forming an evolutionary theory of organic life. In this explanation, he was certainly among the leaders, if not the very first.

Because of the poetic side of his nature he desired to translate these scientific truths into images or mind pictures. Thus, having performed the needed pioneering work in his theory of the development of man and having made the necessary abstractions, he was ready to undertake the pictorial representation in poetry. Had he not an idea big enough to appeal to the imagination and enlist it in the cause of Science?

This he attempted to do in *The Temple of Nature, or the Origin of Society*.[17] After acknowledging God the First Cause, he proceeds:

>Nursed by warm sun-beams in primal caves,
>Organic life began beneath the waves.

The process of generation, however, was spontaneous.

>First Heat from chemic dissolution springs
>And gives to matter its eccentric wings.

The atoms were brought together mechanically through attraction.

>And quick contraction with ethereal flame
>Lights with life the fibre-woven frame,
>Hence without parent by spontaneous birth
>Rises the finest specks of animated earth.

---
[17] Published in 1803, the year after his death.

He next explained how these "specks" developed:
> In branching cones the living web expands,
> Lymphatic ducts, and convoluted glands;
> Aortal tubes propel the nascent blood,
> And lengthening veins absorb the refluent flood;
> . . . .
> Next the long nerves unite their silver train
> And young sensation permeates the brain.

Finally he traced the gradual development of the mind from the first actions of "excited sense," through the voluntary repetitions that resulted from a pain and pleasure economy sponsored by Recollection, aided in the act of choosing by Reason and by the mystic power of suggestion and association of ideas.

If his science was too far in advance of his time to be understood or even dimly appreciated, his poetic style, on the other hand, was thoroughly conservative, and for a short time it was very widely praised. In 1803, the critic of the *Edinburgh Review*, could call his verses "immortal," because they were in the style of Pope, full of the machinery of sylphs, gnomes, and sprites; very rhetorical with their periphrases, personifications, elaborate similes and metaphors. Possessing none of the novelty of Burns, Cowper, Young, Gray, or Collins, and being, moreover, completely conventional, his was a style which soon lent itself to travesty, such as that accorded to it by George Canning in the "Anti-Jacobin Review":
> Let Hydrostatics, simpering as they go
> Lead the light Naiads on fantastic toe;
> Let shrill Accoustics tune the tiny lyre;
> With Euclid sage fair Algebra conspire;
> The obedient pulley strong Mechanics ply,
> And wanton Optics roll the melting eye!

It is not the Popeian style alone that Canning is parodying in his "Loves of the Triangles." It is also, and very much more, Darwin's attempt to put contemporary science into poetry, a principle which a little later furnished the basis for some amicable disputes between Coleridge and some of his friends—discussions which served, so he tells us, to render his "own thoughts more and more plain," and to deliver him from the "painted mists that occasionally rise from the marshes at the foot of Parnassus." To him Darwin's work was a "Russian palace of ice, glittering, cold, and transitory." And the thing which grew clearer to him was that Poetry and Science are mutually exclusive.[18]

This issue came more and more into prominence in the generation of Coleridge and Wordsworth. While the scientific attitude of mind was gaining ground in many quarters, the concept of a growing and developing world was also finding expression in the work of some of the poets. Much of the new poetry tended to devote itself to revealing man's inner nature,—the well-springs of his emotion rather than the full fruit of his rational nature. The naïve element became prominent. This position tended to make poetry and science antagonistic, or to render one a continuation of, or development from, the other. The former point of view was supported by Coleridge and his followers, who regarded these spheres as entirely antithetical. Wordsworth, on the other hand, felt that even, "the remotest discoveries of the chemist, the Botanist, or Mineralogist, will be as proper objects of the Poet's art if the time should ever come when these things shall be familiar to us . . . as enjoying and suffering beings."[19] For him, this was in the future, and he made no effort to utilize the current concern in chemistry, electricity, geology, or biology, which a large portion of mankind was then feeling and thinking about.

One is inclined to raise the question at this point, did the growing scientific interest tend to find a reflection in some of the poetry in the early years of the nineteenth century? We can, as a matter of fact, detect an increasing respect among the poets

[18] *Biographia Literaria*, Chap. I.
[19] Preface to the *Lyrical Ballads*.

for the little differences between one man's experiences and another's. We find some of these poets aiming to express the singularities rather than the idealized generalities, as the classical age had tried to do. Does this characteristic owe anything to the growth of scientific interest? When we find these differences being examined with something of the keenness of discernment which characterized the scientist—as Wordsworth for example, studies the Cumberland rustics and analyzes with minute care the growth of his own mind (in "The Prelude"), and as he exhibits a thesis-like quality of mind in making the ordinary seem extraordinary and in expressing "emotion recollected in tranquility"—we cannot help feeling that something of the method of the scientist has carried over into poetry.

It is, of course, obvious that the intellectual result of a poet who has been touched by the concept of evolution may be very different from that of Erasmus Darwin, who curiously enough used a vehicle of expression which had been conditioned, in part at least, by the Newtonian idea of science, to preach the philosophy of development. Wordsworth and Coleridge, on the other hand, employed a style which was occasioned to a certain extent by this same idea of growth and development, even though they themselves eschewed the doctrines. It is fitting, therefore, that we should consider in the next chapter the work of a greater poet, whose medium is influenced in part by the new philosophy, and who consciously upholds these doctrines in the subject matter of his poetry,—Johann Wolfgang von Goethe.

Chapter VII

POETRY CHAMPIONS EVOLUTION
GOETHE

Goethe is an important figure in any consideration of the relations of science and poetry in the latter part of the eighteenth century and the first part of the nineteenth, because in him, we have perhaps as near a union between science, poetry, and philosophy as we can find throughout that period. More thoroughly imbued with the Nature Philosophy of his time than Erasmus Darwin, he was fully as much of a scientist and a very much better poet.

His long life (1749-1832) spans a period of rapidly changing ideas and ideals. Born at a time when the stage was set for a secession from French classicism and the way was being prepared by the more radical thinkers for a philosophical revolt from French Cartesianism and a reaction from the mathematico-mechanical conception of Newton, the youth exhibited something of the spirit of the Encyclopedists combined with the desire to experience and to unify.

At the University of Leipzig, however, he heard expounded for the most part the orthodox views on metaphysics, logic, and theology, derived from Cartesian principles, as these were interpreted by Thomasin and Wolff; and a spirit of rebellion stirred within him. He turned to writing light anacreontic lyrics and some plays, to taking drawing lessons and to studying art. He went out much in society and fell in love. Indeed, the distractions of student life proved too great a strain on his strength, and on account of illness he was compelled to return to the home of his parents in Frankfort-on-Main. Even at that time he must have been dimly aware at least of the ideas that were rippling the surface of intellectual life in Germany. One of these disturbing currents emanated from Lessing and the group of thinkers who had gathered about him in Berlin. These, prompted by the teachings of Shaftesbury, were laying great emphasis upon the importance of the moral feeling as the main spring in human conduct. Another current issued from France and bore on its surface the influence of Voltaire and the French Encyclopedists, placing the emphasis upon reason. But the most important eddy of all was that in which the ideas of Shaftesbury and Rousseau, exalting the "natural" man at the expense of the "rational" man, giving more attention to the impulses, the yearnings and the strivings of the individual, swirled against the older bulwarks and threatened to undermine them. To this reaction from Cartesianism and from the French Enlightenment and even from the thoroughgoing English Empiricism, Goethe very early began to respond, if not positively at first, yet with a restlessness that is characterized as "divine." There seemed to be something in his inmost being which craved understanding, not of a series of isolated details, such as science had been content with in the first half of the eighteenth century, but of all being and all existence. This need grew with his years, and his experiences in themselves served to strengthen it.

Upon his enforced return to Frankfort he had time, during his convalescence, to consider some of these matters. Another influence, however, overshadowed these more somber considerations, after he had been cured very mysteriously, at least so it seemed to him, by Dr. Metz in the city of his birth. Thus, he became interested in the speculations and researches of Dr. Metz and Fraulein von Klettenberg, and with them he dipped into the semi-magical works of Paracelsus, the half-mythical, half-scientific way of viewing nature in the *Aurea Catena Homeri*. From his interest in alchemy and in the Neoplatonic philosophy, he began to seek by way of experiments to discover the mysterious interrelation of things. By means of a wind furnace, alembics, and retorts he attempted to produce natural salts and to extract virgin earth from liquor silicium and observe its transition into pregnancy. From these mystical studies he proceeded towards a more methodical chemistry, the chemical compendium of Boerhaave serving as his guide. Even in his youthful days he came to feel that by experiencing the world, the poet and the artist experience the eternal, the genuine, and the typical.[1]

This conviction deepened in his subsequent life and especially when he went to Strassburg, in 1770, to complete his law course, and found himself in a new environment. It seemed to him to be symbolized in the Gothic architecture of the minster, offering something entirely opposed to the classical and rationalistic atmosphere which he had known at Leipzig. Here too he met Herder, who taught him the underlying significance of the Gothic art and the charm of the simple and the naïve. When the youth found that he had much time on his hands he proceeded to broaden his knowledge of medicine, anatomy, and chemistry, thus supplementing the deepening of his aesthetic appreciation and understanding. But even though his natural curiosity was being directed into more scientific channels and was consequently less mystical, the idea of an inner unity still persisted. Nor did this conviction lessen in his more practical life at Weimar. Indeed, from 1775, when he first went there to live, his interest in science grew more definite and concrete. "Road-making and mining led him to mineralogy and geology, forestry and agriculture to botany, while his lectures on the human figure at the Weimar School of Drawing occasioned his more careful anatomical studies."[2] Notwithstanding the fact that with Frau von Stein he read Spinoza's *Ethics* and Buf-

[1] Bielschowsky, III, 251.
[2] *Ibid.*, I, 360.

fon's *Epoque de la Nature,* "demonstrated to her conic sections and microscopic preparations, became absorbed with her in the bony structure of man, in the orbits of the stars, and in the history of the earth's crust, read with her the literature of ancient and modern times,"[3] he never slackened his search for unity.

Up to this time his personal experiences and emotions had colored all his literary endeavors. His works from 1770 to 1785 show this especially. Thus, *Götz von Berlichingen,* written in Strassburg, gave expression to his more unrestrained propensities; the titular hero of *Clavigo* comes to a tragic end through his want of character; Werther's sorrows are occasioned for the most part by his lack of moral strength. In all these there is a defiance, not only of the literary conventions, but also of the static conception of life. These heroes and the other characters are acted upon by their environment, and they change, either developing or deteriorating. The author very strongly emphasizes this changing process. Indeed, his characters appear to be experimenting with the forces of life, seeking not merely to adjust themselves to their surroundings, but also to realize their latent possibilities. Tragedy results in their failure to accomplish this. They are trying in fact to achieve the same thing as their creator. If Goethe has been at times discouraged, if he has thought of suicide, if he has felt weak and weighed down by circumstances, he has nevertheless pressed on, with the aim of experiencing and realizing something more. After he settled in Weimar he still persisted in his scientific investigations. He studied anatomy under Loder at Jena. In 1784 he demonstrated that the intermaxillary bone in man existed and that its reputed absence had been due to the fact that it had grown together with the adjacent bones. Two years later, just previous to his Italian journey, he was entertaining the idea that all organs of plants are merely specialized leaves. In addition, he experienced along with his many other sensations and speculations the responsi-

[3] *Ibid.,* I, 308.

bilities and duties of state in Weimar, as he concerned himself with agricultural, horticultural, and mining problems.

The next experience that came to him was probably the most potent one of his life, bringing a fuller revelation of the true significance of beauty. His Italian journey (1786-88) served to reveal the meaning of antiquity rather than the Renaissance, and initiated him into the austere charm of the classic ideal of restraint, an ideal he ever after cherished and attempted to adapt to the newer conception of growth and development. He returned to a Germany still under the influence of the *Sturm und Drang,* a movement which now appeared to him thoroughly uncongenial. With his new interests and the vast field for thought and speculation which his Italian experience had opened up, he lived a quieter and more contemplative life. Yet the divine restlessness did not desert him entirely. Once, in the clutches of such a turbulent mood, he sought peace in Venice; but his trip failing to satisfy him; he studied painting there and occupied himself with thoughts of the metamorphosis of the animal body. Upon his return to Weimar he utilized a few of his superabundant energies in directing the ducal theatre as well as continuing his scientific investigations, which included at that time some experimenting with optics and the evolving of a theory of light and color.[4]

The French Revolution apparently stirred him but little, for he could not see how anything really salutary could come out of violence. It seemed to him at this time that man's most profitable activities lay in pursuing truth through science and through beauty. So he continued to study botany, zoology, comparative anatomy, chemistry, and astronomy. He planned a poem on nature which was never written. All this time he was turning over in his mind a theory of art, much of which found expression in the *Propyläen,* the periodical which he established. In *Die Metamorphose der Pflanzen* (1797), and *Die Metamorphose der*

[4] "Beitrage zur Optik."

Tiere (about 1806), he definitely sought to combine poetry and science. His friendship with Schiller, which had ripened since 1794, just at the time when Schiller was deeply engaged with the problem of reconciling poetry and philosophy, tended to stimulate in Goethe a renewed interest in verse and to focus his attention more persistently upon its possible relations with science. This problem continued to interest him throughout the twenty-seven years he survived Schiller, who died in 1805. In the second part of *Faust* it is evident in his ethical and moral conclusions, and also in the prose works *Wilhelm Meisters Wanderjahre,* and *Die Wahlverwandtschaften.*

Unless we understand the evolution of Goethe's mature thought, it is difficult to comprehend why science and philosophy held such a prominent place in his long active life. His philosophy was derived in the main largely from the pantheism of Spinoza. The sparks of the divine which he felt to exist in his own soul were ever seeking union with the Infinite or the One. Through the restless striving occurred that growth or development of the innermost self, which he termed culture. Of the various ways of approaching this Unity, one way is through Science. But this, in the Newtonian sense, cannot give the final word. There are however, several other avenues of approach, all involving some form of experience derived through activity.

He wrote *The Sorrows of Werther,* he declares, in order to "preserve my internal nature according to its peculiarities, and let external nature influence me according to its qualities, . . . and to allow all beings from man downwards, as low as they were comprehensible, to act upon me, each after his own kind. . . . There arose a wonderful affinity with the single objects of nature," he adds.[5] According to this conception the whole course of the world is a development, an unfolding of the divine plan. Many of these experiences may be achieved vicariously through

---

[5] *Dichtung und Wahrheit,* John Oxenford's trans. Lond., 1873, I, 470.

literature and the arts. Indeed, another way to pursue the desired unity is by seeking beauty. Whether experiences in general be sought for, or beauty, or any other specified knowledge, before harmony or anything approaching unity can be achieved, a certain amount of limitation and discipline is necessary. Thus, he finds a definite place for science again. In this restless search for unity, therefore, both the feelings and the intellect are intimately involved.

His final, or mature, concepts of reality were the product of slow growth and development, built up from a whole series of experiences, which first sought to emphasize the feelings, and later the rational side. Each step had advanced him, he felt, to a position nearer his goal. Therefore each individual moment in the process—the irrational moment, quite as much as the rational—had something of a sacred character. Toward the shaping of that final philosophy went much of the thought of the romantic philosophers—Herder, Fichte, and Schelling. They regarded as real only that inner self, or divine spark, which controlled the facts of external nature. Only with these so-called "facts"—mere outer coverings or trappings—did natural science deal. Indeed, according to this interpretation, the Newtonian concept of the world was merely the phenomenal and not the real view. Schelling supported this conception by the argument that the study of nature and the study of intelligence lead us to the same conclusions. In brief, nature and mind are the expression of the selfsame principles and are merely two aspects of the same thing. Thus the importance of the imagination, or of the will, is doubly secured; it may be merely another aspect of reality, but it can transcend the physico-mechanical aspect of the universe.

Goethe, not content with the Encyclopedic or the empiric points of view as a final explanation, champions occasionally the position that recognizes many different ones, all of which may be equally valuable in a growing world.

> Seele des Menschen
> Wie gleichst du dem Wasser!
> Schicksal des Menschen.
> Wie gleichst du dem Wind.[6]

Goethe had, however, after his induction into the beauties of classical art, and after his association with Schiller, found also a certain value in the restrained imagination. This side of his character is reflected especially in the second part of *Faust*, in Mephistopheles' scene with the Student, which is evidently intended for a satire on Fichte's philosophy of the unrestrained imagination.

The student has progressed far in learning and experience since he came a humble suppliant in Part I. Now he knows that "knowledge . . . is nothing worth," but "Man's life is in the blood," and hence in youth. Mephistopheles, disguised in the robes of Faust, remarks ironically, "The devil here has nothing more to say." The student continues:

> Wenn ich nicht will, so darf kein Teufel sein,
> . . . .
> Die Welt, sie war nicht, eh ich sie erschuf;
> . . . .
> Ich aber frei, wie mir's in Geiste spricht,
> Verfolge froh mein innerliches Licht.[7]

Mephistopheles then comments upon this attitude:

> Original fahr' hin in deiner Pracht!
> Wie würde dich die Einsicht kränken:

---

[6] Spirit of man,
Thou art like unto water!
Fortune of man
Thou art like unto wind.
"Gesang der Geister über den Wassern." Bowring trans., p. 219.

[7] Save through my will, no devil dares to be
. . . .
The world was not, till it I did create
. . . .
But I am free, as speaks my spirit-voice
My inward light I follow, and rejoice.

Wer kann was Dummes, wer was Kluges denken,
Das nicht die Vorwelt schon gedacht?[8]

The two parts of *Faust* are autobiographical in respect to the changing philosophy which is there depicted. This poem, it ought to be remembered, is really the life work of the poet. He began it about 1773 and worked at it intermittently until its completion in 1831, just the year previous to his death. Necessarily, during that time, his conception of Faust and of his philosophy underwent many changes. In the "Urfaust," for example, written by 1775, a product of the *Sturm und Drang* period, there is much rebellion and little philosophy. His initial inspiration came from some of the popular old books on Dr. Faustus, a character of the sixteenth century, and from the old puppet play of that name, and also from Lessing's appreciative remarks upon the theme. His purpose was not merely to reproduce the sixteenth century scene and setting. That was not at all Goethe's way. What he sought to express was the yearnings of Dr. Faustus in terms of late eighteenth century ideals, as reflected largely through his own inner experiences.

Goethe's conception is seen more clearly by contrasting it with that of his near contemporary Lessing, who, in his fragmentary "Faust" makes his hero become the type of a high-minded scholar, possessed with an unquenchable thirst for knowledge. Lessing, the thinker, holds that God cannot have given man an irresistible desire for knowledge merely to ruin him forever, and a voice from above consequently calls out to the devils: "Ihr sollt nicht siegen!"

Goethe's *Faust,* as Santayana points out, is imbued with the spirit of Rousseau, Hamann, Herder, and Swedenborg. "It is the drama of rebellion against convention; a flight to nature, to

---

[8] Part II, Act II, l. 226 f. Trans. by Swanwick, Lond., 1914.
Go, in thy pride, Original, thy way!
True insight would, in truth, thy spirit grieve;
What wise or stupid thoughts can man conceive,
Unponder'd in the Ages pastaway?

tenderness, to beauty; and then a return to convention again, with a feeling that nature, tenderness, and beauty, unless found there, will not be found at all.⁹

Santayana is, of course, referring to the final version: and it is upon this same version that I shall base the brief analysis that follows.

Before the opening of the play, Faust had been directing all his energies towards arriving at an understanding of the universe through rationalism, just as the Encyclopedists had attempted to do earlier in the eighteenth century. In the first act of the drama we find him in a very sceptical and disheartened mood. He has come to the pessimistic conclusion "That we in truth can nothing know!"¹⁰ So he resolves to give himself to magic

> Ob mir durch Geistes Kraft und Mund
> Nicht manch Geheimnis würde fund,
>
> . . . .
>
> Dass ich erkenne, was die Welt
> Im Innersten zusammenhält.¹¹

Like Goethe himself, Faust desires to embrace unity. He opens a huge volume to the sign of the Macrocosm, but he finds that he is no longer satisfied with symbols.

> Welch Schauspiel! aber ach! ein Schauspiel nur!
> Wo fass' ich dich, unendliche Natur?¹²

He desires to penetrate to reality itself, but when he summons the Earth-spirit through magic, he cannot endure the sight of

---

⁹ Santayana. *Three Philosophical Poets*, p. 142.
¹⁰ *Faust*. I, l. 11.
¹¹ In hope, through spirit-voice and night,
Secrets now veiled to bring to light
. . . .
That I the force may recognize
That binds creations inmost energies.
Faust. l. 34 f.
¹² A wonderous show! but ah! a show alone,
Where shall I grasp thee, infinite nature, where?
Faust. ll. 102-103.

it at first, and the Spirit declares: "Du gleichst dem Geist, den du begreifst, Nicht mir!"[13]

Rationalism and science have failed to satisfy this inner craving for unity. They have brought him only a spirit of denial (symbolized in the figure of Mephistopheles), who now offers him, however, the romantic consolations of a free will and an unrestrained imagination. But these, while giving him the love of Marguerite, bring disaster and even threaten disintegration to his personality, and hence no real satisfaction. In that love, however, there was the transient sense of beauty; and Faust determines to seek henceforth the desired unity, through the pursuit of ideal beauty. But he finds that without a certain amount of restraint tempered by wisdom and knowledge, he can do no more than grasp at the mere shadow. At length, guided by knowledge in which science has a vital part, he is able to realize for a short time this sense of ideal beauty (symbolized in the person of Helen of Troy), but at the last it eludes him. Then finally, accepting the principle of further limitation, he enunciates the gospel of work and of social service. And as the Angels bear his soul aloft they sing:

> Gerettet ist das edle Glied
> Der Geisterwelt vom Bösen
> Wer immer strebend sich bemüht,
> Den können wir erlösen[14]

Such, in brief, is the growth and development of the mind of Goethe. Life is a flux and change; the life history of an individual is a series of experiences, in which the beautiful soul seeks for highest self-realization. In this process are involved the

---

[13] Thou'rt like the spirit thou dost comprehend,
Not me! . . .
Faust. I, l. 164.

[14] Saved is this noble soul from ill,
Our spirit-peer. Who ever
Strives forward with unswerving will,
Him can we aye deliver.
Faust. II, Act V. l. 895 f.

will, the imagination, the ideal, the intellect and its systematic organization of phenomena, which is science. The exercise of any one of these activities, if pursued far, will involve the others. And this brings us more directly to a consideration of how poetry is related to Goethe's philosophy of growth and development.

In 1802 Goethe wrote Schiller: "I can never conduct myself in a purely speculative manner, but immediately I must see, for every proposition, an intuition, and thus I return forthwith to nature." In poetry, he looks through intuition, for the revelation of nature's truths before they arise clearly into rational thought. Any subject, he insists, science as well as any other, may lend itself to poetical treatment.

Goethe looked upon art as an expression of man's needs and desires in relation to his experience. So in heeding the inner promptings, one is led back to nature and to science. In this sense mankind is enclosed in an endless circle: if he would know nature, he must needs observe the effects of natural phenomena upon himself and more especially upon his emotions and his volitions (things which art revealed); but on the other hand, if he would know art, he must know also how nature works. Hence, art and nature are really two aspects of the same thing, whereby such a doctrine as the metamorphosis of plants would have a direct bearing upon art as well as upon nature.

In the practice of art we can compete with nature, [he declares], only when we have learned from her, to some extent at least, the manner in which she proceeds in the production of her works. . . . Therefore, in the highest sphere it is not really what has come into being, what is, as such, that is a subject for art; but in so far as in it a trace of growth, evolution, and living motion is observed, and the relation of the parts to one another and to the whole is visible.[15]

Here we have a direct declaration of the principle of development or evolution applied to art. Beauty, he defines accordingly as "an adequate realization of a hidden law of nature."[16] The

[15] Quoted from Bielschowsky, III, 99.
[16] *Spruche in Prosa,* No. 197. See Bielschowsky, III, 101.

law of development in organic nature is indeed just such a hidden law. Furthermore, since the process of development implies activity, Goethe feels that there should be a principle of activity, not merely in the work of creating, but also in the appreciating. He gives an emphatic expression to this idea in the fragmentary "Pandora." "Pandora" is undoubtedly symbolical of beauty. She is both the mother of the sciences (which seek truth with understanding) and of the arts (which represent it to the senses). When she comes to live upon Earth, she is spurned by Prometheus, symbolical of strength of mind, body, and will, and also, of prodigious activity. But his brother Epimetheus, whose mind is fixed on the ideals of life and is athirst for beauty and love, marries her. Epimetheus, lacking the very essential virtue of activity, is merely receptive, and seeks to enjoy life passively, until he falls into pessimism. At length, Pandora parts from him, leaving their daughter Epimeleia with him, who when she grows up fittingly marries Phileros, the son of Prometheus. And thus when the ideal of activity is joined with a love of beauty, the dawn of a new era appears.

Goethe, therefore, sees nothing antithetical between science and poetry. As "science has developed out of poetry," he asserts, "science and poetry may be combined."[17] At the same time he cautions the poet against an over-critical attitude, as witness, for example, the little poem called "Joy," in which the dragon-fly in flight delights the poet, its colors especially, but when it alights and he examines it more closely:

> Und nun betracht' ich sie genau,
> Und seh' ein traurig dunkles Blau-
> So geht es dir, Zerghedrer deiner Freuden![18]

While all poetry should furnish an element of instruction, this factor should not be obtrusive. Didactic or schoolmasterly

[17] Morphologie MS, VI, 139 and 167.
[18] 'Tis of a sad and dingy blue
    Such, joy-dissector, is thy curse indeed!
    Parabolisch. Die Freude.

poetry, he regards, as "a hybrid between poetry and rhetoric." His belief in the power of beauty is further demonstrated in *Faust* as the hero is liberated more and more from sensuousness through his pursuit of ideal Beauty, and as through the death of Euphorion his attention is directed more and more towards moderation and self-restraint, which are at their best in Hellenic art. Thus, by pursuing beauty, man acquires moral culture.

Poetry, moreover, is to be distinguished from science by its selective character. Indeed, he considers Byron's fault to be a too great concern with the empiric.[19] "Byron tells us truths, but truths so disagreeable that we should love him better if he held his peace. There are things in this world, which the true poet rather conceals than discloses."[20]

Goethe does not in any sense of the word identify science and poetry. While they are not antithetical in their materials or in their deep underlying principles, yet poetry as an art must observe a certain technique of inclusion and exclusion, and a certain development of thought and idea. It is symbolic rather than abstract; it is intuitive rather than rational. It does offer, however, another means of approach towards truth. This point of view comes out into bolder relief, when we compare his conception of the relationship of science and poetry with the conceptions of contemporary or near-contemporary critics.

A. W. Schlegel, for example, one of the spokesmen for the romantic movement in Germany, consecrates "the impressions of the senses" at the expense of the rational.[21] Novalis gives omniscience to the poet, who can peer behind "the veil [of Nature] and mysterious garment of the Unseen."[22] Therefore, there is more truth, he claims, in the romance of the poets than in a learned chronicle. Thoroughly imbued with the nature philoso-

[19] *Eckerman's Conversations*—trans. by S. M. Fuller, Boston, 1839, p. 170.
[20] *Ibid.*, p. 171-72.
[21] *Lectures on Dramatic Art and Literature.* I, 17.
[22] Carlyle's essay, "Novalis."

phy of his time, he too expressed the idea of metamorphosis or evolution in nature, which was "once an uncouthly teeming rock —now a quietly thriving plant, a silent human artist."[23] According to both of these views the poet with his all-seeing eye, so mysterious, and with his spark of the divine, can transcend the scientist. To the poet, as it were, belonged the final word.

By contrast, we note a quite different conception in Schiller. Although he also insists that the poet is essentially concerned with the sensuous and not the rational, and is "everywhere the guardian of nature,"[24] he is inclined to imply that art and science have rather different realms of activity. For example, beauty for him does not depend upon an understanding of natural laws.[25] He separates aesthetics entirely from ethics. Rationalism (and he undoubtedly includes Cartesianism and the Newtonian physics) has proved entirely inadequate to bring happiness to man. The freedom of the will, championed by the romantic philosophers, has not succeeded either. What is needed is not so much enlightenment of the mind as discipline of the feelings. Man must establish and preserve a perfect equipoise between his sensuous and his rational nature. As Kant had suggested,[26] he accepts for this office the aesthetic sense, the love of beauty. The discipline necessary to the accomplishment of this and the final adjustment and harmony may take place, he believes, through a surrender to the illusion of art, which he terms the Spieltrieb (play-bent). In this sense poetry should concern itself with the ideal rather than with the actual or the historical. He would not exclude scientific subjects if they can be treated imaginatively, but they must not make too great a demand upon the reader, or deter him from entering into the illusion. There is just a hint in this theory that Art is in one aspect an escape

[23] *Henry of Ofterdingen*, p. 113.
[24] "In Simple and Sentimental Poetry," quotation from Introduction to *Aesthetical and Philosophical Essays of Schiller*, pp. 299-300.
[25] *Ibid.*, p. 268, 297.
[26] *Critique of Judgment*, 1790.

from reality, but only for the purpose of readjustment between the rational and the sensuous.

The separation between science and poetry, which is barely implied in Schiller's treatment, receives a more definite statement at the hands of Hegel. He attempted in his philosophy, it will be recalled, to express reality in terms of the rational rather than of volition. Naturally he drew a sharp distinction between art and science. Poetry is a naïve attempt to seize "the True," in which the general aspect of things is not yet separated from the individual existence. . . . The poet is to keep himself separate from scientific and religious thought and not borrow their methods."[27] Yet since no better criterion has been discovered for art than imitation, the artist ought to strive to know all he can about nature. The object of art, he agrees with Schiller, is the representation of the Ideal. Since the Beautiful is the Platonic Idea under a particular form, he can concur with Goethe that beauty is a manifestation of a hidden law of nature.

The idea that art offers an escape from reality, hinted at by Schiller, finds its completest expression in Schopenhauer.[28] While holding that the function of art is to repeat the eternal ideas, he finds these opposed to the actions of science (a systematic form of knowledge which remains, as a rule, subordinate to the service of the will). "Science considers things in their relations. Art is concerned with that which is outside and independent of all relations."[29] Science, dealing with the so-called world of reality consists of Will of Force. This will, which Faust-like is incapable of finding satisfaction, may find a release from the tension of existence through self-renunciation and through the creative imagination.

We note in these critics whom we have cited a tendency vary-

[27] *Hegel's Aesthetic. A Critical Exposition.* By J. S. Kedney. 1897. p. 270 f.

[28] *Die Welt als Wille und Vorstellung*, 1819.

[29] *Arthur Schopenhauer: The World as Will and Idea.* Trans. by R. B. Haldane and J. Kemp. 3 vols. Lond., 1883. Vol. I, pp. 238-39.

ing all the way from an assertion that imagination as typified in the arts, poetry included, transcends the scientific view of the world, or presents a different aspect from science, but one equally true; to the position that the truth of poetry, while of a different order, has the very practical purpose of diverting the mind from the scientific aspect of things. It is obvious, however, that not all these critics mean the same thing exactly by the term "science." We have noted that Goethe feels that the statistical results of empirical science cannot be put into poetry. But is his idea of science, merely that, or does it include other elements?

J. S. Robertson, in his *Goethe and the Twentieth Century*,[30] points out, "No man, whose main business in life was poetry, has ever manifested so wholehearted an interest in natural science, and in politics." We can understand this in a measure when we recollect that according to Goethe's theory all these activities are really very intimately connected. One of his biographers, referring to the general condition of science at that time, writes, "Natural science was on the one hand devoting itself more and more to accurate special investigations, and on the other hand was turning more and more to the deepest and ultimate relations of things, thus transforming itself into a philosophy of nature."[31]

Another critic aptly finds that in his scientific work as a whole, it is the romantic rather than the classic Goethe who triumphs. "His method as a man of science was organic, philosophical, poetic, anything rather than precise and mathematical."[32] To this charge Goethe himself bears witness in his "Conversation with Falk":

Our scientific men are too fond of details. They count out to us the whole consistency of earth in separate lots, and are so happy as

---

[30] "Cambridge University Manuals," p. 128.
[31] Bielschowsky. I.
[32] *Quarterly Review*. Jan., 1900. "Goethe and the Nineteenth Century."

to have a separate name for every lot. . . . But what am I the better if I am ever so perfect in all these names? . . . I want to know what it is that impels every several portion,—either to rule or to obey it,—and qualifies some for the one part and some for the other, according to a law innate in them all, and operating like a voluntary choice. But this is the precise point upon which the most perfect and universal silence prevails."[33]

For this same reason he was impatient with the classifications made by Linnaeus, who, he says, exerted a great influence upon him, because of the discord which his work produced in his breast. What Linnaeus "sought with violence to keep out, I had to strive after to satisfy the innermost requirements of my being."[34] These requirements, as we have said before, were dominated by the ideal of unity. Therefore, Goethe had faith that the various genera and species of plant life might be shown to have developed out of one primordial form. He may be said to have studied plant life, as he did animal life later, with the urgent desire to establish this theory through scientific proof. At any rate, he concluded at length that "plants and animals in their most rudimentary stage . . . are hardly to be distinguished."[35] He felt that there may have been a gradual development from the simple to the more complex forms by a process of continuity, in which process man is now the highest development, but ultimately he may be supplanted by a superbeing. This method, according to a thoroughgoing empiricism, was not really scientific. Instead of speculation coming after a prolonged investigation, the speculation in some instances preceded first hand investigation, or at the most, after a brief period of observation and experiment. Goethe believed that he was holding to the principle of a postiori reasoning—a method which he very frequently upheld in his correspondence with Schiller—but in actual practice, as we have seen, he would begin with

[33] B. Taylor. *Goethe's Faust.* I, p. 342. Trans. by Mrs. Austen.
[34] Quoted by Bielschowsky, III, p. 107.
[35] NS VI, 13—Quoted by Bielschowsky, III, p. 107 f.

a theory, which he would try to substantiate experimentally. Furthermore his theorizing had none of the Newtonian mathematical exactness.

From the modern point of view, at any rate, Goethe's science was lacking in a regard for details, in the requisite degree of detachment, as well as in its lack of mathematics. Notwithstanding these deficiencies, he made some contributions which have been of very great importance in the history of science. He was certainly among the first to restore to botany and zoölogy their ancient rank as real sciences. He helped materially to give to science the doctrine of metamorphosis. He accounts for the variation and transformation of species by many of the same means as our modern theories of evolution employ—adaptations, use and disuse of organs, inheritance, and even the idea of the struggle for existence. "Everything that comes into being," he declares, "seeks room for itself and desires duration, hence it crowds another out of its place and shortens its duration."[36]

Besides pointing out the existence of an intermaxillary bone in man, the metamorphosis of plants, and the vertebral nature of the skull, he proposed a theory of light and color which challenged the classical theory of Newton. He was unable to meet the defenders of the older theory on their own ground, however, that of mathematics. Indeed, the method of his attack shows his fundamental weakness as a scientist and his unmistakably "romantic" temper in the field of science. Yet, taking science as he understood the term, in the sense of a "nature philosophy," was he not to a certain degree a forerunner of the science that was founded on the organic conception instead of the type founded on the mathematico-mechanical idea? At any rate, believing that science (so conceived) was one avenue of approach to a comprehension of the unity of things, he sought to give expression to it in his verse. Since his literary method itself was derived from a study of nature, of which he believed science was

[36] NS XI, 156: *Spruche in Prosa.* No. 981.

merely a rationalized expression, he could see no logical reason why poetry might not be utilized, provided certain limitations are recognized, for the embodiment of those truths in a beautiful form. So, among his minor poems, we find the whole idea of the metamorphosis of plants, as well as that of animals, put into verse. His general method in these is somewhat similar to that employed by Erasmus Darwin, it will be observed; only his style is free from the ornateness and the poetic paraphernalia with which the diction of the English poet abounded.

The Metamorphosis of Plants begins:

> Dich verwirret, Geliebte, die tausendfältige Mischung
> Dieses Blumengewühls über dem Garten umher;
> Viele Namen hörest du an, und immer verdränget
>   Mit barbarischem Klang einer den andern im Ohr.
> Alle Gestalten find ähnlich, und keine gleichet der andern;
>   Und so deutet das Chor auf ein geheimes Gesetz,
> Auf ein heiliges Rätsel. . . .[37]

The poet insists that the mystery can be explained and he proceeds to elucidate the process by which "the plant, little by little progressing, step by step guided on, changeth to blossom and fruit,"[38] how

> Aus dem Samen entwickelt sie sich sobald ihn der Erde
> Stille befruchtender Schoos hold in das Leben entläszt,
> Und dem Reize des Lichts, des heiligen, ewig bewegten,
> Gleich den zärtesten Bau keimender Blätter empfiehlt.
> Einfach schlief in dem Samen die Kraft; ein beginnendes Vorbild

---

[37] Thou art confused my beloved, at seeing the thousand fold union
   Shown in the flowery troop, over the garden dispers'd;
   Many a name dost thou hear assign'd; one after another
   Falls on thy list'ning ear, with a barbarian sound.
   None resembleth another, yet all their forms have a likeness,
   Therefore, a mystical law is by the chorus proclaim'd.
      Die Metamorphose der Pflanzen. Trans. by O. E. Bowring.
[38] Werdend betrachte sie nun, wie nach und nach sich die Pflanze,
   Stufenweise geführt, bildet zu Blüten und Frucht.

Lag, verschlossen in sich, unter die Hülle gebeugt,
Blatt und Wurzel und Keim, nur half geformet und farblos;
Trocken erhalt so der Kern ruhiges Leben bewahrt,
Quillet strebend empor, sich milder Feuchte vertrauend,
Und erhebt sich sogleich aus der umgebenden Nacht.[39]

He then describes the process of growth, arguing, according to his theory, that the shoot becomes the leaf, the leaf the flower and so on. In the opening lines of the *Metamorphosis of Animals* the poet demands:

Wagt ihr, also bereitet, die letzte Stufe zu steigen
Dieses Gipfels, so reicht mir die Hand und öffnet den freien
Blick ins weite Feld der Natur. Sie spendet die reichen
Lebensgaben umher, die Göttin . . .[40]

He then proceeds to explain how this metamorphosis takes place,

Sie das höchste Gesetz, beschränkte jegliches Leben,
Gab ihm gemess'ness Bedürfnisz, und ungemessene Gaben,
. . . und ruhig begünstigt
Sie das muntre Bemühn der vielfach bedürftigen Kinder,

. . . .

Also bestimnt die Gestalt die Lebensweise des Tieres.
Und die Weise zu leben, sie wirkt auf alle Gestalten
Mächtig zurück. . . .
Doch im Innern befindet die Kraft der edlern Geschöpfe

. . . .

---

[39] First from the seed it unravels itself, as soon as the silent
Fruit-bearing womb of the earth kindly allows it to escape,
And to the charms of the light, the holy, the ever-in-motion
Trusteth its delicate leaves, feebly beginning to shoot,
Simply slumber'd the force in the seed; a germ of the future
Peacefully lock'd in itself, 'neath the integument lay,
Leaf and root, and bud, still void of color and shapeless;
Thus does the kernel while dry, cover the motionless life.
Upward then strives it to swell, in gentle moisture confiding.
Metamorphose der Tiere. Trans. from *Goethe: with Special Consideration of his Philosophy.* By Paul Carus.

[40] Durst ye ascend to the peaks, to the highest heights on the summit?
Well, then, I proffer my hand, and here you behold from this outlook
O'er the wide province of nature a view. Oh see, how the goddess
Spendeth so richly her gifts!

Doch im Innern scheint ein Geist gewaltig zu ringen,
Wie er durchbräche den Kreis . . .[41]

But this aspiration is in vain, adds the poet, for if it swells one part, the other parts of the organism must suffer. He concludes:

Dieser schöne Begriff von Macht und Schranken von Willkür
Und Gesetz, von Freiheit und Masz von beweglicher Ordnung,
Vorzug und Mangel erfreue dich hoch: die heilige Muse
Bringt harmonisch ihn dir, mit sanftem Zwange belehrend.
Keinen höhern Begriff erringt der sittliche Denker.[42]

Goethe sums up his scientific experiences in the verses:

Freudig war, vor vielen Jahren,
Erfrig so der Geist bestrebt,
Zu erforschen, zu erfahren,
Wie Natur im schaffen lebt.
Und es ist das ewig Eine,
Das sich vielfach offenbart;
Kein das Grosze, grosz das Kleine,
Alles nach der eignen Art.[43]

---

[41] This is her highest decree: Nature limits the scope of each creature
Gives it a limited want, yet supplies it with means without limit.
She favors "those of her children who earn her affections by daring endeavor. . . ." The shape of a creature determines its life and its habits, while vice versa the habits of life will react on the organs.

But in the innermost self of the noblest of nature's creations
Lieth their power . . .
Yet in the innermost self a spirit titanic is also stirring,
Which fain would arbitrarily break through the circle.

Metamorphose der Tiere. Trans. from *Goethe: with Special Consideration of his Philosophy.* By Paul Carus.

[42] 'Tis a beautiful thought to have power and self limitation,
Liberty and moderation, free motion and law and all plastic,
Preference offset by want! O rejoice that the Muses have taught thee
Gently for harmony's sake to yield to a wholesome compulsion,
For there's no ethical thinker, who finds aspirations sublime.
Metamorphose der Tiere.

[43] Joyous, as it me behooveth,
Did for years, my soul aspire
To experience and inquire

A considerable portion of the Second Part of *Faust* is given over to the Neptunist and Vulcanist controversy in the field of geology. Inasmuch as this controversy had only a transitory value, has long since been outdated, and has no vital relationship to the literary qualities of the poem, it has impressed many literary critics as being a blot on the artistic merit of the work. In Goethe's sight, however, it undoubtedly seemed to be one of the most fundamental things in the whole composition, for it really furnished a basis for his conception of metamorphosis, and we have already noted how he applied that to his literary theory. He upheld the Neptunists, because they allowed for the principle of continuity, whereas the Vulcanists' idea of the creation of the earth meant a series of violent upheavals, and was therefore opposed to the opinion of a slow organic form of development.

Although not written in verse, *Wilhelm Meisters Wanderjahre* and *Die Wahlverwandtschaften* offer a further valuable commentary on the invasion of contemporary science, or what the poet believed to be science, into the field of literature. In the *Wanderjahre,* for example, Markerie the beautiful Soul, is deeply interested in Astronomy. Here also we have a debate on the Neptunist and Vulcanist theories. In the Third Book of this work there is a discussion of the spinning machines of Hargreave and Arkwright and Cartwright's power loom, with their attendant social effects.

It is especially interesting to note how Goethe employs the current scientific ideas and theories in *Die Wahlverwandtschaften* (Elective Affinities). The very title itself is suggested

---

How creative nature moveth.
'Tis the eternal one and all
Which appears as manifold,
Small things great are, great things small,
Everything has its own mould.
"Parabase," Trans. by Paul Carus. *op. cit.*

by chemistry. Edward and Charlotte, recently married, are entertaining a friend of Edward's known as the Captain, who, in the course of a conversation about chemistry, explains the meaning of the term "elective affinities": how a certain substance, when brought into proximity with some chemical compound, will break up that compound, combining one or more of its elements with a constituent part of itself. Charlotte and Edward apply this in fancy to their own married life; and the plot proceeds to work out this suggestion. Charlotte's niece Ottilie proves one of the disturbing elements in attracting Edward, while on the other hand the Captain and Charlotte find themselves growing very fond of each other. Charlotte, however, is gifted with a large amount of moral resistance. So she, with the respectful assistance of the Captain, resists the attraction, but Edward and Ottilie fall victims to this apparently mysterious power. The power, after all, is not mysterious, says Goethe in effect, for it can be explained by magnetism or mesmerism, terms which the poet was willing to accept as scientific, or nearly so. An Englishman, a chance visitor to the castle, belongs to the contemporary philosophers of nature who were convinced of a mutual influence between inorganic nature and peculiarly organized people. When he hears that Ottilie always suffers from headache when passing along a certain road, and after he has observed that there are plain traces of coal in the near vicinity of that road, he employs the pendulum test. In her hands the pendulum swings, whereas in Charlotte's it is not moved from the position of rest, thus showing, he insists, that Ottilie is entirely a victim of the magnetic fluid. She struggles bravely against her feeling for Edward, but finds no escape except through death.

It is to be noted that here, as well as in some other instances of Goethe, we have a scientific theory or speculation used in much the same way as the magic wand, the enchanted cup, or the mystical formula which is employed in the medieval romances. Science here is not used for the purpose of teaching scientific truth or for celebrating its achievements. It is utilized more or less as an incidental part of the paraphernalia of the literary artist. To be sure, it has to be some particular achievement, something which in itself has appealed to the imagination of the reader. But by the early part of the nineteenth century there were many things in science, especially those connected with electricity and magnetism, which could make such an appeal.

The type of science of which Goethe approved was the speculative-morphological variety, freed from mathematical limitations and with a minimum of mechanical explanation. With the Newtonian type he was rather impatient, for it cramped his active mind in its search for unity. Like Erasmus Darwin, who was more empirical perhaps, more practical, less impatient of details, but who ardently desired unity, he found satisfaction in theories of development. The concept of growth intrigued the imagination of these two poets. The verse was very different to be sure—Darwin's thoroughly conventional, Goethe's masterly, its rhythms and patterns better suited to the new philosophy. Goethe saw the principle of design at work in the universe and science fitting into this general pattern. Erasmus Darwin, on the other hand, pursued his philosophic speculations without referring to any harmonious design or plan, desiring nevertheless to realize unity.

Obviously this type of science, which leaves so much scope to the imagination, untrammelled by mathematics and mechanical principles, is much more acceptable to the poet than the Newtonian conception.

It remains now for us to evaluate this kind of science. It is clearly not in the main line of development of the scientific spirit. But it contributed, nevertheless, to that main line of development the important principle of growth or evolution. This principle of evolution was as a matter of historical record soon annexed to the traditional science, which came down from Galileo and Newton—the type which attempts to measure everything in terms of mathematics and seeks a mechanical principle at work in every process—for by the Darwinian hypothesis of natural selection, all willing, all initiative upon the part of the individual count for nothing in the process of evolution. The selection is one pursued by nature, dependent in the last analysis upon the fitness of the individual to combat the environment to which it is subjected. Thus, to a very great extent, Biology itself is subject to a mechanical principle and lends itself to tabulation and mathematical measurement. Having conformed to the requirements of a true science, and having freed itself from the vague speculative element which had characterized so much of the Nature Philosophy of the latter half of the eighteenth century and the first half of the nineteenth, Biology, along with Geology, might then be reckoned among the reputable sciences.

Some of the reactions of poetry to this change, we shall note in the chapter which follows.

Chapter VIII

NATURE RED IN TOOTH AND CLAW
TENNYSON'S PROBLEM

The particular aspect of the new conception of evolution which troubles Tennyson is expressed in the line from *In Memoriam* "The stars," she whispers, "blindly run."
This poem was printed in 1850, nine years before Darwin published his *Origin of Species,* which tended, as we have noted, to put biology upon very much the same plane scientifically as the physical sciences—that is, upon a mechanical basis. This is the problem that had been greatly troubling the poet since he had begun to speculate upon these matters after the death of Arthur Hallam in 1833. In one sense we may say that he was reacting from the mechanical conception of nature, just as we have noted that some of the seventeenth and eighteenth-century poets did. Tennyson, however, was thoroughly alive to the idea of metamorphosis, of change, of growth and of development, which had seized upon the imagination of the poets through the romantic period. These earlier writers, as we have already seen, tended in a measure to exclude man from the full rigor of mechanism. Through his powers of willing and his imagination he was able, within prescribed limits, to wield those powers which were advancing civilization and ushering in a state of perfection. It had seemed to them that there was a vast plan being worked out, too intricate for the restricted vision of mankind to comprehend in its entirety, but nevertheless there, in the divine order of things. For Tennyson, however, there was no such assurance, as he pondered over the questions: What if the stars did "blindly

run"? What if there was no benevolent system or order behind their movement? What if that which we termed "development of man" was only an accidental happening? What if man himself, with all his powers of imagination, his idealism and his hopes, was merely subject to mechanical principles over which he had no control?

Lucretius had faced these same questions nearly two thousand years before, and had derived certain cold comfort from the thought that the universe was a mechanism: but the nineteenth-century poet felt a paralysis creeping over him at the prospect. Indeed, if the world was simply a mechanism and if the so-called "advance and progress" were due entirely to mechanistic principles, then how could the poet wax eloquent over these blind forces? There remained, of course, for poetry, the field which had inspired his own early poems, pictorial representations, pretty and ornamental; but now in the face of these much more serious questions, those attempts seemed trivial and not at all vital. The implications of much of the new science tormented his peace of mind, while intriguing his curiosity and upsetting his early ideas about poetry.

In the first place, there was something very interesting about the idea of development, as modern science was explaining it. He realized, too, that many contemporary astronomical, geological, and biological scientists were tending more and more to emphasize the factor of time.

To what extent, he wondered, ought a poet to concern himself with these new scientific facts? He knew that in the past there had been a decided tendency to escape from them. Therefore he makes the narrator in *Locksley Hall* speculate as to whether he would not find more enjoyment in "summer isles of Eden lying in dark-purple spheres of sea" than in the march of mind:

> In the steamship, in the railway, in the
> thoughts that shake mankind.

But he concludes at length, that
>Not in vain the distance beacons; Forward,
>forward let us range.
>Let the great world spin for ever down the
>ringing grooves of change.[1]

In the second *Locksley Hall,* written sixty years later, after the Darwinian hypothesis had raised a violent storm of protest in many quarters and its implications had become increasingly clear, he still preserved his faith in the theory of evolution. His enthusiasm now, however, is seasoned with greater moderation, and while Science is "creeping on from point to point," he cautions youth to "remember how the course of Time will swerve, Crook and turn upon itself in many a backward streaming curve."

>Hope the best, but hold the present fatal
>daughter of the Past,
>Shape your heart to front the hour, but dream
>not that the hour will last.

Tennyson always stood ready to modify his ideas in relation to the latest scientific findings. He was well aware of the tendency upon the part of scientific thought to curtail the power of man's will and to seek for an underlying mechanical principle as the ultimate explanation. He did not ignore this tendency, but he inquired anxiously into the meaning of it and all its dire implications. In *In Memoriam,* upon which he worked intermittently from 1833 to the date of publication (1850), he advanced an explanation of evolution which is perfectly in harmony with the Darwinian theory of natural selection, though the latter was not officially announced until nine years later.

>Are God and Nature then at strife,
>That Nature lends such evil dreams?
>So careful of the type she seems,
>So careless of the single life.[2]

---

[1] *Locksley Hall.*
[2] *In Memoriam,* Sec. 55.

He notes
>... that of fifty seeds
> she often brings but one to bear.

Nay, even more than that, further consideration shows that she is not even careful of the type:
> From scarped cliff and quarried stone
> She cries a thousand types are gone:
> I care for nothing, all shall go,[3]

God and Nature do appear to be at strife; and man,
> Who trusted God was love indeed,
> And love, creation's final law

seems to find
> Nature, red in tooth and claw.

Notwithstanding that the poet sensed the import of these facts upon ethical and religious thinking, he did not try to minimize them in the slightest degree, but sought rather to restate the problem in terms of the new science. Courageously he declares that he fears not the fact that Nature is "red in tooth and claw." The very principle of evolution and its struggle makes it possible for man to "move upward, working out the beast" and letting "the ape and tiger die."[4] In this struggle he sees the very law of progress itself.

> The solid earth whereon we tread
>
> In tracts of fluent heat began,
> And grew to seeming-random forms,
> The seeming prey of cyclic storms,
> Till at the last arose the man.
>
> Who throve and branch'd from clime to clime,
> The herald of a higher race,
> And of himself in higher place.
>
> . . . .
> Crown'd with attributes of woe
> Like glories, move his course, and show

---
[3] *Ibid.*, 56.
[4] *In Memoriam.* Sec. 118.

That life is not an idle ore.
But iron dug from central gloom,
And heated hot with burning fears,
And dipt in baths of hissing tears
And batter'd with the shocks of doom.

To shape and use . . .

Indeed, everything is in process of change. In the *Morte d'Arthur*, the dissolution of the Round Table is in this respect "an image of the mighty world," and Arthur's last words from the barge,

The old order changeth; yielding place to new,

gives expression to this same law of progress.

The more important of the progressive steps of evolution are indicated in the following quotation from *The Princess* (1847):

This world was once a fluid haze of light,
Till towards the centre set the starry tides,
And eddied into suns, that wheeling cast
The planets: then the monster, then the man,
Tattoo'd or woaded, inter-clad in skins,
Raw from the prime, and crushing down his mate.

Again, he gives expression to the view of Laplace:

Regions of lucid matter taking forms,
Brushes of fire, hazy gleams,
Clusters and beds of worlds, and bee-like swarms
Of suns, and starry streams."[5]

This process of evolution however, he declares in 1855,[6] is continuous.

A monstrous eft was of old the Lord and Master of Earth,
For him did the high sun flame, and the river billowing ran,
And he felt himself in his force to be Nature's crowning race.

---

[5] "Palace of Art."
[6] *Maud.*

> As nine months go to the shaping an infant ripe for his birth,
> So many a million of ages have gone to the making of man:
> He now is first, but is he the last? is he not too base?

Something of his own adventurous attitude towards the facts and the mystery of life is expressed in some lines from "Ulysses."[7]

> I am a part of all that I have met;
> Yet all experience is an arch wherethro'
> Gleams that untravell'd world, whose margin fades
> Forever and forever when I move.

And in the lines from *In Memoriam;*

> So then were nothing lost to man;
> So that still gardens of the souls
> In many a figured leaf enrolls
> The total world since life began.[8]

Later, in 1869, after the idea had been expressed by Darwin, Spencer, and others, he gave a graphic description of the stages of the evolution of man, in his account of the sculpture girding the hall at Camelot:

> In the lowest beasts are slaying men,
> And in the second men are slaying beasts,
> And on the third are warriors, perfect men
> And on the fourth are men with growing wings.[9]

These quotations offer testimony of the poet's knowledge of the movement of contemporary science, some factors of which we ought to bear in mind if we would understand his interest in evolution.

During the first half of the century science continued to extend its exact methods of measurement into the realm of the biological sciences, where fancy had been more or less free to speculate upon the possibilities of evolution. But coming into

[7] 1842.
[8] Sec. 43.
[9] *The Holy Grail.*

contact with this new body of material, science itself underwent a reaction, its scope broadening so as to allow more room for imagination and speculation. We can see this conflict being waged towards the middle of the century in regard to spiritualism, mesmerism, and clairvoyance. Science, however, always seeking a materialistic basis, tended gradually to exclude these from the list of reputables.

Whereas, after the publication of Lyell's *Geology* (1830), it was more or less recognized in scientific circles that everything in the inorganic world was moved by mechanical causality, man and organic nature in general were regarded as being exempt from this and under a special teleological dispensation and in no way subject to a blind materialism. But gradually as the halfway mark in the century approached, scientists were forced to recede from this position. With Wohler's synthesis (1828) and with the enunciation of the conservation of energy in 1842 by Mayer, von Helmholtz, and others, it became increasingly evident that the organic was in no way essentially different in chemical composition from the inorganic. Hence, a firmer basis was established scientifically by the middle of the century for a naturalistic explanation of life itself.

In the meantime, the fact was demonstrated through the microscopic studies of Schleiden (1838) and Schwann (1839) that plants and animals have the same cellular structure. It only remained, therefore, for Darwin to show, as he endeavored to do through a study of the breeding of domestic animals, how organic structures adapt themselves to the service of the organism in which they occur, and that organic nature is subject to definite natural laws, no less rigorous than those governing inorganic nature.

In November, 1844, Tennyson wrote Edward Moxon, asking him to procure a book which he had seen advertised in the *Examiner*. "It seems to contain many speculations with which I have been familar for years, and on which I have written more than one poem. This book is called, *Vestiges of the Natural History of Creation.*"[10] Although published anonymously, this remarkable book is now universally attributed to Robert Chambers. When it was first published in 1844, the same year that Tennyson read it, it created a great sensation; and within the next nine years there were ten editions of the book. In this book, the poet, along with those other inquiring minds, saw gathered together from geology, chemistry, botany, and zoology, those facts which had been gradually accumulating during the previous hundred years or more, and beheld them presented in such a striking sequence that they seized upon the imagination of most of the readers and bade them revise many of their ideas in accordance with the findings of science and be prepared for further startling revelations along the same line.

The author points out that the forms of the heavenly bodies have been determined by the law of gravitation, and as he examines the various forms of organic life which are revealed through geological remains, he feels that these are in some way connected with the production of the physical. At any rate, he notes a progression of animal life, a progress from the simple to the complex, and that in larger groups there is traceable a fundamental unity of organization. Since all organisms, both vegetable and animal, commence and develop from a single cell he concludes that the organic rests also upon a single law, not that of gravitation, but of development.

"An innocent little bird in the claws of the cruel hawk—a poor stag grasped by the ruthless boa—a lamb in the fangs of the wolf—upon no theory can this be understood except upon that of an economy governed by general laws."[11] The author holds, however, that "the pursuit of science is but the seeking of a deeper aquaintance with the Infinite."[12] "Such is the way to

[10] Memoir. I, 223.
[11] Quoted from ed. of 1884, pp. 407-08.
[12] *Ibid.*, p. 13.

happiness. . . . Obedience is not selfishness . . . it is worship."[13]

Huxley's *Man's Place in Nature* (1863) was the first work to extend "frankly and undisguisedly" the Darwinian doctrine of natural selection to man.[14] Sir Charles Lyell, however, as well as many other scientists, could not adopt the theory of the descent of man from brutes; and Darwin himself did not specifically declare it until 1871 in *The Descent of Man*.

In the face of these facts we can make even a stronger assertion than merely that Tennyson was well versed in the movement of contemporary science. It is evident that in many instances he grasped the essential facts even before they received scientific promulgation. Indeed, this interest in science was one that was present from childhood. We know from the *Memoir*, that in his very early years he keenly observed "the habits of birds and beasts and ants and bees"—an observation which had been encouraged by his mother and shared with his two older brothers.[15] While extremely young he wrote:

> The quick-wing'd gnat doth make a boat
> Of his old husk wherewith to float
> To a new life! All low things range
> To higher! But I cannot change."[16]

Also:
> The rays of many a rolling central star,
> Aye flushing earthwards, have not reached us yet.

His interest in Natural History was probably stimulated further by reading Buffon's *Histoire Naturelle,* which was in his father's library.

The three years he spent at Cambridge served also as a spur, though not so much through the medium of the university curriculum, as by the association with other eager, youthful, inquiring minds—especially in the famous Apostles Club, of which

[13] *Ibid.,* p. 412.
[14] Walker, *Literature of the Victorian Era,* p. 236.
[15] *Memoir.* I, 16.
[16] *Ibid.,* I, 18.

he was a member. This club founded in 1820, eight years before Tennyson went up to the university, had for its object the open-minded and tolerant discussion of social and literary questions. Here the teachings of Coleridge still continued to exert a marked effect, for while Frederick Denison Maurice was no longer in residence at that time, his admiration for the author of *Aids to Reflection* still made itself felt, especially through Richard Trench, who was intimate with Tennyson, and through Arthur Hallam, who at the time of his death was looking up to Coleridge as his master. J. S. Mill has called Coleridge's the greatest "seminal mind" of his time. Through that mind had passed the currents of rationalism, unitarianism, Voltairianism, biblical criticism from Germany, and the German idealistic philosophy. Yet Coleridge had preserved his Christian faith. It was no wonder that his views in such an age of intellectual turmoil should have received earnest attention, and that his purpose stamped itself upon the receptive mind of the young Tennyson. Here too he became acquainted with the growing social and political problems which were finding expression in the Reform Bill agitation. It is said also that he advanced the theory that "the development of the human body might possibly be traced from the radiated, vermicular, molluscous, and vertebrate organisms."[17]

Another association that tended to strengthen his interest in philosophical and scientific questions was that with Arthur Hallam, interrupted only by the sudden death of the latter in 1833. Arthur Hallam dead, however, was certainly no less a potent influence, for the problems which science was dimly propounding now became much more insistent and thought-provoking.

Back in Somersby again, he continued his studies more seriously than ever. We know that besides German, history, Italian, and Greek, the youthful poet was interested in chemistry, bot-

[17] Sir Oliver Lodge: "The Attitude of Tennyson towards Science." In *Tennyson and His Friends*. Ed. by Hallam, Lord Tennyson. 1911.

any, electricity, animal psychology, and mechanics.[18] In 1837, he was occupied with Lyell's *Geology*.[19] At just about this same time he met at Park House—the home of his brother-in-law, Edward Lushington—the precocious William Thomson (later Lord Kelvin).

With the opportunity that came from being in proximity to London, after he had moved to Boxley in 1841, he found himself drawn into more intimate contact with current scientific, philosophic, social, and literary activities. He renewed acquaintanceship with many of his fellow "Apostles," and he joined the Sterling Club. Much of his talk centered about "politics, philosophy, theology, and the new speculations rife on every side."[20]

In 1852 we find him taking a marked interest in the formation of the cliffs at Whitby and in the shellfish found along the shore, as well as in reading Herschel's *Astronomy*.[21] After he moved to Freshwater and was at home at Farringford, he continued his geological studies with the local geologist, Keeping, as his mentor.[22] Two years later there is an entry in his journal that he stopped over at Bowchurch to see some "double stars thro' a telescope of Dr. Mann's." "Also," the poet adds, "he showed me things thro' his microscope."[23] Again, he stays in the New Forest with his friend Lord Lilford to observe the bird life there.[24]

Almost as soon (November, 1859) as Darwin's *Origin of Species* was published, he sent "by his own desire" for an early copy.[25] It was indeed an easy matter for him to accept the main

[18] Memoir. I, 124.
[19] *Ibid.*, I.
[20] *Ibid.*, I, 185.
[21] *Ibid.*, I, 351.
[22] *Ibid.*, I, 366.
[23] *Ibid.*, I, 384.
[24] *Ibid.*, I, 414.
[25] *Ibid.*, I, 443.

tenets of the theory of natural selection. Darwin he did not meet, however, until nearly ten years later, in 1868.[26] At about that same time he wrote an Epigram entitled, "By a Darwinian":

> How is it that men have so little grace,
> When a great man's found to be bad and base,
> That they chuckle and chatter and mock?
> We come from apes—and are far removed—
> But rejoice when a bigger brother has proved
> That he springs from common stock.[27]

He apparently accepted the animal descent of man from the time of those verses in *In Memoriam* in which evolution of man signifies "the working out of the beast" and letting "the ape and tiger die." But after the controversy which the Darwinian hypothesis produced, and after its theological and ethical implications had been pointed out, he did not change his views. "The Making of Man" testifies to that fact:

> Where is one that, born of woman, altogether can escape
> From the lower world within him, moods of tiger or of ape?
> Man as yet is being made, and ere the crowning age of ages,
> Shall not aeon after aeon pass and touch him into shape?

Indeed, in 1887, he could look back upon "fifty years of ever-brightening Science."[28] He liked the law and order which science prescribed; he gloried in the opportunity for improvement which was offered by the principle of organic evolution. He was perfectly well aware of the materialistic trend implied by the theory of natural selection. Intellectually he craved the truth which science was revealing; and he was never so busy with his own reflections and his poetry that his ear was not attuned to sounds of scientific activity. Always he desired to know the latest news; and upon learning it his active mind set to work to weave it into the texture of his daily thinking. This interest continued unabated until the closing years of his life.

[26] *Ibid.*, II, 57.
[27] *Ibid.*, II, 58.
[28] *Poems.* Macmillan, 1894, p. 805.

Despite his leaning towards mysticism, which we shall have occasion to note later, his real interest in science has won the admiration of some of the scientists of his own time as well as those of more recent date. Huxley declared that he was "the first poet since Lucretius who has understood the drift of science."[29] Perhaps this view scarcely does justice to Dante, Erasmus Darwin, or Goethe. But obviously Huxley means here a recognition of mechanical natural law, without appealing to mystical powers as a vital part of the process. Scientific leaders like Herschel in astronomy, Owen in anatomy, Sedgwick in geology, and Tyndall in physics and natural philosophy, all hailed him as a champion of Science and addressed to him words of genuine admiration "for his love of Nature, for the eagerness with which he welcomed all the latest scientific discoveries, and for his trust in truth."[30] They also strongly commended his scientific references as being true to the facts. Professor Sedgwick wrote in 1860 of Tennyson that he regarded him as "pre-eminently the Poet of Science."[31]

Such stanzas as these from *In Memoriam* must have delighted the heart of the geologist:

> There rolls the deep where grew the tree
> O earth, what changes thou hast seen!
> There where the long street roars, hath been
> The stillness of the central sea.[32]
> . . . .
> The hills are shadows, and they flow
> From form to form, and nothing stands;
> Like clouds they shape themselves and go.[33]
> They melt like mist, the solid lands,
> . . . .

---

[29] *Life of Huxley.* II, 338.
[30] Memoir. I, 298-99.
[31] *Ibid.*, I, 298-99.
[32] *In Memoriam.* CXXIII.
[33] *Ibid.*

> The moanings of the homeless sea,
> The sound of streams that swift or slow
> Draw down Aeonian hills, and sow
> The dust of continents to be . . .[34]

Professor Sedgwick makes clear what he means by "poet of science" in contrasting Tennyson with Wordsworth, who dealt with "nature as known by simple observation and interpreted by religious and sympathetic intuition." For Tennyson, "the physical world is always the world as known to us through physical science; the scientific view dominates his thought."

This view of Tennyson, Sir Oliver Lodge, writing in 1911, thoroughly endorses. He "assimilates the known truths of Science and Philosophy, through the pores so to speak, without effort and with intuitive accuracy, one who bears them lightly and raises them above the regions of bare facts into the realm of poetry."[35] Another modern testimonial comes from the hand of the celebrated astronomer Norman Lockyer, who declares that Tennyson's mind was "saturated with astronomy."[36] Similarly W. N. Rice, a professor of geology, finds him, "an observer of nature at first hand and . . . his descriptions are always phenomenally true." Many of the descriptions referred to depended upon microscopic and telescopic knowledge. But what makes him more in harmony with the modern spirit, according to Professor Rice, is that "he views nature materialistically rather than pantheistically as Wordsworth did."[37]

It has become customary at the present time to decry Tennyson's state of mind and to point out that he failed to accept the "facts." Whatever his shortcomings may have been philosophically or theologically, he was evidently thoroughly alert scien-

---
[34] *Ibid.* XXXV.
[35] "The Attitude of Tennyson towards Science." From *Tennyson and His Friends.* Ed. by Hallam, Lord Tennyson, 1911, p. 284.
[36] *Quarterly Review.* Jan., 1907.
[37] W. N. Rice: *The Poet of Science and other Addresses.* Abbingdon Press, 1919.

tifically—so sensitively attuned, in fact, that he seized upon implications involved at even the vaguest hint from the scientist. In this respect he challenges comparison with Erasmus Darwin and Goethe.

He is unlike the older Darwin in the fact that he is not content to adopt the detached scientific attitude of mind; but he concurs with him in the belief that the mechanical explanation is not the whole truth and that a unity may be achieved. Each welcomes a mechanical explanation for material phenomena, within certain bounds; but to both of them the mechanical explanation as the ultimate one is unthinkable. To Erasmus Darwin, the human will is a vital factor in the process. To Tennyson, the infinite process of evolution is determined very much more largely by external circumstances than by the force of the individual will. And yet he insists that the human will, within certain boundaries, is free.

Again, like Goethe, Tennyson believes that scientific truth is but one aspect of the whole truth. It was for this, it will be recalled, that Faust so restlessly strove and decided finally that the greatest wisdom lay in trusting to the interconnection of things and striving whole-heartedly along one line of activity, valuing it in terms of the social service rendered. This subtle interconnection of things involves, Goethe believes, the pursuit of science, of beauty, and of the welfare of mankind. These tenets were accepted also by the Victorian poet, who sees them working themselves out in an ever changing universe—with the earth, the flora, the fauna, all subject to the great law of evolution. But he cannot accept the principle as thoroughly as did Goethe. In a phenomenal world of flux and change, Tennyson desires ardently to cling to something which is changeless—to what seems to him the fundamental truths of Religion—God, Immortality, and Free will.

Goethe, like Erasmus Darwin, sees man evolving through striving towards his ideals; but to Tennyson he is subjected to a much greater extent to scientific laws, though partaking also of a vision, which tends unhappily to set God and Nature at strife.

This brings us to the second main point in our consideration of Tennyson. His understanding of the scientific currents of his time was forcing upon him the painful question whether Nature as revealed in science was not utterly opposed to the idea of a benevolent and just God. Here he found himself facing a very unpleasant dilemma. He could not, like Wordsworth whom he very greatly admired, be satisfied in assuming that there was a divine spark in every living thing—at least, not without an examination of the evidence, nor like Coleridge, with seeing in the visible form only a shadow of its inner essence. It did, however—especially later in his life—make a great difference whether the object causing the emotion was essentially material or fundamentally spiritual. He saw that science declared it was material; the traditional religion insisted that it was in its inner essence spiritual or else a mere delusion. He was not willing to turn his back upon the scientific evidence, which impressed him as being very strong, but on the other hand, it was not easy for him to give up the orthodox religious training of his youth.

Brought up in a religious environment, his father a clergyman and his mother the daughter of a clergyman, he naturally had strong religious leanings. While his father in his theological tenets was considerably in advance of his age[38] the boy grew up in an atmosphere of piety, both at the rectory in Somersby and at his grandmother's in Louth, until in his nineteenth year he went up to Cambridge. This early religious environment left an enduring trace upon his character and gave to his mind a bent which helped to shape the whole future course of his thinking.

His associations at Cambridge, especially in the Apostles Club, awakened him to the fact that many of the beliefs which he had

[38] *Memoir.* I, 14.

been taking as a matter of course were really being challenged by modern science, and particularly by the scientific temper of mind which it was engendering. Although it was then too early for the rationalistic theses of Strauss and Feuerbach, a more critical interpretation of the Scriptures had long ago been advocated by Hume and others, and the materialistic bias of modern science was making itself felt in this direction also. Such a critical spirit was disquieting to orthodoxy, and was constantly demanding a restatement of theological doctrine.

He found his companions enthusiastic "for the modern schools of thought" and despising the "rhetoric and sentimentalism" of the old.[39] Experiencing some unhappy hours as these ideas assailed him, along with the social and political problems of the age, he felt that the University at that time (1830) stood apart from these vital matters and taught "nothing feeding the heart."[40]

The crisis was precipitated in 1833, when, with the death of Arthur Hallam, Tennyson, so sensitive to impressions of every kind, sustained a shock that tended to render a temperament naturally reflective more introspective, and made him ask, as never before, what was the meaning of life.

The three main aspects under the guise of which life had hitherto presented itself to him—a world which allowed for religious faith, a world filled with "fairy tales" of science, and a world that presented an opportunity for beautiful expression upon the part of the poet—these now drew together, and out of the confused image which confronted him he sought to make a synthesis, and thus present to his own mind, and to those other minds who were also struggling with the doubts of the age, a clear picture, with its elements distinct and definitely proportioned.

[39] From Lord Houghton's address in 1866—quoted from *Memoir.* I, 36.
[40] *Ibid.*, I, 67.

The sudden loss of his friend served to bring all his doubts and fears to a crucial test. It became of the utmost importance to arrive at a solution to the questions: What of God? Immortality? And the meaning of life?

The desired perspective did not come at once. His first reaction was naturally despair and the fight that ensued between faith and hope is recorded in "The Two Voices," with faith the victor. But after that, there was still to be fitted into the picture the jarring elements from the realm of science, and especially the idea that nature has progressed by the method of struggle and "the red tooth and claw." If everything was to be put upon the basis of materialism, where then was a loving God, and immortality, and the free will of man? What saved man from being a mere plaything of the forces of nature? What was there to hope for, if the old faith was swept away? He desired most ardently to cling to the supports which that had afforded him; and he loved truth too well to turn his back upon the scientific temper. So he proceeded to take a new inventory of both science and his religious faith, in the hope of arriving at a satisfactory synthesis.

He feels that he must admit first of all that science is necessarily limited in its outlook.

> All the tracks
> Of Science making toward thy perfectness
> Are blinding desert sand: we scarce can spell
> The Alif of Thine Alphabet of Love.[41]

At the same time, God's ways are difficult to understand,

> Our planet is one, the suns are many, the
> world is wide.[42]

The scientist, in spite of his glorious calling, is subject to the failings of humanity. The surgeon, for example, might be happier using his knife than in trying to save the limb.[43]

[41] "Akbar's Dream."
[42] *Maud.* IV; VIII.
[43] "In the Children's Hospital."

The man of science himself is fonder of glory, and vain,
An eye well-practiced in nature, a spirit bounded and poor.[44]

He resolutely states the case for science in his "Lucretius (1868). Here the titular character, with his steadfast belief in molecules and atoms, desires to commit suicide, when in a feverish state of mind produced by the elixir administered by his wife, he beholds airy spiritual beings that have no part in his materialistic ideal.

In *In Memoriam* (1850), which had been seventeen years in the making, he attempted to answer the ever pressing problem of the relation of evolution and its implications to religion. He questions the existence of God, of immortality, and of freewill in general. He turns to science for light on the subject, but there he finds little hope, he honestly admits, as he courageously faces the facts which that science reveals to him. Intellectually he feels himself impelled to the stygian blackness of skepticism. And then comes the mystic vision by which he senses the presence of Arthur Hallam, and once more is restored to him his faith. He believes that through this mystical experience he has seized hold upon the Truth, which resides beyond where all the powers of intellect can penetrate.

Again he finds, in this mystic vision, the answer for which he has been seeking, and the very principle of synthesis. No longer do God and Nature seem at strife. Nature is too limited to comprehend God: it merely points the way. "This is a terrible age of unfaith," he wrote, "I hate utter unfaith, I cannot endure that men should sacrifice everything at the cold altar of what with their imperfect knowledge they choose to call truth and reason."[45]

As he read more philosophy—Spinoza, Berkeley, Kant, Schlegel, Fichte, Hegel, Ferrier—after 1850, he asserted ever more strongly that "nothing worth proving can be proven," and that

[44] *Ibid.* IV; VII.
[45] *Memoir.* I, 309.

even in the great scientific laws, "we have but faith; we cannot know."[46] He came to look at nature in general through the eyes of science; but of the human soul, he insisted an exception must be made. "Whatever is the object of Faith," he declared in a conversation with Locker-Lampson in 1869, "cannot be the object of Reason. In fine, Faith must be our guide—that Faith which we believe comes to us from a Divine Source."[47] Indeed, Tennyson says of "The Holy Grail," written at that same time, "I have expressed there my strong feeling as to the Reality of the Unseen. . . . The Spiritual is the real."[48] We note, in brief, a growing mysticism, which extends the idea of God fulfilling "Himself in many ways"[49] to seeing in the process of evolution itself a reflection of "the glory of God."

> God is law, says the wise; O Soul, and
> let us rejoice,
> For if he thunders by law the thunder is
> yet his voice.[50]

Matter, then, is "merely the shadow of something greater than itself, and which we poor short-sighted creatures cannot see."[51] In brief, everything culminates in God. This is the idea of the "Flower in the crannied wall."

> . . . If I could understand
> What you are, root and all, and all in all,
> I should know what God and man is.

He believed that "the further science progressed, the more the Unity of Nature, and the purpose hidden behind the cosmic process of matter and motion and changing forms of life, would be apparent."[52] To Tyndall he once said: "No evolutionist is

[46] *Ibid.*, I, 311.
[47] *Ibid.*, II, 69.
[48] *Ibid.*, II, 90.
[49] *Morte d' Arthur.*
[50] "The Higher Pantheism."
[51] *Memoir.* II, 69.
[52] *Ibid.*, I, 323.

able to explain the mind of Man or how any possible physiological change of tissue can produce conscious thought."[53]

The second *Locksley Hall* (1887) furnishes us with some interesting side lights on how the poet felt in regard to this problem of faith and reason towards the end of his life. Here the old man of eighty is revisiting Locksley Hall, sixty years after his previous visit, when he had been full of righteous indignation because his cousin Amy who had loved him forsook him to marry an older and richer man. Then he had cursed "the social wants that sin against the strength of youth, the social lies that warp us from the living truth;" but nevertheless he had cried "Forward, forward let us range,"

> Let the great world spin forever down the
> ringing grooves of change.

Now the old man, in the later poem, chides his grandson for his weaker faith, and especially his doubts concerning a future life.

> Gone the cry of "Forward, Forward!" lost within
> a growing gloom,

he complains. Even the faith in science and the "triumphs over time and space,"

> Staled by frequence, shrunk by usage into
> commonest commonplace!

And he admonishes him,

> Read the wide world's annals, you, and take
> their wisdom for your friend.

Instead, you

> Do your best to charm the worst, to lower
> the rising race of men;
> Have we risen from out the beast, then back
> into the beast again?

The old man feels—and in his attitude cannot we sense something of the poet's attitude also, from the vantage point of nearly four score?—that science is now being considered too much from a materialistic standpoint, and that the spiritual meaning which

[53] *Ibid.*

he as a young man had read into the idea of evolution is now lost, or if alive at all, the later generation expects science to bring about quickly, through some mechanical means, very radical social and political changes. Does the younger generation hope, he asks, for a Utopia with
> All diseases quench'd by Science, no man
> halt, or deaf or blind;
> Stronger ever born of weaker, lustier body,
> larger mind?

and that earth will be "a warless world, a single race, a single tongue?" They do well to be "grateful for the sounding watchword, 'Evolution,' "
> ... ever climbing after some ideal good
> And Reversion ever dragging Evolution in
> the mud.

But they ought to remember too that it took
> Many an Aeon to mould earth before her
> highest, man, was born,
> Many an Aeon too may pass when earth is
> manless and forlorn.

He concludes with the thought that there may be much in the world which we cannot experience with our senses.
> There may be those about us whom we neither
> see nor name.

Yet we can
> Follow Light, and do the Right—for man
> can half control his doom.

In fact, it is man's duty, the poet says in effect, "to rule thy Province of the brute," so that when old age comes he will stand "on the height of his life with a glimpse of a height that is higher."[54]

For all his faith in the supernatural his attitude towards spiritualism was one of suspended judgment. He thought that if there was anything in such manifestations, "Pucks not the

[54] "By an Evolutionist."

spirits of dead men reveal themselves."⁵⁵ In 1868 he talked much with the Longfellows about such manifestations⁵⁶ and again nearly twenty years later when he visited his brother Frederick, who had become an ardent spiritualist, accepting table-rappings, et cetera, he declined to take a vital interest in the subject. He was too scientific-minded in one respect to accept these so-called signs from the spirit world, even while he ardently defended the existence of the spiritual and regarded it as the ultimate reality.

His position finally, then, is like that of Carlyle and the other Transcendentalists who regard the natural laws as only the manifestations of spiritual force. He is opposed to reducing man ultimately to the position of an automaton. Man's limited understanding prevents him from knowing the All; and it is the recognition of that principle which furnishes him with his basis of faith. This faith is as real to him as anything in the field of scientific evidence. Indeed, the sense of Arthur Hallam's presence at that crucial moment of doubt in "In Memoriam" was as true for him as if he had actually seen his friend with his own eyes. It is this fact more than anything else perhaps, which makes so many modern readers decry Tennyson. Having accompanied him so far upon his journey, and having found him trustworthy in his science, they feel that the poet suddenly betrays them, by taking them into the realm of mysticism and asking them to accept this experience, with exactly the same confidence that they have accepted the demonstrable facts of science.

When Tennyson tried to reconcile the three areas of interest—science, theology, and poetry—he found a double conflict going on in the depths of his nature. First there was this conflict between science and religion, which, as we have already noted, helped to bring science prominently into his poetry. Sooner or later, in all probability, science must have found expression in his verse, because the new scientific theories with their emphasis

---
⁵⁵ *Memoir.* II, 56.
⁵⁶ *Ibid.*

upon vastness in both space and time stirred his imagination deeply; and as his attention was directed more and more to social and political questions, the fruits of science must have been reflected there also. It was his desire, however, to show that neither religion nor ethics was negatived by the findings of science and that the Unseen was just as vital to humanity as the Seen. To prove this he had continually to reckon with the latest scientific theories.

In the second place, came the conflict between science and the traditions of poetry. For Tennyson, despite his intellectual interest in science and his more or less instinctive interest in religion, was first and foremost a poet, who desired to speak to the heart primarily and to appeal to the intellect secondarily.

The third and last point which we shall make about Tennyson is: while the new conceptions which science forced upon the poet tended somewhat to change the character of his poetry, they did not work a revolutionary change in his style. Tennyson thought of poetry at first as something rather apart from the activities of life itself. In his boyhood, he first admired Byron very much, then his allegiance shifted to Keats, and for a time he made the search for beauty his chief literary interest; but he did not, like Goethe, search for a hidden law. Instead he was content with rather a pictorial, decorative art. We note this conception of poetry displayed in many of his poems of 1830, in "Mariana," for example, the idea of which was suggested by a line from Shakespeare's *Measure for Measure*. This brought to his mind a picture, which he attempted to set forth in great detail and by means of the refrain to suggest a mood. This art, very characteristic of his work for that period, was marked by detailed description and by ornate diction.

The tendency to description and ornateness deepens in the volume of 1832. One poem in this edition, however, "The Palace of Art," shows an attitude of questioning his whole-hearted devotion to the pursuit of beauty, whether it was right to build, "a lordly pleasure house, Wherein at ease for aye to dwell," and to "make merry and carouse."

Like Keats, he feels that bursting into the "lordly pleasure house,"

> A sense of real things comes doubly strong,
> And like a muddy stream, would bear along
> My soul to nothingness.[57]

That is precisely what is beginning to trouble the young Tennyson. Would it be nothingness? And should he, as his teacher prescribed, "strive against all doubtings to keep alive"

> The thought of that same chariot, and the strange
> Journey it went . . .[58]

Whereas he might agree with Keats, that much of the poetry of the eighteenth century was too mechanical, and that the poets "with a puling infant's force sway'd about upon a rocking horse, and thought it Pegasus,"[59] yet the muse in Tennyson's poem found

> Full oft the riddle of the painful earth
> Flash'd thro' her as she sat alone,
> Yet not the less held she her solemn mirth,
> And intellectual throne.[60]

She was painfully aware that "in dark corners of her palace stood"

> Uncertain shapes; and unawares
> On white-eyed phantasms weeping tears of blood,
> And horrible nightmares,[61]

It seemed to her that her soul was

> A star that with the choral starry dance
> Join'd not, but stood, and standing saw
> The hollow orb of moving Circumstance
> Roll'd round by one fix'd law.

---

[57] "Sleep and Poetry."
[58] *Ibid.*
[59] *Ibid.*
[60] "Palace of Art."
[61] *Ibid.*

Finally,

> She threw her royal robes away
> "Make me a cottage in the vale," she said,
> "Where I may mourn and pray.
> Yet pull not down my palace towers, that are
> So lightly, beautifully built;
> Perchance I may return with others there
> When I have purged my guilt."[62]

Thus the conflict, as to whether poetry should seek beauty apart from the activities of life or within those same activities, was warring in his mind, before the death of Arthur Hallam in 1833. This tragedy served to make the problem very much more acute, however, and to raise the question, to what extent the Muse might concern herself with Science; but no satisfactory answer came for a long time. He felt vaguely then what came out into clearer consciousness in the second *Locksley Hall:* "Science grows and beauty dwindles." He was confronted with the paradox of desiring to have science continue growing and yet at the same time wishing to preserve beauty. It thus became more and more apparent to him that his conception of poetic beauty needed renovating and enlarging. But it was not easy to sail away from the accustomed moorings, especially when he had so painstakingly acquired an almost perfect mastery over his technique. Hence, in the 1842 volume we find poems built upon the descriptive and ornate ideal of the older model, with little or no regard for the problems of life; many from the 1830 volume republished, with only a few minor changes; several from the 1832 collection with more modifications and changes; and a few, such as *Locksley Hall* and "The Two Voices," reaching out towards a new ideal of expression, that of giving voice to problems in current life. On the whole, however, the poet is seeking more for perfection of expression than for innovations.

After the publication of the 1842 volumes, he was haunted

[62] *Ibid.*

more and more with a sense that his earlier idea of beauty had been too limited. He began to base his poetry on the "broad and common interests of the time and of universal humanity."[63] His friend Venables suggested, at about this same time, that "the solution of the problem was not to be sought in any transient fashion of thought but in the 'convergent tendencies of many opinions' on religion, art, and nature."[64]

> O leave not thou thy son forlorn;
> Teach me, great Nature: make me live,

was the burden of the poet's prayer at this time.

The poems which came after 1842 tended to deal more with some of the intellectual problems of the age. "The Princess,"[65] for example, attempted to discuss the place of woman in the new order; *In Memoriam*,"[66] as we have seen, tried to reconcile the new scientific theories with theology; *Maud*[67] expressed the unrest of the times; *The Idylls of the King*, extending from 1859 to 1872, became more and more allegorical as the poet sought, through the medium of medieval story, to depict the conflict between soul and sense, which was raging in the life of his time. Much of his later work sought to justify religious faith, while accepting the truths of science.

Indeed, by 1869 he had definitely decided that the idea of "art for art's sake" was not for him.

> Art for art's sake! Hail, truest Lord of Hell!
> Hail Genius, Master of the Moral Will![68]

Similarly, he had no kind of sympathy with the idea that would divorce art from morals.[69] His art creed, Lecky declared, is expressed in the lines:

[63] *Memoir.* I, 123.
[64] *Ibid.*, I, 123.
[65] 1847.
[66] 1850.
[67] 1855.
[68] *Memoir.* II, 92.
[69] Lecky-Memoir. II, 203.

> As when a painter, poring on a face,
> Divinely, thro' all hindrance, finds the man
> Behind it, and so paints him that his face,
> The shape and color of a mind and life,
> Lives for his children, ever at its best.[70]

We get a further inkling of his matured conception of art in "Merlin and the Gleam."[71] Here we have in allegorical form a representation of the progress of poetry. Merlin, who is now dying, calls upon his companions:

> Launch your vessel
> And crowd your canvas,
> And ere it vanishes
> Over the margin,
> After it, follow it,
> Follow the Gleam.[72]

("The Gleam" signifies the higher poetic imagination.)

He is not willing, however, to sacrifice any of the musical quality of poetry. "It often seems to me that music must take up expression at the point where poetry leaves off, and expresses what cannot be expressed in words.[73] He is equally unwilling that art should concern itself too much with realism. He has no sympathy for Zola's method, because it "shows the evils of the world with the ideal. . . . In the noblest genius there is need of self-restraint."[74] Toward the very end of his life he declared, "This modern realism is hateful and destroys all poetry." Yet he is very desirous of expressing the modern spirit in his art, a desire that increased as he grew older. To this end he was urged by Benjamin Jowett, among others, who said that he did not see why the "Dogma of Immortality" should not be put into verse, or the Greek mythology. "Have not many sciences, such as

---

[70] *Memoir.* II, 205.
[71] 1889.
[72] "Merlin and the Gleam."
[73] *Memoir.* II, 394.
[74] *Memoir.* II, 337.

Astronomy or Geology a side of feeling which is poetry?"[75] Tennyson, however, was never quite sure how far this idea might be carried. The adaptation of his art to his age was just what that age required to rescue poetry from the subordinate position which it had occupied in England from 1830 to 1842.[76] There was a feeling then that poetry's "visionary conceptions had rendered cheap and vulgar the wonders of the imagination."[77] Thus, Tennyson and some of his contemporaries, helped to make poetry again a live and vital art.

The introduction of science into poetry was one way by which this interest was reawakened; for it was the growth of science, and more particularly of the scientific temper, that had been a potent factor in turning people away from poetry in the first place.[78] Therefore by broadening his conception of the art of poetry so that it included science and the other current interests of the time, he naturally appealed to a wider audience. The method he first employed resembled in its underlying principle that used by Erasmus Darwin, which aimed to give pictorial expression to scientific abstractions.

Tennyson's early idea of the art of poetry, as we have noted, was pictorial; and therefore when his poems began to deal with science, he still sought, as was natural and also most effective, to express these thoughts in that method. Hence we have such expression as Science "reaching forth her arms, to feel from world to world."[79] "Nature red in tooth and claw."[80] "Man . . . working out the beast" and letting "the ape and tiger die."

As he gave more and more attention, however, to reconciling science and religion, and to conveying a social or ethical message

[75] From a letter to Mrs. Tennyson. *Memoir.* I, 433-34.
[76] Thomas R. Lounsbury: *The Life and Times of Tennyson.*
[77] *Ibid.*
[78] *Ibid.*
[79] *In Memoriam.*
[80] *Ibid.*

to his reader, this pictorial quality tended to recede to the background. We find him employing more frequently a generic or abstract term, instead of a specific, concrete one. In the second *Locksley Hall* he asks:
> Have we risen from the beast, then back
> into the beast again?

And in "Despair":
> Come from the brute, poor souls—no souls—
> and to die with the brute—

Again in "By an Evolutionist":
> "Hold the sceptre, Human Soul, and rule thy
> province of the brute."

In these examples it is beast or brute—any beast or any brute —no longer a specific term such as "ape" or "tiger" which he employed so effectively in his earlier poems.

This tendency to employ a general term instead of a pictorial one may further be seen in the concluding lines to "De Profundis," in which he urges the reader to live:
> Nearer and ever nearer Him, who wrought
> Not matter, nor the finite-infinite,
> But this main-miracle, that thou art thou,
> With power on thine own act and on the world.

Tennyson employed, of course, a different medium of expression from Erasmus Darwin, because between them had intervened the romantic period, with its changes in style and conception. He experimented at first with these various modes and even attempted what he believed to be a new one, in the versification of *In Memoriam*. Although he desired variety, on the whole he was content with the traditional forms, or at the most, with a slight modification of these. He did not feel the need, as Goethe did, or as his contemporaries Browning and Walt Whitman did, for a new technique.

Unlike Erasmus Darwin or the French poets among the Encyclopedists, he did not seek to explain science for the mere sake of teaching scientific truth. Nor was his purpose quite that of

Lucretius, who taught science in order to establish a definite mental attitude and thereby deliver mankind from the fear of superstition. Though, perhaps, a little more in harmony with Goethe, who was interested in science merely as one aspect of reality and as a step in the direction of the cultural ideal, he could not accept the German poet's viewpoint and see Nature and man as entirely harmonious.

He was not in harmony, moreover, with many of his more immediate predecessors who tended either to ignore science or to subordinate it to a minor position. He could not whole-heartedly endorse the sentiment of Wordsworth, who wrote in 1798:

> One impulse from a vernal wood
> May teach you more of man,
> Of moral evil and of good,
> Than all the sages can.

Or that, "we murder to dissect," and therefore,

> Enough of Science and of Art;
> Close up those barren leaves;
> Come forth, and bring with you a heart
> That watches and receives.[81]

This receptive attitude of mind, Tennyson regards as very delightful, if the poet can stop there; he cannot. What if science is but "a succedaenum, and a prop to our infirmity,"[82] that is no reason for ignoring it. And while he too can find delight in meditating upon how Nature's laws,

> Those immaterial agents bowed their heads
> Duly to serve the mind of earth-born man,[83]

he cannot help being very much concerned at the same time with the effect which those laws have upon man himself. For him science is not merely a record of achievement, nor is it something that can be dismissed lightly, as a curiosity or as something of no consequence. Its impact upon human thought

---

[81] "Tables Turned."
[82] *The Prelude.*
[83] *The Prelude*, I, 667.

he feels is too momentous, too fraught with disturbing consequences and possibilities for both good and evil, not to be of very vital import to the poet. While Wordsworth did not deny the possibility of scientific thought finding expression in poetry, he was insistent that it could do so only through an emotional appeal, and that must be sometime in the future. Tennyson, on the other hand, felt that scientific thought must find expression in his own time, because scientific facts were becoming "the natural material of thought on the part of modern man."[84]

With the attitude of Coleridge that science and poetry are antithetical, Tennyson could not therefore sympathize. He doubtless felt the force of it in one respect, for to admit science into poetry meant, to a certain extent at least, a compromise with his earlier conception of poetry; but with the dogma that poetry must not seek to express scientific truth, he could not agree in the least.

Although it might be true, as Keats suggested in "Lamia," that at the touch of cold philosophy the charms of poetry and romance vanish, yet Tennyson apparently realized that if Poetry itself was to survive, in his age, it must take account of philosophy and science. Furthermore, these did not seem to him so forbidding as the earlier poet had thought.

More akin with Shelley in this respect, he could praise natural law because of the necessity and invariability of it; but he could not stop there—without a personal loving God. With Shelley, he could echo the complaint of Demogorgon:
> If the abysm
> Could vomit forth its secrets. . . . But a voice
> Is wanting, the deep truth is imageless.[85]

As he grew older, he tended to arrive at some of the solutions of Shelley, as set forth in *A Defense of Poetry* (1821-24), to the

[84] Raymond M. Alden. *Alfred Tennyson, How to Know Him.* 1917, pp. 287-88.
[85] *Prometheus Unbound.* (1820) II, Sc. 4.

effect that Poetry "comprehends all science and is that to which all science must be referred": and Science is the "Sister of Poetry."

It is obvious that Tennyson could have little sympathy with the merely flippant attitude towards science manifested by his early love, Byron, who wrote:

> . . . Immortal man hath glow'd
> With all kinds of mechanics, and full soon
> Steam-engines will conduct him to the moon.[86]

Or with the more contemporary attitude of Aytoun's hero in *Firmilian* (1854), when he declares that a

> . . . jagged streak
> Upon the surface of a harmless stone
> May be the Helen to some future host
> Of glacier-theorists![87]

He has much more sympathy with the more serious treatment of "Festus" Bailey, who in his attempt to bring the Faust story up to date, is also wrestling with the problem of knowledge and faith.

> Nothing can be antagonist to God. . . .
> Necessity, like electricity
> Is in ourselves and in all things.[88]

Also, Festus has no fear of knowledge, for

> There is no danger now of knowing aught
> Which ought not to be known.[89]

Like Tennyson, he too accepts the mystical conception of reality. It is only in Heaven that the sage

> Masters all mysteries, more and more, from day
> to day, watching the thoughts of men and angels
> Through moral microscopes.[90]

---

[86] *Don Juan.* Canto X.
[87] Sc. XIII.
[88] *Proem.* 1845.
[89] *Festus.*
[90] *Ibid.*

But unlike Tennyson, Bailey's hero concludes that "knowledge is a doubtful boon, Root of all good and fruit of all that's bad."[91]

Tennyson, in attempting to make a compromise between a mechanical universe and a spiritual realm, in which man enjoyed immunity from the limitations imposed upon him by scientific determinism; in sensing the implications of the new sciences built upon the evolutionary idea, and in accepting the newest scientific truths and putting these into musical verse, deserves the epithet that has frequently been applied to him, "the poet of science."

[91] *Ibid.*

CHAPTER IX

THE POET'S DILEMMA—REASON OR MYSTICISM

The question which a study of Tennyson leaves with us, and one seconded by many poets in the latter half of the nineteenth century, is: to what extent can a poet, in the face of the science of that time, rely upon reason and to what extent must he resort to mysticism? Tennyson, as we have noted, found a refuge in mysticism. Matthew Arnold and George Meredith, on the other hand, both ardently championed the cause of reason.

Of course there were some poets of the period who steadfastly refused to ally themselves with either party. The Pre-Raphaelites, for example, tended to react from mechanism by shutting themselves in a world of their imagination, freed from the restraints of the phenomenal world. This is a position which Tennyson, in his maturity at least, even in his most mystical mood, declined to take. Likewise, the "Spasmodic School" (including Gilfillan, Bailey, Bigg, Dobell, and Alexander Smith), had, through the disillusionment caused by the materialistic trend of science, abandoned the mystical attitude and had been rendered feverish and restless. Their cry was to live

To love and flush and thrill—or let me die.[1]

Similarly, Fitz-Gerald, in his *Omar Khayyám* (1859), suggests, by implication at least, that Wine and the Song of Life should serve as an opiate, as it were, against the mechanical and materialistic tempers which modern science has helped engender. Arthur Clough decries the standardization that science causes and the fact that it is depriving man of the old props and ideals, for:

[1] Alexander Smith: *A Life Drama.*

> The lever finds its fulcrum:
> On what it then o'erthrows; the homely spade
> In labour's hand unscrupulously seeks
> Its first momentum on the very clod
> Which next will be upturned. It seems a law.[2]

Although both Robert Browning and Walt Whitman were well aware of the encroachments of science upon the field of poetic imagination, both welcomed in a measure these encroachments and sought to make adequate provision for them, but each of them—in order to make such a provision—like Tennyson resorted to mysticism. Their poetic style, moreover, was influenced by the new thought much more than was Tennyson's.

Although Browning's attitude towards science came to much the same as Tennyson's, the former poet passed through no such struggle before he could formulate the distinction between religion and science. For him, even from the beginning, religion was a matter of faith and love—a conviction that was deepened in the experience of his own happy married life and in the almost miraculous cure which the power of love seemed to bring in the life of his invalid wife. Science, on the other hand, was entirely of the intellect. He well knew that this was capable of illuminating one only to a certain point, beyond which faith and love must lead the way.[3]

Blessed with a healthy and robust nature, one that felt a glowing delight in the exuberance of his animal spirits and a keen zest for life and experience, he was confident that the highest truth one could know was revealed through emotion and feeling. Indeed, for him the Infinite Himself is a being who feels. Therefore, if the intellect attempted to negative this emotional truth, so much the worse for the intellect. Naturally this led to a certain distrust of knowledge in and for itself and tended to bring

---

[2] *Dipsychus.* Pt. II. Sc. VIII.

[3] Compare his treatment of God and Immortality in his "Christmas Eve" and "Easter Day" with Tennyson's *In Memoriam.*

a dualism between feeling and intelligence which became the corner stone of his philosophy.

If love was thus capable of transcending scientific truth, the implications in the new science naturally did not trouble him as they did Tennyson, Clough, and Matthew Arnold. He was confident that:

> God's in His heaven—
> All's right with the world!

With a faith more robust and just as sincere as Tennyson's, he had none of the mental struggles and harassing doubts that beset the author of *In Memoriam*.

Just as Tennyson, however, had found occasion for optimism in the idea of evolution, so we find Browning employing evolution to bolster up his optimistic philosophy. So sure is he that evolution is the law of life, that he looks upon evil as due merely to arrested development. What cause is there then for pessimism in the fact that Nature is "red in tooth and claw"? For out of strife with the evil comes the good.

Browning shows in many instances evidences of scientific knowledge and an interest in scientific procedure. Perhaps some of his power of careful, painstaking psychological analysis is not without its debt to the scientific movement of the time. The dying speech of Paracelsus, for example, shows the poet's familiarity with the idea of evolution in geological, plant, and animal forms—a process which is depicted as not stopping with man but going forward towards Superman and God. In "Evelyn Hope," we have an expression of the conservation of matter and energy in the description of the disintegration of atoms and their recombinations, until the "beautiful Evelyn Hope" and the old lover are once more together. The idea that everything is subject to the law of change is hailed in "James Lee's Wife":[4]

> Nothing can be as it has been before;
> Better, so call it, only not the same.

---

[4] Stanza VI.

Even beauty cannot be kept changeless.
> ... Rejoice that man is hurled
> From change to change unceasingly,
> His soul's wings never furled![5]

Browning has, furthermore, the insatiate curiosity which goes with the scientific seeker after knowledge. He is curious about spiritualism and the type of men who practice it. In "Mr. Sludge, the Medium" he exhibits the mental processes of just such a man.

This habit of analysis, almost scientific in its method, grows upon him with the passing of time "to the detriment of the artistic," until most of his later poems, complains Professor Walker, "are conscious and deliberate discussions of problems, ethical, or religious."[6]

As a matter of biographical record we know that Browning had not the personal interest in science that Tennyson had. And while "there are allusions many and exact to show his familiarity with the growth of various objective sciences during his life," he does not, like Tennyson, deal with "problems growing out . . . of such sciences as astronomy, geology, physics, chemistry, or biology."[7]

As a matter of fact, his very attitude of separating feeling and intelligence and of pinning his own faith to feeling and volition, naturally made these details of science, which seemed of such vast import to Tennyson, of very minor significance to him. The great forces behind these details were important, especially the power of development, for these reacted in turn upon man's volitional nature. But before a scientific concept could assume any special significance for him, it must in turn be translated into terms of the emotions. This was one function of art which

[5] *Ibid.*
[6] Walker: *Victorian Literature*, p. 433.
[7] H. A. Clarke: *Browning and His Century*. N.Y., 1912. p. 45.

REASON OR MYSTICISM

> . . . May tell a truth
> Obliquely, do the thing shall breed the thought.[8]

In fact,

> . . . Art remains the one way possible
> Of speaking truth, to mouths like mine at least.[9]

Browning did not, however, even in his earliest work, regard the ideal of beauty as something apart from actual life. Thus, in two of his early long poems, *Paracelsus* (1835) and *Sordello* (1840), we find him propounding to himself these questions: To what extent may the artist detach himself from everyday life and from reality in general? To what degree may he avoid philosophical and scientific questions, and, *vice versa*, to what extent may he include these?

In *Paracelsus* we have the titular character seeking truth by way of the intellect, eschewing human joys and love; and we have the poet Aprile "consumed by a creative passion which is always akin to love," disregarding entirely the intellectual activities.[10] The poet dies from his excess of the passion, and Paracelsus upon his deathbed exclaims:

> Love, hope, fear, faith—these make humanity;
> These are its sign and note and character
> And these I have lost!

Each life has been incomplete, because it has concentrated too exclusively upon one line of activity, and also paradoxically because it has refused to acknowledge the principle of human limitation in each field of endeavor.

In *Sordello* we have the question proposed in the contrast between the poets Sordello and Eglamore. Sordello, not refusing knowledge as Aprile does, but deeming the imaginative life as something entirely independent of the actual conditions of life

[8] *Ring and the Book.* XII.
[9] *Ibid.*
[10] Mrs. Sutherland Orr. *A Handbook to the Works of Robert Browning.* p. 22.

and bestowing upon the Will the power to transcend both the artist and the thinker, is presented to us at first as egotistical and thoroughly selfish. By way of contrast, Eglamore, the other poet, while regarding art as an end in itself and therefore no part of reality, considers poetry as limited and thoroughly prescribed. Browning makes it clear in these poems and in his later works that he cannot accept the principle of divorcing art from science, or science from art (as Paracelsus and Aprile tried to do); or sanction the idea of looking upon the utterances of the poet as sancrosanct, unless those utterances concern themselves also with the moral problems of the individual and his relations to society. Equally unacceptable to him is the principle which would limit art to an expression entirely consonant with the powers of the artist. Poetry cannot ignore the realistic aspect of life, nor can it afford to devote itself exclusively to reporting merely what the eye and ear reveal. The artist should aspire to accomplish that which lies even beyond his reach. This is the meaning of his "Andrea del Sarto," in which the painter is depicted as a failure because he has not aspired sufficiently. That too is the tragedy of Eglamore in *Sordello*.

For Tennyson the poet was primarily a literary artist expressing himself in moulds that tradition had more or less fixed. For the poet to undertake to express more than his artistic equipment would permit with facility was a betrayal of his trust. His problem, then, was to reconcile the traditions with the material which his century had brought.

Perhaps in one sense the scientific spirit made a deeper impression upon Browning's literary methods than it did upon Tennyson's, perhaps the underlying philosophy of evolution entered more intimately into the texture of his thinking. For Browning, who was also thoroughly well aware of this new material and believed that the poet must take it into account, went much further than Tennyson in the direction of modifying the existing traditions. His poetic style, therefore, even from the earliest times, with its variety of rhythms, its element of the grotesque and its analytical quality, contrasts very markedly with the more conventional and ornate style of Tennyson. To express some of these complex ideas Browning feels neither at ease artistically nor satisfied intellectually with either the conventional, classical, or the freer romantic modes of expression. Desirous of depicting some of the ethical, artistic, religious and more especially the psychological problems of his age, he reaches out for a suitable vehicle. He desires a style, in brief, which will adequately express the new conceptions to which the principle of evolution and its implications are giving birth. That mode of expression must be freer, must be dynamic, giving the impression of change and growth, providing not the basis for a versified science but utilizing the great scientific principles while depicting the development of a personality—a development which takes place not merely through growth of intellect, but also, and primarily, through the aspirations and the emotional reactions of the individual.

Walt Whitman, like Browning, also felt that the traditional mode of expression in poetry was not adequate to his needs. He, too, sought a vehicle for some of the new ideas. Foremost among these was the celebration of American democracy. Feeling that the traditional forms had grown out of the feudal system of government, he desired to discard them entirely and to seek forms which would be suitable to embody the ideals of a democratic government.

"Poet," wrote Whitman, "beware lest your poems are made in the spirit that comes from the study of pictures of things—and not from the spirit that comes from the contact with real things themselves." This new poetry was to take account of everything. "Nothing in the created universe," he declared, "was devoid of interest, or unfit for mention at any time or place, and all were suitable material for the poet."[11] Indeed, there had

[11] Cairn. *Yale Review.* Vol. 8, p. 743-44.

been too much of a distinction, he thought, between prose and poetry, and he believed that the time had come "to essentially break down the barriers of form between them."[12]

Although theoretically there was no limit to the amount of science which could go into poetry, yet speaking more practically the poet says, "You must not know too much, or be too precise or scientific about birds and flowers and trees and water-craft; a certain free margin, and even vagueness—perhaps ignorance, credulity—helps your enjoyment of these things, and of the sentiment of feather'd, wooded, river or marine, Nature generally."[13] But as a rule the question as regards the difference between the emotional nature of the poet and the intellectual nature of the scientist did not trouble him, as it did both Browning and Tennyson. There was no such struggle in Whitman's soul, as there was in Tennyson's concerning the material and the spiritual. Indeed, the American poet seems to glory in materialism.

> I am the poet of the Body;
> And I am the poet of the Soul.[14]

> I accept reality and dare not question it;
> Materialism first and last imbuing.
> Hurrah for positive science! long live exact demonstration.[15]

He is filled with wonder at the mechanism of the moving earth:
> It is no small matter, this round, and delicious globe, moving so exactly in its orbit forever and ever, without one jolt, or the untruth of a single second.[16]

The problem of the mechanical and materialistic aspects of science did not exist for him. Given in the early part of his

[12] *Ibid.*, p. 746.
[13] From *Specimen Days*.
[14] "Walt Whitman."
[15] *Ibid.*
[16] "Who Learns My Lesson Complete."

life to seeking emotional experience and thoroughly undisciplined in the philosophical and religious problems of his age, having received only a more or less haphazard education, which included, however, the reading of Dante, Shakespeare, the Iliad, the Bible, Epictetus, the novels of Scott, and later the poems of Tennyson, some of the Orientals and the Germans, particularly Hegel whose ideas of evolution played such an important part with him, he early found a formula, which more or less satisfied him, in the Transcendentalism of Emerson. This, it will be recollected, made the spiritual the real, and all material things but a representation of the spiritual. Hence, he was not bothered in his religious beliefs, as was Tennyson, by the mechanical and materialistic aspects of science; and he was not in the least troubled as was Carlyle, that so many men were accepting these principles along with the corollary Mammonism.

According to his scheme of philosophy the universe is completely good, and everything that happens is according to a prearranged scheme, in which love takes a very important part. "I hear and behold God in every object," he writes, and adds with a characteristic note of mysticism, "yet understand God not in the least."[17]

> I swear I think now that everything without
> exception has an eternal Soul!
> . . . .
> I swear I think there is nothing but immortality.[18]

He can thus truly feel that

> A morning-glory at my window satisfies me
> more than the metaphysics of books.[19]

He can sense no real antagonism between Science and Religion. "The soul is the divinest thing that science discovers in the universe."[20]

[17] "Walt Whitman."
[18] "To Think of Time." 1855.
[19] "Walt Whitman."
[20] From his "Manifesto."

There is nothing which alarms him in the conception of a universe ruled by natural law. On the contrary, he sees in that a representation of the Divine Will manifesting itself in various ways—in "the procreant urge of the World,"[21] for example. There is hope in the very inexorable quality of these laws.

> The law of the past cannot be eluded,
> The law of the present and future cannot be eluded,
> The law of living cannot be eluded—it is eternal,
> The law of promotion and transformation cannot be eluded.[22]

He saw everything, both the beautiful and the ugly, existing in accordance with natural laws. Like Browning, he believed there was only cause for optimism in the principle of development or evolution. In the first place, the fact that everything is so interconnected with everything else means that as one part progresses every other part feels the good effects, "For every atom belonging to me, as good belongs to you."[23] Furthermore, the process of development means an unfolding of the divine truth. This interconnection of things, of course, implies man's kinship with animals, with plants, and with all nature. This fact does not lessen his enthusiasm, in the slightest degree, and he proceeds to chant the praises of the principle of evolution.

> I am an acme of things accomplish'd, and I
>   an encloser of things to be.[24]

> > Rise after rise bow the phantoms behind me;
> > Afar down I see the huge first Nothing—I
> >   know I was even there;
> > I waited unseen and always, and slept through
> >   the lethargic mist,
> > And took my time, and took no hurt from the
> >   fetid carbon.
> > Long I was hudd'd close—long and long.
> >   .   .   .   .

---

[21] "Walt Whitman."
[22] "To Think of Time."
[23] "Walt Whitman." [24] *Ibid.*

REASON OR MYSTICISM

> Cycles ferried my cradle, rowing and rowing
>   like cheerful boatmen;
> For room to me stars kept aside in their own
>   rings;
> They sent influences to look after what was to
>   hold me.
>   . . . .
> For it the nebula cohered to an orb,
> The long slow strata piled to rest it on,
> Vast vegetables gave it sustenance,
> Monstrous sauroids transported it in their
>   mouths, and deposited it with care.
>
> All forces have been steadily employ'd to
>   complete and delight me;
> Now on this spot I stand with my robust soul.[25]

This idea of development, however, involves a conception of Infinite Space and Time, and this Whitman succeeds in conveying better perhaps than any other poet of his time. When he looks out at the stars at night he realizes that all the starry systems he can see,

> . . . multiplied as high as I can cipher, edge
>   but the rims of the farther systems.
> Wider and wider they spread, expanding always
>   expanding,
> Outward and outward, and forever outward.[26]
>
> See ever so far, there is limitless space
>   outside of that;
> Count ever so much, there is limitless time
>   around that.[27]

He asks his Spirit:
> When we become the enfolders of those orbs,
>   and the pleasure and knowledge of everything in them, shall we be fill'd and
>   satisfied then?

---
[25] *Ibid.*
[26] "Walt Whitman."
[27] *Ibid.*

And my Spirit said, No, we but level that lift,
    to pass and continue beyond.[28]

He sings the praises of the human body, because:

For it the globe lay preparing quintillions
    of years, without one animal or plant;
For it the revolving cycles truly and steadily roll'd.[29]

With both Browning and Tennyson he insists that evolution has not stopped with man—but is going on in the future.

There is no stoppage, and never can be stoppage;
If I, you, and the worlds, and all beneath or
    upon their surfaces, were this moment reduced
    back to a pallid float, it would not avail
    in the long run;
We should surely bring up again where we now stand,
And as surely go as much farther—and then farther
    and farther.[30]

He believed, therefore, that science cannot be hostile to poetry. Although he was deeply moved by the idea of evolution and was intellectually curious about all facts of nature, he did not weigh or test these facts as the man truly devoted to science does, or even as Tennyson did. He did not possess the scientific temper, even to the degree that Browning displayed it in the analysis of human motives, or in sensing the implications of the new science like Tennyson. In the last analysis his interest in the objects of nature was grounded in the faith that they made the unseen visible through the seen. He did not hesitate, however, to employ whatever scientific imagery he could lay his hands upon. "All truths," he writes, "do not need the obstetric forceps of the surgeon,"[31] and goes on to mention the "many-cylinder'd steam printing-press . . . the electric telegraph."[32] He also speaks of the cable:

[28] *Ibid.*
[29] "I Sing the Body Electric." 1855.
[30] "Walt Whitman."
[31] "Walt Whitman."
[32] "Starting from Pawmanok." 1860.

> See, through Atlantica's depths, pulses
> American,
> Europe reaching—pulses of Europe duly
> return'd.[33]

And again:
> See, the strong and quick locomotive, as it
> departs, panting, blowing the steam-whistle;
> . . . .
> See, mechanics, busy at their benches, with tools.[34]

But for all his absorption in the idea of development, he does not make clear how this evolution takes place. He is not troubled, as is Tennyson, with the Herculean task of reconciling the conflicting motives of a struggle for existence and a loving God.

Not all poets in the second half of the nineteenth century, however, resorted to mysticism when they met the scientific issue, or built an ivory tower far from the reach of mundane considerations. Some of them met the implications which lay behind the scientific temper courageously. Matthew Arnold was one of these.

Like both Clough and Tennyson, he was very much concerned about the strife between the church and natural science. He regretted the passing of the old values and felt disconsolate over the religious props and standards which his intellect now assured him were no longer tenable. While he lacked a detailed knowledge of science, yet the spirit of inquiry was very strong in him; and he was just as ready as Tennyson to give full acceptance to the results of scientific research. His training in the classics had nourished in him an understanding of the Greek love of intellectual pursuits. Hence, his faith in the powers of the human mind was more thoroughgoing than Tennyson's and did not falter when he realized the limitations of those powers or seek a compromise in mysticism.

[33] *Ibid.*
[34] *Ibid.*

> Mind is the spell which governs earth and heaven,
> Man has a mind with which to plan his safety:
> Know that, and help thyself.[35]

Indeed, it is through this mind that man frees himself from fears. Furthermore, he "gets no other light, search he a thousand years."[36] Like Tennyson, however, he finds that his intellect leads him to an attitude of doubt, even of pessimism.

> Limits we did not set
> Condition all we do;
> Born unto life we are, and life must be our mould.[37]

In spite of the fact that it is our will to know all the world, and

> We map the starry sky,
> We mine this earthern ball,
> We measure the sea-tides, we number the sea-sands.[38]

we must conclude ultimately,

> Man's measures cannot mete the immeasurable All.[39]

But having once committed himself to the powers of the mind, he is willing to abide by the consequences. He refuses to view the world mystically.

> Fools! that in man's brief term
> He cannot all things view,
> Affords no ground to affirm
> That there are Gods who do![40]

Furthermore, man

> ... hast no *right* to bliss,
> No title from the Gods to welfare and repose.[41]

The greatest wisdom, then, is the acceptance of the inevitable:

> I say: Fear not! Life still
> Leaves human effort scope.

---

[35] "Empedocles." I, ii, 26.
[36] *Ibid.*, l. 144.
[37] *Ibid.*, 184.
[38] *Ibid.*, 319.
[39] *Ibid.*, 341.
[40] *Ibid.*, 347.
[41] *Ibid.*, 160.

> But, since life teems with ill,
> Nurse no extravagant hope;
> Because thou must not dream, thou need'st
> not then despair![42]

He advocates, just as ardently as the Encyclopedists in the eighteenth century had urged, entire reliance upon the human reason; but he cannot draw their optimistic conclusions. The progress of science since then has served to make known the limitations of the human mind and has brought in its wake, he feels, complete disillusionment.[43] Man must indeed resign himself to what is apparently the stern law of nature.[44] In fact, this refusal upon Arnold's part to compromise marks his chief difference from Tennyson and is his most original note.

"We mark not the world's course, but would have *it* take *ours*"[45] is the attitude of mind he believes, which is keeping man so restlessly striving, and prevents him from realizing the ideal of the Scholar Gipsy, *"one* aim, *one* business, *one* desire"[46] and "Free from sick fatigue, the languid doubt,"[47] but because we refuse to face the facts and become resigned to them we have

> ... this strange disease of modern life,
> With its sick hurry, its divided aims,
> Its head o'ertax'd, its palsied hearts ...[48]

And

> England ... Stupidly travels her round
> Of mechanic business, and lets
> Slow die out of her life
> Glory, and genius, and joy.[49]

Precisely because of "this strange disease of modern life," poetry has a unique mission. It should serve as "a criticism of

---

[42] *Ibid.*, 422.
[43] "Dover Beach."
[44] "Resignation."   [45] *Ibid.*, 221.
[46] "Scholar Gipsy." I, 152.   [47] *Ibid.*, 164.   [48] *Ibid.*, 203.
[49] "Heine's Grave."

life." This criticism, he thought, could be found in the Hellenic ideal. There would be furnished a "vision of spiritual ends,"[50] and a liberation from a state of mind which has been "mechanized by the expansion of trade and manufacture," and from "a superstitious faith in the machine."[51]

In this criticism of life however, there is needed the scientific spirit, frank and courageous enough to meet the logical consequences with a smile. There is needed also the Hellenic vision to give us the necessary sense of values. Then "more and more," he declares, "mankind will discover that we have to turn to poetry to interpret life for us, to console us, to sustain us. Without poetry our science will appear incomplete."[52]

Like Tennyson, then, he would furnish ideas in his poetry which would serve the ethical purpose of interpreting life, consoling and sustaining us from the ravages of a too rationalistic attitude and from a mechanized science. Tennyson, however, sought to harmonize the older religion with the new facts of evolutionary science; he relied upon mysticism for a blending of the two and declared that from such an experience mankind can *know* the truth. Arnold, on the other hand, felt that the older religion was incompatible with the new science, though this had its limitations. These must be manfully acknowledged; but concerning the ultimate problems of God, immortality, and free will, man should admit, he argued, that he did not and could not know the answers.

If this conclusion is the logical one to be drawn in pursuing the scientific spirit to its ultimate end, then it may be said that science exerted a profound influence upon Matthew Arnold. At the same time it must be admitted that Arnold had little detailed

---

[50] Stanley T. Williams, *Studies in Victorian Literature*. N.Y., 1923, p. 133.

[51] *Ibid*.

[52] Matthew Arnold. "The Study of Poetry," in *Essays in Criticism*, 2d Ser., N.Y., 1924.

knowledge of any of the sciences. He felt no interest in science for its own sake.

But though he met this issue much more courageously than the other poets we have been considering in this chapter, he was not entirely happy in the position of agnosticism to which it forced him. He was mentally honest somewhat at the expense of his peace of mind.

Another English poet, George Meredith, writing most of his poetry just after Arnold had turned to the essay form, also accepted the implications which lay behind the Darwinian hypothesis and found therein occasion for optimism. Like Arnold, Meredith championed the cause of reason, and a greater part of his poetry was devoted to the glorification of man's intellectual power. Nevertheless like the physician Melampus, in his poem of that name, he loved all the things "that glide in grasses and rubble of woody wreck."[53]

> For him the woods were a home and gave him the key
> Of knowledge, thirst for their treasures in
>   herbs and flowers.
> The secrets held by the creatures nearer than we
> To earth he sought, and the links of their
>   life with ours.[54]

Meredith very early made the same fundamental assumption that had informed so much of the work of Erasmus Darwin and Goethe, that all Nature is a unity. But after 1859 this was no longer such an assumption as it had been in the lifetime of those earlier poets. Science had indeed demonstrated rather effectively that all forms of life, including animals, plants and mankind, were somehow concerned in a great concord, which could be explained in part at least, by a process known as natural selection. In 1888 the poet declared that even though Nature did give

[53] "Melampus." I, 1883.
[54] *Ibid.*, II.

> Breath which is the spirit's bath
> In the old Beginnings . . .⁵⁵

it is man who furnishes it with "mind." Indeed he gave a humorous expression to this same idea much earlier, in 1861, in "By the Rosanna,"

> The roaring voice through the long white chain
> Is the voice of the world of bubble and brain.

The poet speculates upon the effect of introducing the Alpine Rainbow to a London cabman.

> It would do him a world of good, poor devil.

But it is difficult, he reflects, to make the spirit of Nature and the spirit of everyday humanity known to each other.

It was his belief that intellectual activity tended to hold men together, while the animal life, the life of the senses, served to separate them. Since Science and Philosophy are both fruits of the intellect, so to speak, he considers them of the utmost significance.

> On strengthened wing forever more,
> Let Science, swiftly as she can,
> Fly seaward on from shore to shore,
> And bind the links of man.⁵⁶

Science helps demonstrate this interconnection of things, and especially the relation between Earth and Man.

> Earth, the mother of all,
> Moves on her stedfast way,
> Gathering, flinging, sowing,
> Mortals, we live in her day,
> She in her children is growing.⁵⁷

Man's intellect must be fed by Nature, for from her are read the greatest truths.

> Loved, enjoyed, her gifts must be,
> Reverenced the truths she teaches,

---

[55] Nature and Life. I, 1888.
[56] "The Olive Branch," 1851.
[57] "Spirit of Earth in Autumn." 1862.

REASON OR MYSTICISM

> Ere a man may hope that he
> Ever can attain the glee
> Of things without a destiny.[58]

This point of view reminds one of Wordsworth's utterances about Nature's "gifts" and the truths she teaches. Wordsworth might have said too that Nature can teach man how

> To kiss the season and shun regrets,

how to live in "the heart of mirth,"[59] and how to think. But one cannot so easily credit him with asserting that Life and Death are one, for

> Whichever is, the other is.[60]

and,

> He may entreat, aspire,
> He may despair, and she has never heed.[61]

The philosophy which Meredith advocates is based upon science and without that philosophy the stars would seem "implacable"

> To us who would of life obtain
> An answer for the life we strain
> To nourish with one sign.
> Nor can imagination throw
> The penetrative shaft:[62]
>
> Yet space is given for breath of thought
> Beyond our bounds when musing:[63]

Therefore when we employ the mind,

> So may we read, and little find them cold:
> Let it but be the Lord of Mind to guide
> Our eyes, no branch of Reason's growing lopped:
> Nor dreaming on a dream; but fortified
> By day to penetrate black midnight; see,
> Hear, feel, outside the senses; even that we,

---

[58] *Ibid.*
[59] *Ibid.*
[60] "Hymn to Colour." 1888.
[61] "Earth and Man." 1883.
[62] "Meditation under Stars." 1888.
[63] *Ibid.*

> The specks of dust upon a mound of mould,
> We who reflect those rays, though low our place
> To them are lastingly allied.[64]

Thus, Earth's secret is read not in solitary nature, nor in the centers of humanity, but

> It hangs for those who hither thither fare
> Close interthreading nature with our kind.[65]

Furthermore, when reason is employed, it is of service in,

> Lighting Pain to its mad source,
> Scaring Fear till Fear escapes.[66]

And it insures the highest pleasures, because then "Blood and brain and spirit . . . Join for true felicity."[67] When these three are one,

> Earth your haven, Earth your helm
> You command a double realm.[68]

For

> Life, the chisel, axe and sword,
> Wield who have her depths explored.[69]

Likewise, Reason supplies man with faith,

> Leaving her the future task:
> Loving her too well to ask.[70]

Indeed, without Reason and Faith, one must take heed, he warns,

> Are you of the stiff, the dry,
> Cursing the not understood;
> Grasp you with the monster's claws;
> Govern with his truncheon-saws;
> Hate, the shadow of a grain;
> You are lost in Westermain.[71]

---

[64] *Ibid.*
[65] "Earth's Secret," 1883.
[66] "Woods of Westermain," 1883.
[67] *Ibid.*
[68] "Woods of Westermain." 1883.
[69] *Ibid.*
[70] *Ibid.*
[71] *Ibid.*

With Reason, and its manifestations in Science and Philosophy, man recognizes that he is part of Nature, that his happiness lies in realizing this, and in utilizing its benefits. Thereby his fears and doubts are quieted, and he comes to feel a great confidence and faith in the forces and powers of Nature. But this reason must be characterized by a courage that dares "enter these enchanted woods."[72]

Meredith himself possessed a vitality and robustness that might well challenge Browning's. Some of this same quality is imparted to many of the characters in his novels. Like Browning too, only perhaps even to a greater extent, he employed a method of almost scientific dissection of motives. "He is always testing human nature with his finger, like a glass, to see if it rings clear and right."[73] To face truth courageously, however, means discarding the sentimental view. We must come, in so far as it is possible, to cherish the hard, cold facts, in and for themselves.

This type of reason condemns an attitude of despair and resignation, such as Matthew Arnold preached. Reason ought not to have led Empedocles to commit suicide by tumbling head over heels into the crater of Aetna:

> Each life its critic deed reveals;
> And him reads Reason at his heels,
> If heels in air the last of him.[74]

Furthermore, in the dialogue between Foresight and Patience, in the poem of that title, Patience declares:

> I am not Resignation's counterpart.
>
> . . . .
>
> Rather a world of pressing men in arms,
> Than stagnant, where the sensual piper charms
> Each drowsy malady and coiling vice
> With dreams of ease whereof the soul pays price;

---

[72] "Woods of Westermain."
[73] Oliver Elton: *George Meredith: An Appreciation.*
[74] "Empedocles." 1892.

> No home is here for peace while evil breeds.
> While error governs, none . . .

In the idea of change and development, which both Science and Philosophy recommend to his serious consideration, he finds cause for optimism rather than resignation or despair.

> Light to light sees little strange,
> Only features heavenly new;
> Then you touch the nerves of Change
> Then of Earth you have the clue;
> Then her two-sexed meanings melt
> Through you, wed the thought and felt.[75]

The conception of development means we are:

> . . . First animals; and next
> Intelligences at a leap . . .[76]

and he goes on to point out that

> . . . old-eyed oxen chew
> Speculation with the cud,
> Read their pool of vision through,
> Back to hours when mind was mud.[77]

There is another cause for rejoicing, because it is,

> An Earth alive with meanings, wherein meet
> Buried, and breathing and to be . . .[78]

and the process is a continuous one; yet his philosophic mind perceives a Permanence persisting beneath all this change and variety.

> Once beheld she gives the key
> Airing every doorway she;
>
> . . . . .
>
> On the surface she will witch,
> Rendering Beauty yours, but gaze
> Under, and the soul is rich
> Past computing, past amaze.

---

[75] "Woods of Westermain."
[76] "Modern Love." 1862.
[77] "Woods of Westermain."
[78] "Youth in Memory." 1892.

> Then is courage that endures
> Even her awful tremble yours.[79]

Having been led to science through his desire for truth, he tries to be faithful to its pronouncements and to weave these into a greater philosophic generalization, according to the conception of Positivism. In his acceptance of science, "he had the courage," declares one writer, "more perhaps than any of his contemporaries, fearlessly to accept in all their fullness and entirety the conclusions of modern science; and not only to accept them, but to find them vitally poetic and inspiring."[80]

He had no hesitation, therefore, in singing about natural selection and its implications, because in the first place,

> The light of every soul burns upwards.[81]

In the second place we should not "dread competitors," because

> My betters are my masters: purely fed
> By their sustainment I likewise shall scale
> Some rocky steps between the mount and vale.[82]

And to complete the trio, man must struggle, for

> . . . he is in the lists
> Contentious with the elements, whose dower
> First sprang him; for swift vultures to devour
> If he desists.[83]

Indeed,

> Contention is the vital force,
> Whence pluck they brain . . .
>
> . . . . .
>
> Earth yields the milk but all her mind
> Is vowed to thresh for stouter stock.[84]

In *Diana of the Crossways* Meredith writes: "There is nothing the body suffers that the soul may not profit by." Like

[79] Woods of Westermain."

[80] S. Law Wilson: *The Theology of Modern Literature.* Edinburgh, 1899, p. 434.

[81] *Diana of the Crossways.*

[82] "Internal Harmony." 1883.

[83] "Earth and Man." 1883.

[84] "Hard Weather." 1888.

Browning he believed that conflict and struggle are important factors in the development of character, but where Browning is silent about the process Meredith grows eloquent in his praises of the principle of natural selection, and he applies it unflinchingly to mankind as well as to the lower animals. Earth prompts man to rejoice,
> Yet scares him on the threshold with the shroud.
> He deems her cherishing of her best-endowed
> A wanton's choice.
> . . . .
> . . . of her he draws,
> Though blind to her, by spelling at her laws,
> Her purest fires.[85]
>> Beneath the vans of doom did men pass in,
>> Heroic who come out; for round them hung
>> A wavering phantom's red volcano tongue,
>> With league-long lizard tail and fishy fin.[86]

Another feature about the law of natural selection which appeals to him is the fact that the "scaly Dragon-fowl," symbolic of man's egotism, is transformed through the process into something nobler and completely able to realize spiritual values. Thus:
> . . . shall the horrid pall
> Be lifted, and a spirit nigh divine,
> "Live in thy offspring as I live in mine,"
> Will hear her call.[87]

The process is thus an asset to the welfare of the race. For behind it is, he believes, a purpose. It is nature's thought "to speed the race."[88] She abhors the weakling.
> All round, we find cold Nature slight
> The feelings of the totter-knee'd.[89]

She loves the strong:

[85] "Earth and Man." 1883.
[86] "Forest History." 1898.
[87] "Earth and Man."
[88] "The Thrush in February." 1885.
[89] "Whimper of Sympathy." 1887.

> Look in the face of men who fare
> Lock-mouthed a match in lungs and thews
> For this fierce angel of the air,
> To twist with him and take his bruise,
> That is the face beloved of old
> Of Earth, young mother of her brood!
> Nor broken for us shows the mould
> When muscle is in mind renewed;
> Though farther from her nature rude,
> Yet nearer to her spirit's hold!
> . . . . . .
> She winnows, winnows roughly; sifts,
> To dip her chosen in her source.[90]

Nature, then, he concludes, is not really cruel. Only to the weak does she appear so. To the strong man she offers a challenge to wrestle with her and thereby improve the racial stock.

Hence, the new biological science comes to have a definite place in his philosophy—a philosophy which makes due allowance for his blood relationship to the other orders of living things. Nor do the religious implications involved frighten him, as they did Tennyson at first.

> But the worst of me is, that when I bow my head,
> I perceive a thought wriggling away in the dust,
> And I follow its track, quite forgetful, instead
> Of humble acceptance: for, question I must.[91]

In brief, he does not turn away from Reason to embrace the supernatural. For faith, he sees a definite need, but even faith is

> ... Reason herself, tiptoe
> At the ultimate bound of her wit,
> On the verges of Night and Day.[92]

It is a "leap of the spirit." He does not profess to be able to solve the riddle of what happens to the soul after death. Indeed, that cannot be solved until his soul has yearned

[90] "Hard Weather." 1888.
[91] "Martin's Puzzle." 1865.
[92] "A Faith on Trial." 1888.

With all her gifts, to reach the light discerned
Her spirit through.[93]

He is very far from denying truth to the supernatural. He simply states he does not know; and he prefers, in a positivistic way, to devote his time and thought to something which can be known. He does not refuse to admit the possibility of life after death. Indeed his reason assures him there is some ground for such a hope.

When we have thrown off this old suit,
So much in need of mending,
To sink among the naked mute,
Is that, think you, our ending?
We follow many, more we lead,
And you who sadly turf us
Believe not that all living seed
Must flower above the surface.[94]

Anyway, whether there is personal immortality or not, the guarantee of such a fact is not vital. Here he differs from Tennyson, who felt that the assurance of immortality made life worth living. Meredith, on the contrary, believes that it is the sense of the worth of life that assures us of immortality—at least, the immortality of the group if not of the individual. Furthermore, natural selection holds forth the promise of a constantly improving racial stock. Therefore he does not say with Frederick Myers:

Oh dreadful thought! if all our sires and we
Are but foundations of a race to be,—
Stones which one thrusts in earth and builds thereon
A white delight, a Parian Parthenon.

Meredith refuses to feel that this is a dreadful thought. On the contrary, because of this,

We children of Beneficence
Are in its being sharers,

---

[93] "Earth and Man."
[94] "The Question Whither." 1888.

REASON OR MYSTICISM

> And Whither vainer sounds than Whence,
> For word with such wayfarers.[95]

For him the "spirit" is the perfect flowering of the natural through the process of evolution. How firmly he believed this was put to the supreme test, when his wife, who was also his beloved companion, lay dying one beautiful spring day. As he then wandered disconsolate along those familiar paths which they had so often trod together, the beauty of the springtime seemed to mock him at first; and it was cold comfort to reflect that Nature is beneficent; his faith was very nearly shaken. But almost as miraculously as in the case of Tennyson, it was restored to him at the sight of "the pure wild cherry" in bloom,

> But this in myself did I know,
> . . . . .
> That nature at interflow
> With all of their past and the now,
> Are chords to the Nature without,
> Orbs to the greatest whole.[96]

We should not expect "her wheels to pause" or for her to be sympathetic with the individual.

> For the road of her soul is the Real,
> The root of the growth of man:
> . . . . . .
> By Death, as by Life, are we fed.
> . . . . . .
> She wrestles with our old worm
> Safe in the narrow and wide:
> Relentless quencher of lies,
> With laughter she pierces the brute.[97]

And her message to man is

> Would humanity soar from its worst,
> Winged above darkness and dole,
> How flesh unto spirit must grow.[98]

---
[95] "The Question Whither."
[96] "A Faith on Trial."
[97] *Ibid.*
[98] *Ibid.*

Thus, through the assurance of unity, of a purpose that includes growth and development in its program, offering the possibility of nature becoming "conscient and sensitive in man" the poet is able to pass through his greatest trial victoriously. By the inexorable quality of natural law, by the very fact that it allows no place for pity or sympathy, he sees cause for rejoicing. Indeed, the brave soul must welcome this discipline, because only through it can the soul obtain its freedom. Hard necessity is "Wisdom's Mother."[99]

> Having knowledge to spur thee, a gift
>   to compare;
> Rubbing shoulder to shoulder, as only
>   the book
> Of the world can be read, by necessity
>   urged,[100]

there is nothing to be feared from Nature's relentless law of natural selection. For men,

> Not forfeiting the beast with which
>   they are crossed,
> To stature of the Gods will they
>   attain.[101]

If Foresight and Patience join hands,

> The world shall know itself and where it stands,
> What cowering angel and what upright beast
> Make man, behold, nor count the low the least.[102]

Thus is progress secured. But Meredith is not at all certain

> Whether Earth's great offspring, by decree,
> Must rot if they abjure rapacity.[103]

Like Goethe he believes "not argument but effort shall decide."[104]

---

[99] "Foresight and Patience." 1894.
[100] "The Empty Purse." 1892.
[101] "Hymn to Colour." 1888.
[102] "Foresight and Patience."
[103] "To J. M." (John Morley), 1867.
[104] *Ibid.*

REASON OR MYSTICISM

At any rate the concern for the next generation is the real proof of our souls:

> The young generation! ah, there is the child
> Of our souls down the Ages! to bleed for it, proof
> That souls we have, but with our senses filed,
> Our shuttles at thread of the woof.[105]

The ethical question behind the Darwinian philosophy is:

> Keep the young generation in hail,
> And bequeath them no tumbled house![106]

With Spencer he could feel that the "acceptance of the doctrine of organic evolution determines certain ethical conceptions."[107] Spencer had given definite expression to this idea in 1892, and while Meredith concerned himself more specifically with ethical questions in the series of poems entitled *A Reading of Life,* he had, as we have already noted in the selection of the poems from which we have quoted, given expression to the ethical implications of natural selection very much earlier. Some of these implications are to be noted as early as 1883 in "The Woods of Westermain," and "Earth and Man," and in 1888 in "Hard Weather" and "A Faith on Trial." Like Huxley, however, he was not entirely certain that biology could be taken ultimately as the foundation of the moral code.[108] At any rate, all must decide

> . . . shall we run with Artemis
> Or yield the breast to Aphrodite?[109]

It is very essential to note that Meredith is not a thorough determinist. He believes that man has the power to choose what he will do, but that he is, of course, limited by the laws of nature. He should be:

---

[105] "The Empty Purse."
[106] *Ibid.*
[107] "Ethics." I, 25.
[108] Huxley, *Lectures in Oxford,* 1893, and Meredith's "To J. M." 1867.
[109] "The Vital Choice." 1901.

> Obedient to Nature, not her slave:
> Her lord, if to her rigid laws he bows;
> Her dust, if with his conscience he plays knave,
> And bid the passions on the Pleasures browse.[110]

He should in brief, seek the golden mean between the two extremes—the Aristotelian ideal.

> Withal his pitch of pride would not disown
> A sober world that walks the balanced mean
> Between its tempters, rarely overthrown.[111]

To do this, something of a philosophical temper is necessary. Faith in a steady growth and improvement of the race comes, as we have previously noted, as a fruit of this philosophical temper.

> Philosophy is Life's one match for Fate.[112]

This is clearly brought out in the debate between Foresight and Patience, in which the first of these declares that this age,

> For neither of us has it any care;
> Its teaching is through Science to despair.[113]

Patience, however, condemns the attitude of despair as being contrary to the true spirit of the age, which "climbs earth"

"To challenge heaven," declares Foresight.

"Not less, the lower deeps," insists Patience. "Yet, what does it matter if it does laugh at Happiness? It serves as a sure goad to prick the wise."[114]

If the cold, stern, relentless facts appear more than mankind can bear, the philosophic temper can always call to its aid the comic spirit, which is also, "the sword of commonsense," and tends always to restore an equilibrium.

Thus, Meredith rallies time and again to the championship of philosophic and scientific truth, the outstanding formulation of

---

[110] "The Test of Manhood." 1901.
[111] *Ibid.*
[112] "Foresight and Patience."
[113] *Ibid.*
[114] "Foresight and Patience."

which seems to him in his age to be Natural Selection. In this he sought his chief justification for his deep faith that good will finally triumph in a perfected humanity.

His poetry shows plenty of evidence that he was a keen and accurate observer of natural phenomena. Grant Allen declared when he went to consult Meredith about a spring flower: "He knows the facts of intimate country-side life as few of us do after the most specific training."[115] Because of his belief in the fundamental unity of everything and that man and nature are therefore very closely related, he was especially eager to understand nature in some of its more humble aspects. Science offered systematized facts about these various fields of nature and about man. Hence, his interest in science, though he agreed with Spencer that it is but a partially-unified knowledge and that the completely-unified knowledge of which he was so desirous was to be found only in philosophy. He was not content, then, to abide entirely with the ideas that experience revealed. In generalizing upon these "partial-truths" of science, even though in the positivistic sense he sought to eschew all metaphysical speculations, there was nevertheless a sore temptation to build up his theory upon a pure assumption: that back of the process of evolution there was a plan which was in its inner essence good. This was as truly a matter of faith as was Tennyson's argument for immortality. Both were built ultimately upon the same irrational basis of mysticism, for it was through the emotional experience which came with the sight of the "pure wild-cherry" in bloom that Meredith perceived the unity of all nature. When one searches in his work for further proof of scientific interests, beyond that of evolution, it becomes evident that Meredith was not very keenly interested in science in and for itself. In the first place he was not a thoroughgoing Darwinist. He was not con-

---

[115] J. A. Hammerton, *George Meredith in Anecdote and Criticism.* Lond., 1909, p. 67.

cerned with the arguments pro and con as to whether evolution could be explained by a mechanical principle. He leaned rather, to the idea of Goethe—of Lamarck and Erasmus Darwin also—that it is a scheme of progress proceeding according to inherent principles. In believing that the process is working out according to a pre-arranged plan, his temper had much in common with the German transcendental philosophy. He was less visionary, however, than many of those nature philosophers, had very much more regard for facts, and was obsessed with the idea of the necessity of accommodating his mature philosophy to the latest scientific.truths.

Meredith did not feel drawn to science as much as Tennyson did; but just as that poet had felt obliged to wrestle with these scientific truths when they threatened his belief in immortality, so Meredith felt it incumbent upon him to take account of them when they tended to set man and nature against each other, and so destroy that unity which appeared so necessary to him. In accommodating these beliefs to each other, there was no such mental struggle as Tennyson suffered. So sure was he of the real unison of everything, so confident that reason and science would justify his faith, that he experienced apparently only a few doubts during the course of his whole lifetime. His robust nature furnished him with an optimistic courage that carried him through the aspects of a "Nature, red in tooth and claw," without shaking his faith in the ultimate triumph of good.

He does not subscribe, in the least, to a science which is too analytical, as for example, when

    Mr. Professor, learned and jocular

calls the Nymph of the Alpine Rainbow merely a "Foam-bow."

    But who shall expound to a hard cold eye
    The infinite impalpable?[116]

Furthermore,

---

[116] "By the Rosanna." 1861.

REASON OR MYSTICISM 223

> Shall man into the mystery of breath
> From his quick beating pulse a pathway spy?
> Or learn the secret of shrouded death,
> By lifting up the lid of a white eye.[117]

His attitude towards science is further indicated in the introductory chapter to *The Egoist*.

> I conceive . . . that the realistic method of a conscientious transcription of all the visible, and a repetition of all the audible, is mainly accountable for our present brainfulness and for that prolongation of the vasty and the noisy, out of which, as from an undrained fen, steams the malady of sameness, our modern malady. . . . We drove in a body to Science the other day for an antidote . . . and Science introduced us to our o'er hoary ancestry. . . . We were the same and animals into the bargain. That is all we got from "Science."

What is needed, he says in effect, is the philosophical mind and not the analytical instrument that simply "peeps and botanises." This philosophical mind can, he believes, be aided and abetted through art, especially in the cultivation of the Comic Spirit. In his fiction he endeavored to do the latter while in his poetry he attempted to give, in a more succinct form, expression to his philosophy in general. "To demand of us truth to nature excluding Philosophy," he wrote, "is really to bid a pumpkin caper."[118] To state more specifically the philosophic truths that Meredith desires to express in his poetry, it is necessary to sum up the following main points: Nature (or Earth) and man are intimately connected, a fact which is clearly revealed through the exercise of reason, without which Nature and man appear to be at war. Reason shows, however, that through this apparent opposition, Nature (of which man is the conscious and sentient part) evolves from sense to spirit through the Darwinian principle of natural selection, and that man and nature are thereby perfected. Man, therefore, should welcome this law of natural

---

[117] "Hymn to Colour." 1888.
[118] Quot. from Mary S. Gretton. *The Writings and Life of George Meredith.* Lond., 1926, p. 11.

selection and determine to stand by the consequences whatever they may demand of him as an individual. To help him arrive at such a spiritual attitude he will have need of his philosophy and of the purging effect of the comic spirit. This will demand a readjustment in his theological conceptions; his faith will shift from a confidence in a divine revelation of individual immortality to a confidence in the natural laws themselves working out a plan by which human society is to reach a point of perfection.

These ideas Meredith desires to express in poetic form. He feels bound, however, by the traditions of nature poetry which have come down from the Greeks, from Shakespeare, Chaucer, Spenser, Wordsworth, Shelley, and Keats. Moreover he has a clear conception of what he feels imaginative writing should be:

> The art of the pen is to arouse the inward vision, instead of labouring with a drop-scene brush, as if it were to the eye; because our flying minds cannot contain a protracted description. That is why the poets, who spring imagination with a word or a phrase, paint lasting pictures.[119]

It is much the same problem with which Browning had been preoccupied.

Meredith told Sidney Colvin that in his poetry he was trying to achieve "concentration and suggestion."[120] Plainly then his problem was how to combine the maximum amount of philosophy with a sufficient amount of emotion or feeling. He seeks to emotionalize his material, and in a more marked sense than most philosophic poets, because he is attempting to a greater degree perhaps than most of them, to transcribe an abstract intellectual form into verse.

Having something of a "disgust of the sermon in rhyme" because "it is not attractive in being too chaste,"[121] he would avoid being too manifestly didactic. Yet he is insistent that his

---

[119] *Diana of the Crossways.*
[120] Hammerton, *op. cit.*, p. 166.
[121] "The Empty Purse."

poetry should have a distinctly intellectual content. His aim is to take the bare facts of nature and to give them back "drenched with a dew of human emotion."[122] He has no interest in art for art's sake, despite the fact that he lived for some time with Rossetti and Swinburne. "I desire to strike the poetic spark out of absolute human clay," he wrote the Rev. Augustus Jessop in 1861. "Of course I do not think of binding down the Muse to the study of facts. That is but a part of her work."[123] He wishes "to cling to earth."[124] Earth must be the source of his material, which of course may be refashioned. But this refashioning, or emotionalizing, he believes, can be achieved through the use of an abundance of effective metaphors, which will call up, by an economy of means, a vivid picture. As regards their use, however, Mr. Hammerton points out that there is little to distinguish Meredith in prose or in poetry, "unless it be that the compression of poetry brings one metaphor on the heels of another more quickly than in prose."[125] The charge of obscurity often laid at his door may perhaps be accounted for, to a large extent at least, by this excessive compression and "foreshortening" of phrase.

It is natural, at any rate, that in his attempt to obtain a union of intellect with the more traditional type of nature poetry the product should frequently give the impression of being experimental. Coming after the Romantic poets he felt of course, the force of the poetic patterns inherited from them. This tradition, it will be recalled, reacted in the main away from the generalized, the conceptual and the mechanized vocabulary of science—a vocabulary which had grown rapidly during the course of the nineteenth century. Whereas for Lucretius it had been sufficient to add a little honeyed sweetness, for Meredith it was necessary to

---

[122] From "Times" on his Eightieth Birthday—quot. Hammerton.
[123] Letters. I, 44-45.
[124] *Ibid.*, I, 157.
[125] Hammerton. p. 268.

move his readers emotionally. His problem therefore was much more difficult, and the poetry which is the product of Meredith's labors can scarcely be said to be entirely satisfactory in all respects. One writer[126] declares that Meredith's poetic reputation suffered because of his too wide interests. The literary man disowned him because he was too philosophic and didactic; the scientist because he was a nature poet; and the philosopher because he was too literary. This is equivalent to saying that Meredith did not succeed in perfectly fusing Nature poetry, philosophy, and science. Perhaps he was, as Arthur Symons has protested, attempting the impossible here; but at any rate the attempt is interesting. That it was easy to give poetic expression to the philosophic, scientific and positivistic aspects of science no one will for a moment maintain.

Professor Jack, who seems to have considered carefully this whole matter of philosophic poetry, sees in Meredith's work a distinct contribution to the poetical movement of the age, which has not yet succeeded, however, in showing that "emotion and matter of thought" are no longer separate.[127]

There is one aspect of Meredith's style, which cannot, it seems to me, be laid entirely to the fact that he falls a little short of his ideal. While it may be true that his style was aptly suited to his method and outlook and that what he was attempting to do must render it obligatory for him to make no less of a demand on the reader than his material made on himself, yet his alleged obscurity appears to be due in part also to a certain mannerism of style. There is a sense of effort in much of his work, which has variously been charged to his early German education, to his continued interest in German literature, and to the influence of the prose style of Carlyle. In addition there is the fact of his

---

[126] William Chislett Jr.: *George Meredith: A Study and an Appraisal*. Boston, 1925, p. 212.

[127] Adolphus A. Jack: *Poetry and Prose*. N.Y., 1912, p. 205.

Celtic ancestry, which may somewhat account for his insistence upon the fanciful, the vague and the obscure.

At any rate the ideal that Meredith held out for himself must still be regarded as worthy, and perhaps possible, even though in its aspiration to unite philosophy, science, and poetry, it may still be searching for a supreme genius.

Chapter X

IN CONCLUSION: JOHN DAVIDSON

While it is my intention in the main to avoid drawing any conclusions about the present state of the controversy between Science and Poetry, there is one poet whose work, commencing in 1886 and continuing through 1908, the year prior to his death, is so significant that we cannot afford to ignore him in this study. He brings to the statement of the problem a new and important element, one which is still offering a challenge to our poets. John Davidson (1857-1909) carries out to a logical conclusion much of the philosophy that lies implicit in biological science and has so much in common with Lucretius, the first poet with whom we began our survey, that he seems a fitting figure with whom to conclude our account.

Like the Roman poet he can lustily sing the praises of materialism:

> Religion, Art, Philosophy—this God,
> This Beauty, this Idea men have filled
> The world with, study still, and still adore,
> Are only segments of the spirit's tail
> We must outgrow, if spirit would ascend,
> (Let Spirit be the word for body-and-soul!
> Will language ne'er be fused and forged anew?)
> And quit the withering life of fear and shame,
> Of agony and pitiful desire
> To reign untailed in heaven hereafter—Laugh!
> The changing image seizes you.
> ... Understand it, you at least
> Who toil all day and writhe and groan all night
> With roots of luxury, a cancer struck

> In every muscle: out of you it is
> Cathedrals rise and Heaven blossoms fair;
> You are the hidden putrifying source
> Of beauty and delight, of leisure hours
> Of passionate loves and high imaginings;
> You are the dung that keeps the roses sweet.[1]

But he cannot draw the comforting conclusion that Lucretius drew from his dogma that the atom is indestructible. Instead, he believes that the atom dies and that this is a "deeply satisfying fact," because "even the atom had to die in order to live,"[2] and that the wonderful experiments of Gustave LeBon, by whose efforts this has been made known, entitles his name to be written in the same line as Darwin's.

In agreement with Lucretius he has no patience with superstition or with those self-deluding characteristics, which refuse to accept the "facts" because these seem too difficult to acknowledge honestly. But he is not thinking so much of the tranquility of mind which Lucretius believed to be the prerequisite of happiness. A long highway stretches between these two thinkers and along it have trod the footsteps of Darwin and Schopenhauer, and more recently those of Nietzsche have left visible traces. The circumstances forbid that man should find happiness when existence itself is perceived to be a tension, when the fundamental law of progress is strife, turmoil, and competition, and when the most that man can do in the face of these facts is to seek to rear a stronger race.

The goal now is not quite so simple as Lucretius and the older philosophers believed. To follow natural law, to accept reality, means to strive for strength and the fullest self-realization in the face of all disillusionment.

"Obey your Nature, not authority,"[3] sings the poet. In another poem he declares that he will have no creed.

[1] "The Testament of a Vivisector." Lond., 1901.
[2] Epilogue to "Mammon and his Message," Lond., 1908.
[3] In his "Smith." 1888.

> Henceforth I shall be God; for consciousness
> Is God: I suffer; I am God: this Self,
> That all the universe combines to quell
> Is greater than the universe . . .[4]

He writes of a musician, of his struggles and of how his wife dies of starvation, but when the musician dies, God welcomes him because he has persisted in self-expression.[5] In his "Ballad of Tannhauser," the hero returns to his first mistress in the Venusberg, not to repent of his sin later, but to live with her in immortal happiness. He pictures the Vivisector as liking his work because it fills him with a pleasing sense of mastery and satisfies his lust for inflicting pain."[6]

One of Davidson's critics refers to him as a "princely decadent,"[7] and perhaps many of his readers will concur in this view. But must we not admit, if we are strictly honest, that all this philosophy is merely the logical working out of some of the implications in the Darwinian theory? If we object to seeing it represented in poetry, may it not be because we are not as strictly logical as the poet, or that we look to poetry for an escape from reality? Or do we have deep and conscientious objections to the materialistic hypothesis that lies behind this attitude?

> I say, this twentieth century begins
> No other age than the Millennium,
> In every time and change the cry has been
> "Escape! Escape!"
>
> . . . .
>
> But now we know escape impossible;
> And on the tolling of that knowledge comes
> The Golden Age, Millennium, Heaven-and-Hell—
> That have been always though men knew it not;
> For knowledge to the subject of it makes

---

[4] "A Ballad in Blank Verse of the Making of a Poet."
[5] "Ballad of Heaven."
[6] "Testament of a Vivisector." Lond., 1901.
[7] W. M. Parker. *Modern Scottish Writers.* Edinburgh, 1917.

>   The character of things. Oh, Matter means
>   That Man shall not escape![8]

"By an advanced process of chemical selection which we do not yet know how to begin to study, but which in time we shall assuredly understand, Carbon, Hydrogen, Nitrogen, and Oxygen were chosen to be the basis of all life."[9] "The brain is further enriched by Sulphur and Phosphorus.[10] "Thought and imagination . . . are as physical and material as digestion and secretion."[11] This surely pictures the position of the scientist who is scientist first and foremost, of the man who insists before all else in reducing cause and effect to a mathematical formula. It is the Newtonian concept combined with the Darwinian idea of a struggle upon the part of the organism to adapt itself to its environment.

An important point to note is that Davidson protests against the idea that poetry is merely the product of chemistry or of any other science. "The efficacy of what appears incompetent for such great results as the music of Wagner or the plays of Shakespeare is not to be decided by the test-tube and the balance."[12] There is involved the element of imagination, and what is required is a renewal of this. "The so-called rise of rationalism was an ejectment of the Imagination."[13] "By Imagination men live."[14] And he proceeds to state his creed as follows: "I devour, digest, and assimilate the Universe; make for myself in my Testaments and Tragedies a new form and substance of Imagination; and by poetic power certify the semi-certitudes of science."[15] There is no attempt to call the poet inspired, or a be-

[8] "The Testament of a Prime Minister." Lond., 1902.
[9] "Mammon and His Message," Lond., 1908. Epilogue, p. 165.
[10] *Ibid.*, p. 166.
[11] *Ibid.*, p. 166.
[12] *Ibid.*, p. 167.
[13] *Ibid.*, pp. 171-72.
[14] *Ibid.*, p. 173.
[15] *Ibid.*, p. 175.

ing who is blessed with supernatural power, for the thought and the imagination that has gone into poetry is matter, more refined to be sure than ordinary matter, but subject to the same laws. The

> ... chief end
> Of Matter—of the Earth aware in us
> As of that greater Matter orbed and lit
> Throughout Eternal Night—is evermore
> Self-knowledge.[16]

For "Man is the universe become conscious, and now approaching self-consciousness."[17] This self-consciousness which finds expression in poetry, however, is not due entirely to rationalism, as Lucretius believed, for Davidson asserts that "ultimate causes" cannot be known scientifically, but that "Man attains to unity with the subconscious universe by raising himself through poetry above experimentation and ratiocination."[18] The Testaments, he declares, "are addressed to those who are willing to place all ideas in the crucible, and who are not afraid to fathom what is subconscious in themselves and others."[19] Hence poetry should not only deal with "something from direct experience and observation of life," but also "express the heart of things."[20] The new poetry is to be constructed out of his emotional moods.

> Heat the furnace hot,
> Smelt the things of thought
> Into dross and dew
> Mould the world anew.[21]

---

[16] "Testament of a Vivisector." Lond., 1901.

[17] "Mammon and his Message." Lond., 1908. Epilogue, p. 147.

[18] See Hayim Fineman: *John Davidson: A Study of the Relations of his Ideas to his Poetry*. Thesis. Univ. of Penn. 1916. Also "Mammon and his Message." p. 173.

[19] From a note appended to "Testament of a Vivisector."

[20] See Fineman, *op. cit.*, "Godfrida," p. 3.

[21] "To the New Men," in *Ballads and Songs*. Lond., 1895.

This moulding of the world anew is not done in a matter-of-fact manner, for the highest poetry should have perfect freedom and an element of spontaneity in it.[22] So important is this factor to him that he even denies that there is an art of literary criticism,[23] and his whole attitude, grounded as it is in the facts of existence and in materialism, is really romantic. Indeed, he refers to his own plays as "romances," but he defines romance as the essence of reality. "Romance does not give the bunches plucked from the stem; it offers the wine of life in chased goblets. I have moulded and carved my goblet to the best of my art; and I have crushed wine into it."[24] Thus even though art should never divorce itself from fact, yet its highest aim is to give delight, and to achieve that goal is "to impart strength most permanently."[25]

"Poetry is Matter become vocal, a blind force without Judgment. . . . When Matter uses a free mind, 'of imagination all compact', like Shakespeare's, then are its happiest moments."[26] Davidson scoffs at the epithets "metaphysical" and "philosophical" when they are applied to poetry. "A poet may employ metaphysics and philosophy as he may employ history and science, but all poetry is poetical."[27] By "poetical" he means, of course, matter which has been refined by the imagination, and the abode of this is the universe itself.

Imagination is the gulf and the retort that swallows and transmutes sight and sound, touch and taste, and all emotion, passion, thought, into beauty and delight, into power and achievement. . . . It is by imagination that religion or any cause lives and prospers.[28]

In this conception of poetry, we note a full acceptance of the scientific point of view, along with the materialistic philosophy

---

[22] "Man Forbid." p. 125.
[23] "A Rosary," p. 185.
[24] Prologue to "Godfrida." Lond., 1898.
[25] *Ibid.*
[26] "On Poetry," in *Holiday and other Poems*, N.Y., 1906, pp. 137-8.
[27] Epilogue to "The Triumph of Mammon." Lond., 1907, p. 166.
[28] "Mammon and his Message." Lond., 1908, p. 149.

that accompanied it at the close of the nineteenth century. The poet was not to attempt to escape from the consequences of this doctrine and its implications. These facts were not merely to be accepted but they were to be woven into the very texture of his poetry, and form the very framework of his imagination. The function of the imagination, however, was none too clearly defined. When he went to London in 1890 to seek his literary fortune, he apparently had no very clear idea of what constituted the imagination. He was then thirty-three years of age, part of his active life having been spent in teaching school, and in working at odd times in a chemical laboratory, his interest being somewhat divided between science and literature. Up to this time very little had been achieved in a literary way, his most notable and significant work being, *Smith; a Tragic Farce*, in which he gives expression to his characteristic attitude towards life and which inherits much from Carlyle.[29] In "Smith" he had written

> ... one must become
> Fanatic—be a wedge—a thunderbolt,
> To smite a passage through the close-grained world.[30]

When he reached London he found many of his associates in the Rhymer's Club, among whom were Ernest Dawson, Edwin J. Ellis, G. A. Greene, Lionel Johnson, A. C. Hiller, Victor Parr, W. B. Yeats, Richard Le Gallienne, Ernest Rhys, Arthur Rhys, Arthur Symons, John Todhunter, all deeply influenced by the French poetry of the time, and all holding that poetry should not concern itself with public interests or with theories and generalizations of the mind, but only with impressions.[31] In so far as this group of writers derived from the French symbolists, they

---

[29] *Poems by John Davidson*, Introd. by R. M. Wenley. N.Y., 1924, XIX.
[30] *Smith*.
[31] See the excellent account by C. E. Andrews and M. O. Percival: *Poetry of the Nineties*, N.Y., 1926, p. 7 f.

believed that imagination has some way of arriving at truth denied to the reason.[32] Davidson reacted against this movement, to the extent that he was greatly concerned with theories and generalizations of the mind, but he held to their idea, in part at least, that the imagination had some unique power for revealing a higher truth than the reason could disclose.

And here it seems to me, we may note something highly significant about the attitude of these poets with whom we have been concerned in this study. They have all, in varying degrees, claimed a transcendency for poetry. Perhaps Lucretius made fewer claims than the rest, for he employed poetry as the most pleasing means for teaching philosophic truth. If John Davidson was next in insisting that poetry must take account of scientific truth, he also believed, as we have noted, that poetry was a product of the imagination and in this respect transcended science. For Matthew Arnold, as well, poetry transcended science and philosophy in offering a criticism or evaluation of life. George Meredith, attempting to uphold an optimistic philosophy while facing the implications of the Darwinian hypothesis, yields finally to a supernatural philosophy that ends in mysticism, closely akin to Tennyson's and Walt Whitman's. The other poets we have considered in this connection all claimed a province for poetry apart from rationalism. Indeed, with the exception of Lucretius, all have rebelled sooner or later against the materialistic philosophy. No wonder then that when science appeared definitely wedded to this same materialism, critics felt that along that way lay ruin and destruction for poetry.

With the twentieth century the solid foundation upon which the older science had been built began to crumble. The earlier conception of space and time had to undergo certain modifications. Man no longer felt so sure about the efficacy of his science. The dissatisfaction of the poets with the purely ma-

---

[32] *Ibid.*, p. 31.

terial explanation of the universe was now reflected in the minds of some of the twentieth-century philosophers, and some scientists, feeling the implications embodied in, and emanating from, the type of thought which had been engendered by the Newtonian science, began to question its power to solve all the riddles of man. They were no longer so sure of what it meant by "matter," which was now defined in new terms of space and time, not merely as extension, but as "events" or "organisms."[33] It is in motion that all modern science finds its root,[34] and the motion of light becomes the standard by which all other motions are measured. The implications which lie beneath these philosophic generalizations have not yet been worked out to any marked extent. Whether the generalizations themselves will be accepted ultimately as fundamental truths or not still remains to be seen. At any rate it is interesting to note that the main objecion of the poets against materialism as it has been interpreted during the latter half of the nineteenth century and their insistence upon something of more vital importance beyond the so-called material universe is apparently receiving serious attention upon the part of many scientists and philosophers. Whether science and poetry will succeed in meeting more amicably in the future than they have done in the past remains to be seen.

At any rate John Davidson was most desirous of coming to terms with the spirit of science. Few poets have had the hardihood to exclaim with one of his characters:

>   Consider how the silent sun is rapt
>   In self-devotion! All things work for good
>   To them that love themselves.[35]

There lies he declares,

>   A ruthless obligation on our souls
>   To be despotic for the world's behoof
>   Ruthless, I say; because the destinies

---

[33] A. C. Whitehead. *Science and the Modern World.* N.Y., 1925.
[34] Baker Brownell. *The New Universe,* N.Y., 1926, p. 12.
[35] Spoken by Urban in *Self's the Man.* Lond., 1917, p. 79.

JOHN DAVIDSON

> Admit no compromise: we must be first,
> Though everlasting war cement each course
> Of empire with our blood; or cease to be
> Our every name and language in dispute.

The drama concludes with the words:

> Learn to forgive yourself
> Though you were Judas, learn to forgive yourself.[36]

Surely the Darwinian theory of natural selection with all its worst ethical implications could go no further than that. Many poets, since Tennyson described his mental struggle in *In Memoriam,* had approximated to that position; but none had expressed it so boldly as Davidson, so entirely without flinching; and yet it seems rather significant that with such a philosophy he was a very unhappy man and ended his life by committing suicide. Intellectual courage we have to allow to the man; but are we to conclude that this philosophy of ruthlessness can offer only despair, unhappiness and dissatisfaction, that man requires more to live by than such a logical application of scientific truth? Have the myriads of poets who have protested against such a conclusion all realized that fact consciously or unconsciously? Have they all sensed that man's nature could not, and would not, be satisfied with an explanation so purely mechanical?

Even Davidson declines to accept the interpretation of determinism that renders man a mere automaton, his will completely enslaved; for it will be noted in the selections quoted above, man is free to determine whether he shall be ruthless and despotic or merely quiescent.

While many of these poets have been able to follow to some extent in the footsteps of Lucretius, in his acceptance of natural law, his reliance upon reason rather than upon superstition, his willingness to face the facts and mould his life in accordance, very few of them have been willing to go farther and relinquish the right of freedom of choice. Indeed the most significant point

[36] *Ibid.,* p. 136.

about the philosophy of Lucretius is, it leaves absolute freedom of choice to the individual as to whether he will let his mind become a prey to superstition and unreason or subject it to the iron discipline of reason. Many of the modern poets draw no such optimistic conclusions about the ultimate power of reason to satisfy the innermost cravings of man. In the first place, the modern poet versed in the scientific thought current at the end of the nineteenth century knows that he is a prey to primitive impulses that are more primary and influential than reason, which is, after all, in the history of the race merely secondary. Furthermore he is no longer so sure that human reason is the only avenue to truth. He is too well aware of its limitations; he has heard the word "sub-conscious" employed in so many different senses that he scarcely knows whether to subscribe to it or not; but at any rate he feels that there is a great motive power back of, and independent of, human reason with which he must reckon.

Such seems to be the impasse which these two attitudes of mind have reached. The two contending armies are marking time, while the terms of the armistice are being discussed. There appears to be reason to believe that a peace conference will result which may succeed in defining the boundaries of science and poetry more satisfactorily than they have ever been defined before. It may be found that the interests of each will be seen to harmonize much better than was imagined in the past. If it can be shown that the ultimate difference between the poet and the scientist is one of degree rather than of kind, such a harmony of interests will surely be discovered. In the meantime we patiently await the terms of the treaty.

BIBLIOGRAPHY

Besides the usual histories of science, poetry, and works of reference, and those books mentioned in the footnotes, the following have proved of especial interest.

ARISTOTLE. The Poetics. Trans. by S. H. Butcher. London, 1911.
ARNOLD, MATTHEW. Essays in Criticism. Second Series. New York, 1924. Essay: "The Study of Poetry."
BABBITT, IRVING. The New Laokoon. Boston, 1910.
BALDWIN, C. S. Poetic and Rhetoric: Classical and Medieval. Two Vols.
BALFOUR, ARTHUR. The Foundations of Belief. New York, 1906.
BARRY, F. The Scientific Habit of Thought. New York, 1927.
BENN, A. W. The History of Modern Philosophy. London, 1912.
BERGSON, HENRI. An Introduction to Metaphysics. Trans. by T. E. Hulme. London, 1913.
BOSANQUET, BERNARD. A History of Aesthetic. New York, 1904.
BROAD, C. D. Scientific Thought. New York, 1923.
BROWNELL, BAKER. The New Universe. New York, 1926.
BUCHANAN, SCOTT. Poetry and Mathematics. New York, 1929.
BUCKLEY, A. B. A Short History of Natural Science. New York, 1902.
BUTCHER, S. H. Aristotle's Theory of Poetry and Fine Art. London, 1911.
CAJORI, FLORIAN. A History of Mathematics. New York, 1910.
CAMPBELL, NORMAN. What Is Science? London, 1921.
CLARK, D. L. Rhetoric and Poetry in the Renaissance. New York, 1922.
CORNFORD, FRANCIS M. From Religion to Philosophy. London, 1912.
CROCE, BENEDETTO. Aesthetic. Trans. by D. Ainslee. London, 1922, also The Philosophy of Benedetto Croce.
――― The Problem of Art and History. Trans. by H. Widson Car. London, 1917.

CUMONT, FRANZ. Astrology and Religion among the Greeks and Romans. New York, 1912.
CURRY, WALTER C. Chaucer and the Medieval Sciences. New York, 1926.
DEWEY, JOHN. Psychology. New York, 1891.
DU BELLAY, JOACHIM. Deffense et illustration de la langue françoyse. From œuvres completes. Paris, 1903-1907, Vol. I.
DUNCAN, CARSON S. The New Science and English Literature in the Classical Period. Univ. of Chicago thesis, 1913.
DUNN, WILLIAM P. Sir Thomas Browne. A Study in Religious Philosophy. Columbia University Dissertation. Menasha, Wis., 1926.
EASTMAN, MAX. Enjoyment of Poetry. New York, 1921.
ELIOT, T. S. Homage to John Dryden. London, 1927.
ELLIS, HAVELOCK. Dance of Life. Cambridge, 1923.
FLETCHER, JOHN GOULD. "Two Elements in Poetry." *Saturday Review of Literature*, Vol. IV, p. 5.
FRAZER, SIR JAMES. The Golden Bough. Abridged. New York, 1922.
GUMMERE, FRANCIS B. The Beginnings of Poetry. London, 1901.
HALDANE, JOHN B. S. Daedalus, or Science and the Future. New York, 1924.
HALLAM, LORD TENNYSON. The Attitude of Tennyson towards Science. London, 1911.
HARRISON, J. E. Ancient Art and Ritual. New York, 1913.
HIRN, Y. Origins of Art, A Psychological and Sociological Inquiry. London, 1900.
HOBSON, E. W. The Domain of Natural Science. Cambridge, 1923.
HÖFFDING, H. History of Modern Philosophy. 2 Vols., London, 1900.
HORACE. Ars Poetica. Epistula ad Persones. De Arte poetica. Paris, 1900.
HOWARD, W. G. Laokoon, Lessing, Herder, Goethe. Selections with introduction and commentary. New York, 1910.
HUNT, T. W. Literary Principles and Problems. New York, 1906.
LECKY, WILLIAM E. H. Rise and Influence of Rationalism. 2 Vols. New York, 1914.
LOWES, J. L. Convention and Revolt in Poetry. New York, 1919.
——— The Road of Xanadu. A Study in the Ways of the Imagination. New York, 1927.

MACKENZIE, A. S. The Evolution of Literature. New York, 1911.
MAHAFFY, J. P. What Have the Greeks Done for Modern Civilization? London, 1909.
MAXIM, HUDSON. The Science of Poetry and the Philosophy of Language. New York, 1910.
MERZ, J. F. History of European Thought in the Nineteenth Century. 4 Vols., London, 1896-1914.
MILLS, JOHN. The Realities of Modern Science. New York, 1919.
OSBORN, H. F. From the Greeks to Darwin. New York, 1924.
PADELFORD, F. M. Essays on the Study and Use of Poetry by Plutarch and Basil the Great. New Haven, 1902.
PEARSON, KARL. The Grammar of Science. London, 1900.
PERRY, BLISS. A Study of Poetry. Cambridge, 1920.
PLATO. Ion, Phaedo, and The Republic. Jowett's trans. London, 1908.
POINCARE. Science and Hypothesis. London, 1905.
PRESCOTT, F. C. The Poetic Mind. New York, 1922.
RANDALL, J. H., JR. The Making of the Modern Mind. New York, 1926.
RICHARDS, I. A. Science and Poetry. New York, 1926.
RITCHIE, A. D. Scientific Method. London, 1923.
RUSSELL, BERTRAND. Icarus, or the Future of Science. London, 1924.
——— Philosophy. New York, 1927.
SANTAYANA, GEORGE. The Life of Reason. New York, 1924: I Reason in Society; II Reason in Art; III Reason in Science.
——— The Sense of Beauty. New York, 1896.
SEDGWICK, W. T. AND TYLER, H. W. A Short History of Science. New York, 1921.
SHELLEY, P. B. Defence of Poetry. Prose Works, ed. by Harry B. Foreman. 4 Vols., Vol. 3, London, 1880.
SINGER, CHARLES. Studies in the History and Method of Science. Oxford, 1917-1921.
SPINGARN, J. E. A History of Literary Criticism in the Renaissance. New York, 1920.
STIMSON, DOROTHY. The Gradual Acceptance of the Copernican Theory of the Universe. New York, 1917.
TAYLOR, H. O. Ancient Ideals. 2 Vols., New York, 1913.
THOMAS, CALVIN. "Poetry and Science," *Open Court,* July 18, 1889.
THOMSON, J. ARTHUR. The Outline of Science, Vol. 4, Science and Modern Thought. New York, 1927.

THORNDIKE, ASHLEY H. Literature in a Changing Age. New York, 1920.
THORNDIKE, LYNN. A History of Magic and Experimental Science during the First Thirteen Centuries of our Era. New York, 1923.
WELLS, HENRY W. Poetic Imagery. New York, 1924.
WENDELL, BARRETT. The Temper of the Seventeenth Century in English Literature. New York, 1904.
WHEWELL, WILLIAM. A History of the Inductive Sciences. 3 Vols., London, 1838.
WHITHEAD, A. N. The Concept of Nature. Cambridge, 1920.
―――― Science and the Modern World. New York, 1926.
WORDSWORTH, WILLIAM. Preface to the Lyrical Ballads. London. 1911.

INDEX

Akenside, Mark, 66
Aquinas, Thomas, 13
Aratus, 29
Arbuthnot, John, 66
Aristotle, 7, 13, 19, 20, 21, 23, 25, 72, 116
Arnold, Matthew, 5, 23, 191, 203-7, 235
Aytoun, William E., 189

Bacon, Francis, 8, 9, 13, 40, 41, 52, 75
Bailey, Philip J., 189
Bayle, Pierre, 81
Berchoux, Josephe, 100-1
Berkeley, Bishop, 11
Blake, William, 74-79
Boerhaave, 10
Boileau, 21
Bonnet, 10
Boyle, Robert, 58
Browne, Sir Thomas, 56
Browning, Robert, 192-97, 202, 211, 213-14
Buchanan, Scott, 14
Buffon, 10, 96, 106, 117, 125, 165
Butler, Samuel (1612-80), 48 sq.
Butler, Samuel (1835-1902), 119, 125, 126
Byron, Lord, 189

Callimachus, 28
Campanella, 116
Campenon, Vincent, 94, 100
Canning, George, 128
Carlyle, Thomas, 179, 199
Chambers, Robert, 164

Chénier, André, 102 sq., 110; his idea of poetry, 106; theory of organic development, 106, 191, 203
Clough, Arthur, 191, 203
Coleridge, S. T., 3, 129, 166, 172, 188
Collins, William, 128
Comte, August, 12
Condillac, 82, 83
Condorcet, 91
Copernicus, 8, 9, 45, 52, 54, 55
Corbet, Richard, 47
Cowley, Abraham, 51, 52, 58-59, 67
Cowper, William, 128
Croce, Benedetto, 2, 4, 24
Cuvier, Georges, 10

Daniel, Samuel, 40, 41
Dante, 20, 24, 53, 55
Darwin, Charles, 12, 120, 125, 156, 157, 159, 163, 167-68, 229
Darwin, Erasmus, 10, 100, 109, 110 sq.; conception of poetry, 111, 112, 118, 121, 127; his philosopher friends, 113; his prose works, 119, 123, 124, 155, 171, 185, 207, 222
Davenant, Sir William, 54, 58
Davidson, John, 228 sq.; compared with Lucretius, 228-29; his Darwinism, 230; conception of poetry, 231-33
Davies, Sir John, 40
Deism, 9, 62, 82
Delille, Jacques, 90, 95, 99
Denham, Sir John, 48
Descartes, 8, 51, 81, 82, 115

Dewey, John, 3, 15n
Diderot, Denis, 86, 93
Donne, John, 42 sq.; scientific imagery, 45 sq.
Dorat, Claude, 95-96
Drummond, William, 55
Dryden, John, 48, 60

Ellis, Havelock, 16
Emerson, R. W., 4
Empedocles, 25, 28, 89, 106, 116
Eratosthenes, 29
Esménard, J., 100

Fichte, J. G., 137, 138
Fitz-Gerald, Edward, 191
Fletcher, Phineas, 47
Fontenelle, Bernard de, 82, 91
French philosophes, 9, 12, 82

Galen, 7
Galileo, 13
Gibbon, Edward, 62
Gilbert, Nicholas, 101
Godwin, William, 62
Goethe, Wolfgang von, 4, 10, 23, 126, 130, 131 sq.; criticism of static conception of life, 134; scientific interests, 134, 135, 147, 148, 149; *Faust,* 138 sq.; applies principle of development to art, 142-43; use of science in verse, 150-53, 154; 171, 187, 207
Gray, Thomas, 16, 128
Greville, Fulke, 40, 41

Habington, William, 45, 56
Haeckel, E. H., 116
Harvey, William, 115
Hegel, G. W., 3, 4, 146
Helvetius, 82, 83

Herder, J. G. von, 116, 137
Herrick, Robert, 55
Hesiod, 28
Hobbes, Thomas, 51, 56, 57, 63, 106
Holbach, P. H. D., baron d', 82, 83, 86
Horace, 20, 89, 94
Hume, David, 11, 62, 64, 107, 108, 114
Hunter, John, 10, 115
Hunter, William, 10
Hutton, James, 10, 116
Huxley, Thomas, 165

Imagination, meaning to the poet, 15

Johnson, Samuel, 73-74
Jonson, Ben, 45

Kant, Immanuel, 4, 10, 11, 23, 107, 108, 114, 116, 145
Keats, John, 3, 181, 188

Lamarck, 10, 106, 125, 222
La Mettrie, 82-83
La Motte, Houdar, 90, 91, 97
Laplace, 10, 116
Leonardo da Vinci, 8
Lessing, G. E., 132, 139
Linnaeus, 10, 99, 111, 126, 148
Locke, John, 9, 61, 75, 82
Lowes, J. L., quoted, 15, 17
Lucretius, 20, 25 sq.; his conception of poetry, 27; Epicurean philosophy, 28; attitude towards science, 30; survival of the fittest theory, 31; science in his poetry, 32 sq.; 71, 89, 94, 103, 158, 186, 225, 228, 235, 237
Lyell, Sir Charles, 116, 163, 165

INDEX 245

Mandeville, Bernard de, 62
Marini, 22
Marvel, Andrew, 47
Meredith, George, 191, 207-27; attitude towards science, 208 sq., 212; Darwinism, 213 sq., 221-22; use of science in poetry, 223-26; 235
Milton, John, 51 sq., use of Ptolemaic theory, 53; reference to Copernican theory, 53, 55, 63
More, Henry, 51, 52, 54
Moro, Lazzaro, 10
Myers, Frederick, 216
Myths, their relation to science and poetry, 18 sq.

Newton, Sir Isaac, 3, 9, 12, 13, 61 62, 67, 71, 75, 76, 82, 84, 105, 145, 155
Nicander, 29
Novalis, 4, 144

Oken, Lorenz, 117

Paine, Tom, 62
Painting, influence of science upon, 23
Paley, William, 62, 118
Paracelcus, 8
Parmenides, 25, 28
Pater, Walter, 16
Plato, 13, 19, 27
Pliny, 7
Plutarch, 20
Poe, Edgar Allan, 3
Poetry, relation to science, 2
Pomfret, John, 52
Pope, Alexander, 62, 63 sq., 69, 72, 128

Pre-Raphaelite movement, effect of science upon, 2
Provençal poetry, 20
Ptolemy, 7, 45, 52

Randolph, Thomas, 45
Richards, I. A., 1 sq., 5, 18
Robinson, J. H., 64
Roucher, 96
Rousseau, Jean Jacques, 106, 107, 108, 114, 132
Royal Society, 51, 58

Saint-Lambert, 90, 93, 97
Santayana, George, 5, 23, 139
Schelling, 4, 137
Schiller, 4, 136, 145 sq.
Schlegel, A. W., 144
Schopenhauer, 3, 146, 229
Servetus, Michael, 8
Seward, Anna, 111, 113, 114
Shaftesbury, 107, 108, 132
Shakespeare, 3, 93
Sheffield, John, 57
Shelley, 5, 188-89
Spencer, Herbert, 12, 219, 221
Swift, 66

Telesio, 8
Tennyson, Alfred, 16, 157 sq.; scientific interests, 166-70; effect of death of Arthur Hallam, 166, 173, 182; attitude towards the supernatural, 178; effect of scientific thought upon his poetry, 180 sq.; his art creed, 183-87; 191, 192, 196, 202, 203, 204, 222
Thompson, J. Arthur, 13
Thomson, James, 67 sq., 71, 73, 94

Vesalius, 8
Virgil, 89, 94, 105
Voltaire, 82 sq.; his idea of poetry, 84; his interest in science, 86-87, 132

Waller, Edmund, 48, 58
Walsh, William, 58
Watt, James, 113

Whitman, Walt, 192, 197-203
Wilmot, John, 56-57
Wither, George, 45
Wordsworth, William, 4, 129 sq., 172, 187-88, 209

Xenophanes, 25, 28

Young, Edward, 69 sq., 128

Date Due

JUN 14 65			

Demco 293-5